Debugging C

Robert Ward

Que™ Corporation
Indianapolis, Indiana

Library of Congress Catalog No.: LC 86-61152

ISBN 0-88022-261-1

90 89 88 87 86   8 7 6 5 4 3 2 1

Interpretation of the printing code: the rightmost double-digit number is the year of the book's printing; the rightmost single-digit number, the number of the book's printing. For example, a printing code of 87-4 shows that the fourth printing of this book occurred in 1987.

About the Author

Robert Ward

A digital design engineer, Robert Ward develops microprocessor-based communications equipment for an international marketer of computer accessories. He has developed programs ranging from dedicated real-time control programs for single-chip microcontrollers to small compilers for large UNIX hosts to massive vertical applications for CP/M hosts. Ward teaches computer science at McPherson College and is president of Dedicated Micro-Systems, Inc.

His quest for solutions to the challenges of programming in C on a personal computer led to his role as international coordinator of the C User's Group. Ward's interests include programming languages, computer architecture, and artificial intelligence.

Product Director
Chris DeVoney

Editorial Director
David F. Noble, Ph.D.

Managing Editor
Gregory Croy

Editors
Kathleen A. Johanningsmeier
Gail S. Burlakoff

Technical Editor
Paul Wilt

Production Foreman
Dennis Sheehan

Production
Joe Ramon
Mae Louise Shinault
Peter Tocco
Lynne Tone

Composed in Megaron and Que Digital
by Que Corporation

Cover designed by
Listenberger Design Associates

Table of Contents

3   Localizing Compile-Time Errors

4   Conventional Trace Methods

5 Managing Trace Facilities

6 Why Is Debugging C Difficult?

7 Stabilizing Pointer Bugs

8   Special Trace Techniques

9   Source-Level Debuggers

10   Interpreters and Integrated Environments

Acknowledgments

There are special people who have contributed significantly to this book. I offer my heartfelt thanks to the following persons:

Chris DeVoney and the technical staff at Que, who have enlightened me about several of my programming parochialisms.

Que's editors, who enhanced the consistency and readability of the manuscripts and brought the entire work to press in a remarkably short time.

David Raanan, of AT&T Information Systems, who reviewed the discussion of sdb in Chapter 9.

The good people at C.L. Publications, who created a forum where the main thesis of this book could be tested.

Jack Purdum of EcoSoft, who offered the special encouragement and advocacy that permitted me to take this work from an idea to a published book.

Trademark
Acknowledgments

Introduction

Why a Book on Debugging?

To write programs that work, you must know how to debug. It's that simple. In fact, if you produce working programs, you will spend at least half your time debugging.

To write programs that work, you must know also how to define problems (systems analysis), how to design solutions (algorithms and software engineering), and how to code in your chosen programming language (syntax and good practice). There are hundreds of books written on these subjects.

Isn't it strange that there are no books on debugging? I think so. All programmers do it, but nobody wants to talk about it and I think that's a mistake. First, you *can* improve your debugging skills. Like design skills, debugging skills evolve from critical analysis and exposure to new techniques and ideas. Second, you *must* improve your debugging skills. Good debugging skills are requisite to successful programming. To grow as a programmer and to tackle increasingly challenging assignments, your ability to debug also must grow. Because you program in C, you'll face peculiar debugging problems that demand enhanced debugging skills.

Debugging Then and Debugging Now

When I began programming in 1969, the teaching language was Fortran IV. A well-designed program was one that got the right answer. Attitudes about program design have changed since then. Today, by means of such carefully designed teaching languages as Pascal and Logo, beginning students are introduced early to modular design. But, when I consider how I learned to debug, my introduction to programming seems rigorously structured by comparison. Except for a vague admonition to "use trace statements to find any problems," I don't remember any classroom advice about how to debug. Sadly, that situation hasn't changed much.

The popular introductory Pascal programming texts (*Oh! Pascal!*, by Doug Cooper and Michael Clancy; *Introduction to Pascal and Structured Design*, by Nell Dale and David Orshalick; and *An Introduction to Programming and Problem Solving with Pascal*, 2nd Edition, by G. Michael Schneider) include debugging tips—usually at the end of each chapter. The Clancy and Cooper sections are called "debugging and anti-bugging." I suggest that a more precise title might be "anti-bugging and anti-bugging." Except for the all-purpose admonition to include trace statements, the book sections cover defensive programming strategies, rather than debugging strategies. The authors nurture a belief that either good programmers won't have bugs or, if they do, programmers know intuitively how to find bugs.

Until I started teaching, I assumed that good debugging skills were a natural outgrowth of good design skills. Not so. A bright student may intuitively decompose a problem into beautifully coherent, cohesive, functional modules. That same student may not be able to find the most trivial syntax errors, let alone discover subtle run-time bugs. Equally bright students turn in working designs that literally defy analysis. While I don't believe that we learn debugging by studying design, I do believe that we can learn efficient debugging.

We can develop a methodological model that directs our efforts toward more productive searches. We can acquire heuristic knowledge (a kind of folk wisdom) about where to look first. We can be deliberately sensitive to the different variables and observable phenomena in different environments. We can become expert at selecting and using appropriate tools. And, through critical analysis of our attempts to find "worthy" bugs, we can learn from our own mistakes.

Debugging = Working Programs

The simple truth is that programs seldom run right the first time. As I pointed out, debugging accounts for at least half of most development project time. Careful, disciplined design and coding won't eliminate the need for debugging; good design and coding simply make efficient debugging possible.

There is no technological relief on the horizon. The design/debug effort ratio remains fairly constant across all language classes. Neither better design nor better languages will eliminate debugging. Although debugging may change shape—we may someday find ourselves debugging specifications rather than procedures—we will need debugging as long as we create new applications.

As a teacher, I've come to believe that the greatest single difference between the person who succeeds in a programming class and the person who doesn't is that the successful programmer develops debugging skills and the unsuccessful programmer does not. While all learners commit the same types of errors in their first drafts, the individual who doesn't understand debugging remains blocked and frustrated, and the individual who does understand debugging finds the errors and goes on to experiment with new and more powerful techniques.

You may discover that your growth as a programmer has been restricted by your debugging skills. Think of a time when you were frustrated by a new operating system or language. Was part of your difficulty caused by your inability to find bugs in the new environment? To restate the question, if I could guarantee that you would find a new bug after only two seconds of searching, would you be willing to tackle almost any project in any environment? Successful debugging supports exploration and refines understanding. The more adept you are at finding bugs in a given environment, the more readily you can master that environment.

Debugging C Is Demanding

You can't rely on debugging techniques borrowed from other programming languages when you program in C. C programmers willingly discard the protection provided by other high-level languages. Too often, newcomers underestimate the impact of this change on the debugging environment. Novices assume that because both C and Pascal are small and well-structured languages, debugging C is similar to debugging Pascal. Nothing could be farther from the truth. Some of the special problems associated with debugging in C are detailed in Chapter 3, and the tools and techniques for dealing with C's special problems are discussed in later chapters.

Who Should Read This Book?

If you've spent hours looking for a bug in a C program only to give up without having gained a clear idea of the nature of the problem, this book is for you.

If you are a moderately experienced programmer recently introduced to C, and have written and debugged several programs of more than 500 lines in another programming language, you'll find the reading comfortable.

If you are a beginning programmer, the first few chapters will be applicable. Later chapters may be more difficult for you.

If you are an intermediate C programmer (almost mastered pointers), you should feel at ease with the material presented throughout the book.

If you are an experienced programmer, the discussion about methodology and commercial products will be particularly interesting. You may be surprised to find one or two new techniques as well.

To read this book, you must know the syntax and semantics of C or you must have access to a good teaching text. You need also a good C compiler or interpreter. Although I hesitate to recommend a beginning text, my students like Jack Purdum's *C Programming Guide* and Tom Plum's *Learning to Program in C*. Some parts of *Debugging C* will be easier to understand if you have the kind of appreciation for computer architecture that comes from attempting to write or modify a small assembly language program.

Throughout the book, I assume that you know how to read a user's manual. With that in mind, I have not rewritten existing manuals but rather, outlined how various pieces of the programming environment affect debugging efforts. With this understanding, you may be more selective about the sections of the manual you choose to read. You also may better appreciate the significance of what you read.

This book is about debugging only. Such singular focus shouldn't imply that debugging skills substitute for design and coding skills.

They don't. I purposely avoid discussing design, coding style and practice, advanced use of data structures, or any other aspect of the programming process because the subjects are covered satisfactorily in other books. This book is devoted expressly to an analysis of bugs and debugging methods, with a "how to" look at representative debugging tools.

Chapter Survey

Chapter 1 encourages the reader to approach debugging scientifically. Chapter 2 looks briefly at testing and develops bug-classification schemes to support later discussions. Chapters 3, 4, and 5 explain conventional bug-searching methods that work for virtually all modern compiled languages. Chapter 6 explains why C is difficult to debug. Chapter 6 also marks the conceptual boundary between the foundations and applications sections of the book. Chapters 7 and 8 adapt conventional debugging methods to the C environment. Chapters 9 and 10 discuss commercial debugging tools. The appendixes include a reading and resource list, source code for several prototype debugging accessories, and an sdb quick reference chart.

1
Foundations

Borrowing a phrase associated with guerilla warfare, the programming team's color-commentator might describe debugging as a "search and destroy mission." The description is appropriate in the sense that bugs can be elusive and difficult to recognize. Debugging begins with reconnaissance, the program-testing phase designed to expose errant behavior. When an error is recognized (the enemy is present), the search begins. After discovering that the program does a specific task incorrectly, the programmer's mission is to determine which part of the program is responsible for the error. Eventually, after narrowing the search to a single line or expression, the programmer exterminates the bug.

Describing debugging as a "search and destroy mission" is, however, deceiving in several ways. The programmer who searches for several hours, only to locate a misplaced semicolon, might find the mission's "destroy" element overstated. Furthermore, programmers seldom battle a designated enemy. Each unique species of bug requires a specialized search technique, and each must be handled individually. Neither hand grenades nor mortars can be used in debugging. The most obvious exaggeration lies in comparing successful debuggers to combat soldiers. Instead, good programmers more closely resemble laboratory technicians who are, through training and exercise, sensitive to the need for the disciplined and methodical searches that are essential for efficient debugging.

Debugging and Scientific Method

Many programmers consider themselves engineers and crafts-men. Both occupations are good models for the discipline and skill necessary to design and code useful programs. Using the engineer's deliberate, knowledgeable approach to design, the programmer creates carefully conceived and cost-effective programs. Drawing on the craftsman's practiced attention to detail, the programmer skillfully builds programs that are practical and durable.

Debugging is a different matter. The programmer creates nothing more than experiments during the debugging process. At this stage, a programmer resembles an FAA crash inspector. The programmer picks up the pieces, studies them to discover why the program crash occurred, and evaluates possible fixes and safeguards. When presented with a prototype that allegedly is worthy of production, the programmer tests and explores the program's behavior, actively seeking any tiny violation of the specifications or hint of instability.

During the design phase, the programmer (with clearly defined priorities) seeks to create an efficient, understandable program. During debugging, the programmer is confronted with a potentially enormous set of unknowns. The task is not one of creative synthesis but of testing and analysis. During the debugging process, the programmer collects information with no assurance that the data is significant to the task. The programmer first tries to find unspecified error behavior and then to discover its cause. The process of debugging demands that the programmer not only be an excellent observer and record keeper but also skilled at testing and experiment design, and knowledgeable about causal mechanisms.

It makes sense that laboratory experimentation based on scientific method is the model for debugging activities, if you consider that

- scientific method seeks to understand the unknown, to explain observable natural phenomena, and to expose cause-and-effect relationships through repeatable experiments

- bugs are an unknown (initially) natural phenomena whose cause we want to understand

The fit between scientific method and debugging is as compelling as the fit between engineering and software design. Recently, software design has benefited significantly from the engineering model. Debugging should benefit comparably from a deliberate effort to adapt the scientific-method model.

Relating debugging to scientific experimentation doesn't change the steps that a good programmer follows while debugging a program, but places new emphasis on certain practices.

First, the programmer must function as a detached observer rather than as passionate creator. Once drafted, the code should be prodded, examined, and understood. ("We wrote the program, but because the code is seldom what we meant it to be, now we must discover what it really is.") This dispassionate attitude, or selective forgetting, is crucial to success.

Second, the programmer must keep extensive, detailed records. The machine can be employed easily as a secretary, but the record-keeping task must be carried out conscientiously.

Third, debugging and design are different tasks and require different ways of thinking. Flipping a mental switch and visualizing a lab coat rather than a craftsman's apron might help.

The Debugging Process

Debugging involves four phases: testing, stabilization, localization, and correction. The distinction between these phases may not always be clear. For instance, in most high-level languages stabilizing a bug is usually a trivial step. In C, however, one almost always needs to focus separate and deliberate attention on each phase. Although each phase is distinct from the others, one is not necessarily completed before the next begins. Usually, debugging is a cyclic, opportunistic activity. Debugging is cyclic because all four phases are repeated for each bug. Debugging is opportunistic because a new bug, or information pertinent to a secondary bug, is frequently discovered when searching for a principal bug. Although the delineation of phases is technically valid and intellectually useful, the separation of phases is seldom as clearly drawn in a working environment.

Phase One: Testing

Testing exercises the capabilities of a new program by stimulating it with a wide range of input values. The testing phase has two objectives:

1. To discover the limitations of a new program

2. To verify that a design meets specifications

The process is analogous to flight-testing a new airplane. Although the primary objective is to verify that the plane meets specifications, the test pilot usually tries also to discover the actual limits of performance. In other words, by seeking out the program's "breaking points," testing serves to verify that a program does what it is supposed to do.

To produce sound results testing must be comprehensive, exercising a program's every capability under a variety of conditions. For reliable results, testing should be conducted in a carefully controlled environment. In languages other than C, controlling the environment simply means controlling input to the program. Controlling the environment in C may require extreme measures. All test results must be recorded and carefully compared with program expectations. Any deviation from the expected results is a potential bug that merits further investigation.

Phase Two: Stabilization

Stabilization is an attempt to control conditions so well that a specific bug can be generated at will, even after special instrumentation has been added to the program. In this instance, *instrumentation* refers to program statements that report only information about program execution, not information contributing to the completion of the program's main task.

Instrumentation, commonly referred to as "trace" or "debugging" statements, consists of print statements that generate a trace, or record, of what happened during program execution. Trace statements are generally removed immediately after debugging. In high-level languages other than C, bugs that can be replicated without instrumentation can always be replicated with instrumentation. Not so in C. Any change in the source code or the linking process can significantly alter a bug's behavior—even make the bug disappear.

The principal problems programmers encounter during stabilization are tightening control on testing conditions and refining test design. The techniques used in stabilization are similar to those used to control the testing environment. One might, therefore, define stabilization as refined testing. However, testing and stabilization differ significantly. During the testing phase, the programmer (like the hunter stalking elusive prey) has no specific target. During the stabilization phase, the quarry has been discovered. Now, sights must be calibrated before taking aim to fire.

With modern ammunition, most of us wouldn't go stalking until we had calibrated our sights. With older, slower moving loads, the hunter made adjustments for "windage" factors before every shot. Because C often seems to require such "manual adjustments," many critics label it old-fashioned or primitive.

In this case, however, it is typical debugging techniques that may be more deserving of the labels old-fashioned and primitive. With slight extensions, the debugging techniques presented here are general enough to be the basis for a comprehensive approach to debugging. Manual adjustments become unnecessary. In other words, if debugging enjoyed the same respect as design and coding enjoy, stabilization (even in C) could be absorbed into testing.

Phase Three: Localization

Only after a bug has been identified, instrumented, and made repeatable can the search for its cause begin. The search advances by narrowing the range of possibilities and by localizing the bug to a specific segment of code or variable in the data.

The localization phase is characterized by intensive data collection and analysis. Like the scientist, the programmer studies the data, constructs a hypothesis about how such data might be created, and modifies the experiment to test hypothesis validity. Sometimes, because the modified experiment doesn't produce reliable data, the programmer must return to the stabilization phase. Each properly designed experiment contributes information that further restricts the range of possible causes for the bug.

Finding the bug (identifying the responsible line of code or variable) is a side effect of the primary objective of this phase of the process. The primary objective is to construct and validate a hypothesis that explains all observed bug symptoms.

To the scientific programmer, corrections that are not based on a thorough understanding of the failure mechanism ("how could that error have generated this output?") will be unsatisfying. Realistically, such haphazard "fixes" aren't corrections; they are guesses waiting to sabotage all earlier work.

Generally, localization is a monotonic process that, when correctly practiced, leads the programmer ever closer to a solution. The process, however, is not monotonic in one variable only. As explained in a later section on the principles of proximity, localization relies on three basically independent types of proximity or nearness. To interpret correctly the clues produced by testing and to construct useful experiments, the programmer needs to have a clear understanding of each kind of nearness.

Phase Four: Correction

After a bug is located, it must be corrected. Usually, the correction is trivial. If the bug reflects an error in design, however, the correction can be costly. But whether the correction is a trivial one or one created through faulty design, it is not within the scope of this book to discuss error correction techniques.

Verifying a correction is important. Every test that produces output suggesting a connection to the corrected bug should be repeated. Additionally, to verify that a correction has not unsettled anything, the careful programmer should rerun a representative selection of all bug-free tests.

Principles of Proximity

Every field draws on fundamental principles. In the field of electronics, it's Ohm's law. In physics it is the laws of conservation of mass and energy. The process of debugging relies also on fundamental principles and properties. The primary, but least helpful, principle is that of causality. Programmers must believe that for every effect there is a cause. Else, why bother? A bug would be a spontaneous irregularity.

A more practical, restricted form of this principle is that of proximity or nearness. Every effect is, by some measure, proximate (near) its cause. Programs exhibit three types of proximity: lexical, temporal, and referential. Thus the first principle of debugging is:

Every effect is near its cause either lexically, temporally, or referentially.

When searching for a bug, we rely on these notions of proximity to guide us, to help us know when we are "getting warm."

Lexical Proximity

Two pieces of code are lexically adjacent if they appear next to each other in the program listing.

Lexical, in this case, means *the way it is written*. Lexical proximity is the physical nearness of one line to another in the printed source listing. Programmers rely on lexical proximity to localize *compile-time* errors (errors that the compiler discovers during compilation). Programmers must rely on lexical proximity when tracking compile-time errors because referential and temporal proximity exist only in a running program. Compilers help by supplying a line number in their error messages.

```
1:      main()
2:
3:      {
4:      int i;
5:
6:      for ( i = 0; i < 5; i++ )
7:          printf( "\nHello World" )
8:      printf( "\nGoodbye World\n" );
9:      }


******* Fatal Error in line 8. Expecting ';'  ********
```

Listing 1.1. A compile-time error.

Because the error message names line 8, the programmer expects to find the mistake in line 7 or 8. This expectation is reasonable in many cases, including this example. Remember, however, that the line named by the compiler is guaranteed only to be the last line capable of generating the mistake. The real error may lurk anywhere between the first line and the named line. In extreme cases, the compiler's message may say

```
******* fatal error: at or before line 742 ******
```

in a program of only 742 lines. All this message tells you is that there's a syntax error somewhere between the first and last lines of the program. Chapter 3 discusses several general methods for forcing the compiler to provide more useful information.

Temporal Proximity

Two pieces of code are temporally adjacent if one executes immediately after the other.

Temporal (related to time) proximity is a *run-time* characteristic. That is, temporal proximity can be observed only while the program is actually executing. During sequential segments of code, lexical and execution (temporal) ordering are identical; but when a control primitive (such as a branch, loop, or function call) is executed, the program's statement execution order will differ from the lexical order.

```
1:        main()
2:
3:        {

            .
            .
            .
40:     while ( k < 7 ){
41:         dotest();

            .
            .
            .
234:        proc1();
235:    }
236: }
```

Listing 1.2. Example of temporal proximity.

In this example, lines 41 and 234 are lexically remote. However, whenever line 234 is reached with k less than 7, lines 234 and 40 become temporally adjacent. In other words, line 41 follows line 234 at run-time because of the influence of the while control structure.

Listing 1.2 illustrates an important difference between lexical and temporal proximity. Lexical proximity is static and determined when the program is created. Temporal proximity is dynamic and determined by run-time conditions. If k was 6 in line 40, but was greater than 7 by line 234, the loop wouldn't be repeated and do-test() and proc1() would remain temporally remote from each other. All conventional trace methods are useful because they expose either temporal or referential proximity.

Referential Proximity

Two pieces of code are *referentially adjacent* to a specific variable (which both reference) if no other references to that variable occur between their references to it.

Programmers respond to the principle of referential proximity when they suspect a line of code because "it was the last operation to change this variable" (a variable that now has a wrong value).

In listing 1.3, lines 5 and 13 are lexically and temporally remote but referentially adjacent. They are the two closest lines (in execution time) that reference the variable i.

```
1:    main()
2:    {
3:    int i, j, k;
4:
5:    i = 0;
6:    for ( j = 0; j < 19; j++ ) {
7:       for (k = 0; k < j; k++ ) {
8:          putchar( " " );
9:          }
10:      printf( "*\n" );
12:      }
13:   printf( "%d\n", i );
14:   }
```

Listing 1.3. Lines 5 and 13 are referentially adjacent.

On single-user machines specific pointer bugs appear to violate the property of lexical proximity. Under certain circumstances, lines of code can change a variable that they don't appear to reference, at least not at the source-code level. When this happens, the principle of referential proximity is effectively removed from the list of "fundamental debugging support properties," causing many conventional debugging methods to become unreliable and unproductive. Later chapters describe the causal mechanism for this behavior and offer debugging tools and trace techniques used in place of the conventional methods.

Debugging Tools and Techniques

The knowledgeable programmer can select tools from a variety of hardware and software aids and trace techniques—tools ranging from the clumsy to the sublime. Even the lowly trace statement, in fact a primary tool, has many variations. Trace statements can be designed to trace temporal or referential relationships, to preserve or disrupt code structure, or to monitor virtual or physical resources.

Virtual resources are those that the machine appears to have when working in a particular programming language. Physical resources are real, tangible devices and structures.

For instance, on an 8086/8087-based system *without* the math coprocessor, floating point arithmetic is a virtual resource. On an 8086/8088-based system *with* the math coprocessor, floating point arithmetic is a physical resource. In both instances, C's apparent capability to evaluate functions is a virtual resource.

Many integrated debugging tools can be used as replacements for the trace statement. Machine-level breakpoint debuggers allow execution to be traced at the machine level in terms of machine (physical) resources without changes in the code block. Similarly, source-level debuggers allow programs to be traced at the virtual machine level in terms of logical (virtual) resources without adding trace statements to the program. Good breakpoint debuggers permit traces to be initiated and varied dynamically. Interpreters simplify the test and localization phases of debugging by offering trace capabilities at the source code level while automatically monitoring logical facilities usage.

Not all software tools for debugging are related to tracing. Cross-reference programs "index" the code to help locate references to specific variables or functions. Other programs supplement the syntax checks performed by the compiler. Examples of syntax checker programs range from the simple curly-brace checker to sophisticated syntax analyzers (like the UNIX®-based utility lint) that identify nontypical or potentially hazardous, but legal, usages.

All hardware debuggers assist in trace-related functions. Logic analyzers don't really analyze logic but instead capture machine-level activities—usually data and code as it transfers across the memory bus. Emulators perform similar captures but allow greater control over the test conditions.

RETURN

Debugging doesn't have to be a risky ad hoc process. Because debugging has an identifiable structure based on explicable principles and properties, the debugging process deserves to be categorized as a science, not as an art or a mystery.

In this chapter, we have outlined the structure of the debugging process, and we have formalized the guiding principles of the debugging process. Building on this foundation of principles and properties, the remaining chapters of the book explain how debugging practices fit into the process and relate to the properties of proximity. Specifically, the foundation we have built will serve as a guide for remodeling debugging techniques to fit the special world of C.

2
Program Testing

All testing involves an analysis of the program based on existing rules, tests, gauges, and standards. Some of the programmer's yardsticks, the syntax rules of a language for instance, are enforced by an external source (the compiler). Other measures, such as the conventions governing how functions use a program variable, must be supplied by the programmer. Prior to testing (usually during the design phase), either the designer or the programmer develops program parameters, as well as expectations about how the program should work. Although beginning programmers don't always appreciate the importance of specifying program expectations, experienced programmers know that clearly stated expectations are critical for efficient and effective testing.

Recognizing Bugs

In *Karel the Robot*, Richard Pattis claims that bugs come in four flavors: lexical, syntactic, execution, and intent. The guidelines (yardsticks) that these bugs violate are the alphabet, syntax, and semantics of the language, as well as the intent of the designer. As Pattis' words suggest, the yardsticks we measure our programs against so strongly influence what we see and learn when testing, that those yardsticks, quite naturally, become the hidden basis for bug-classification schemes.

Lexical Errors

Lexical errors are compile-time errors that occur when a programmer uses symbols that are not legally part of a language. The equivalent mistake in English is using a nonexistent or misspelled word. Testing is simpler for this class of errors than for any other. The test applies a single rule (or lookup table) to each symbol in the program. Symbols that cause lexical errors always cause an error, no matter where they appear. In C, *#12joe* is always an illegal symbol (strings in comments don't count here) because there is no preprocessor directive named *12joe*.

If this error seems contrived, it's because constructing a lexical error in C is difficult. C offers programmers a great deal of freedom with symbols. C also obligingly applies reasonable interpretations to superficially faulty symbols. Other languages are more rigid. Early dialects of BASIC, for instance, allow only reserved words, constants, and two-character variable names for easy-to-identify lexical units and symbols.

If the compiler issues the error message `Illegal symbol` without identifying what was expected, it can be a subtle clue that a lexical error has been discovered. To find a lexical error, look only at the spot named in the error message. Focus carefully on the legality of the individual symbol.

To recognize lexical errors, the programmer must know all the language's reserved words (or have a table handy). The programmer must have also a clear description of the rules for constructing variable names, function names, preprocessor symbols, statement labels, and various constants (character, string, and numeric). To understand a specific error, you must know which rule it violates.

Syntactic Errors

Syntactic errors occur when legal symbols are combined in illegal ways. The English-language equivalent of a syntactic error is a mistake in grammar, such as "he don't got no shoes."

Each word exists and is spelled correctly, but combining these words in this order isn't "legal." Syntactic errors are the most common C compile-time errors. They usually produce an error message of the form:

```
Illegal symbol <until> in line 23, expecting while.
```

or

```
Expecting while in line 23, encountered until.
```

Such an error message might be generated by my favorite mistake:

```
do {
   .
   .
   .
} until ( .... );
```

(I teach a lot of Pascal.)

The language's syntax rules are used to guide the programmer in identifying this kind of error. If a syntactic error is suspected, use a concise syntax specification and be prepared to apply it again and again until the deviation is located. Keep in mind that, although a programmer may be able to point to the last spot where the error might be, he or she won't know exactly where the error is until appropriate testing measures are applied.

Understanding syntax as a compiler understands syntax is helpful. Programmers generally cannot understand compiler error messages until they understand language design and compiler mechanics and design. Learning to read BNF or an equivalent notation will provide some insight. (BNF, or Backus-Naur Form, is a formal notation for describing syntax.) Learning how the lexical scanner of a modern compiler classifies program symbols into token types will increase also the programmer's level of understanding.

The "railroad track" drawings presented in Pascal books are a nice intuitive representation for syntax specification. They represent the parsing process in a natural way. And there are several good compiler textbooks and a series of nice articles ("The Mechanic's Guide to Grammar") in *Computer Language* as well. (See Appendix A at the end of this book.)

Execution Errors

Execution errors occur when the programmer requests, in perfectly acceptable grammar, something impossible or illogical. In a compiled environment, execution errors cause a running program to abort. In conventional languages, execution errors are detected by run-time type checks, bound checks, and by hardware fault detection mechanisms. The following fragment of Pascal, for example, would abort in line 7 because the reference to arry[19] is impossible. arry has only 10 elements.

```
1: VAR
2:   k: INTEGER;
3:   arry: ARRAY [1..10] OF INTEGER;
4:
5: BEGIN
6:   k:=19;
7:   arry[k] := 7;
8:   .
9:   .
```

This example is presented in Pascal because it cannot be constructed in C. The C equivalent would, quite possibly, run to completion with no indication of error, other than incorrect output. In C, arry[19] isn't always nonsense, and even when it is nonsense, there is no run-time range check or bound checking to flag it as unreasonable. However, the memory-protection hardware of multiuser systems will frequently (but not always) detect this type of error and generate an error message.

```
***** memory fault: program aborted *******
```

Sophisticated machines often provide hardware detection for certain arithmetic errors. Systems that have hardware divide, for example, will detect

```
 8:   k = 0;
 9:   j = 22;
10:   m = j/k;
```

as a divide-by-zero error.

In conventional languages, execution errors are fairly easy to locate. The program almost always aborts at a spot that is lexically, temporally, or referentially near the error. In C, because of the lack of run-time range checking, a program can run for several thousand lines before the error becomes serious enough to be detected by a hardware mechanism. In many cases, the program will run to normal termination. The important binding of program abort to error has been lost.

To recognize an error in conventional languages, a programmer need only be familiar with the high-level semantics of the language (the effect of operations). In other words, the testing yardstick that exposes execution errors is a given language's semantics. To recognize the cause of an error in C (even after the error has been located), the C programmer frequently needs to understand high-level and machine-language semantics as well as the subtle interaction between the language and the operating system.

Such semantic differences create the most serious problems for the programmer debugging C. At the very least, the C programmer is forced to use more disciplined techniques to search for errors. Chapters 7 and 8 present applicable "home brew" techniques, and commercial products are discussed in Chapters 9 and 10.

Intent Errors

In a conventional language, an intent error occurs whenever a program runs to normal termination but produces incorrect results. Intent errors often are referred to as "logic errors."

The testing yardstick for intent errors is the original program specification. Intent errors can be errors in design and errors in design implementation.

If a programmer designs and codes a program providing for five types of input only to discover, during testing, that there are sometimes seven types of input, he or she has designed a program containing an error. Unlike all other kinds of errors, design errors can be extremely painful to correct—especially in large programs. Programmers try to avoid intent (program design) errors by implementing methodical design strategies.

This book focuses on debugging correct designs. The assumption is that the reader is skilled enough in design to avoid serious design problems or to recognize design errors if they do exist. For those who haven't been exposed to formal design methodologies, several sources are listed in Appendix A.

An error in design implementation occurs when programmers fail to write what they intended to write. This routine to compute *n!* is an example:

```
1:      int fact(n)
2:      int n;
3:
4:      {
5:      int i, temp;
6:
7:      temp = 1;
8:      for (i#=#0; i <= n; i++)
        temp = temp * i;
9:      return temp;
10:     }
```

This code always runs to completion (unless there is hardware detect of multiply overflow), and it always returns zero. The design is correct, but because the programmer really meant to write *for (i#=#1;...)*, the implementation is incorrect.

Remember that C blurs the boundary between execution and intent errors. Many execution errors are invisible except for their indirect impact on program output. Programmers can be misdirected easily by execution bugs. Before assuming that incorrect output is the result of a "logic error," the possibility of an obscure execution error should be eliminated.

There are yardsticks that can be applied to intent errors. First, the programmer must have a clear idea of what correct output is. Second, the programmer must have a specific idea of what correct operation is.

It may be helpful to think of intent yardsticks as questions about "internal output." What values should the variables assume as a correct implementation of the design executes? What portions of the program should be executed with defined input? Without specific expectations about the program's "internal" behavior, it is possible to focus directly on the source of the problem, and not recognize the source of an error.

Other Yardsticks

The bug-classification scheme presented in the preceding section is designed with an eye to the kinds of tests used to recognize errors. The classification scheme begins with the bug easiest to automate and moves to the bug most difficult to automate.

For instance, the programmer without access to a compiler might choose a simple table-lookup program to test for lexical errors. Automating the test for syntactic errors requires, at least, the parser from a compiler that leaves out the code generation routines.

Execution errors require a code generator sophisticated enough to carry out run-time checking, and hardware testing. Tests that uncover intent errors are extremely difficult if not impossible to construct. They are the subject of an area of advanced research known as "verifiability."

Alternatively, one could classify bugs by how difficult they are to localize. The following arrangements are based on this notion of apparent "bug mobility."

Some Bugs Stand Still

Generally, bugs that "stand still" and are independent of everything around them such as lexical errors, are easy to localize. The procedure that tests for them locates them. As the bug's symptoms become more dependent on its environment, the bug appears to "move around" or to "change clothes." The error becomes more difficult to locate.

Lexical and syntactic bugs always stand still, but so can all other kinds. In fact, all the examples in the discussion of syntactic, execution, and intent errors are of bugs that stand still. These bugs exhibit the same symptoms, no matter what happens in their environment. A bug that stands still will exhibit a symptom regardless of

- any input the program receives
- the invocation sequence used to start the program
- trace statements or debugging support added to the program

Some Bugs Are Input Dependent

Some bugs exhibit symptoms that change when input changes.

"Input bugs" are difficult to identify and localize unless the input that caused them can be identified and replicated. Ordinarily, it is not difficult to re-create the input in file processing applications.

For most applications, conventional trace and other source level techniques are quite effective. In real-time applications, identifying the input is not just difficult; without adequate hardware, it's virtually impossible.

Some Bugs Are Code Sensitive

Some bugs exhibit symptoms that change whenever the code changes.

A classic example is the bug that causes a program to crash, but disappears completely when a trace statement is added. When the trace statement is removed, the bug reappears. Programmers who come to C from conventional high-level languages, and C programmers who have always worked on memory-protected multiuser systems, are thoroughly unprepared for these creatures.

Some Bugs Are
Environment Sensitive

Some bugs exhibit symptoms that seem to change randomly.

In fact, the symptoms change in response to subtle changes in the hardware environment. Consider the program that runs perfectly one time following each compilation but, until it is recompiled, blows up on all subsequent executions.

The programmer whose experience is limited to BASIC or Pascal will be unprepared for these intriguing errors. Assembly language programmers probably are familiar with similar problems. "Random" bugs are largely a by-product of uninitialized variables. In a single-user environment, they can be "stabilized," usually by initializing memory. On multiuser systems, they may be extremely difficult to manage because the user's direct control over hardware resources is severely constrained.

Before Attempting To Localize, Stabilize

This classification scheme highlights an often overlooked step in the debugging process: stabilizing the bug to be localized. In conventional programming environments, stabilizing the bug requires only that identical input be used on each test. The step is trivial and not particularly visible.

In C, stabilization sometimes requires major effort if conditions are to be controlled well enough to stimulate a bug at will. Each successive entry in the classification scheme demands that the programmer control a progressively larger set of environmental variables.

Although BASIC and Pascal programmers need to control only program input before taking aim at a bug, C and assembly language programmers must, occasionally, control the entire hardware environment. Debugging a C program is not just different from debugging an equivalent Pascal or BASIC program; it is intrinsically more difficult. More variables are involved.

Testing Strategies

"You certainly can't find a bug and correct it if you are unaware that it even exists."

An effective and efficient approach to program testing underlies all successful debugging efforts. Structured testing methods support test control by encouraging the programmer to work step by step through the program. Good testing methodology also encourages a programmer to test programs in manageable segments. Generally, testing in controllable increments produces a more thorough test of each segment.

Short of no test at all, the worst testing method the progammer can adopt (at least for projects of more than 200 lines) is to write a program, type it in, and sit back to see what goes wrong. Using this strategy to test a large project (3,000 lines of C on a personal computer, for instance) will probably produce a program with many "undiscovered" errors. Or, it will force the programmer to give up because some bug or complex of bugs defies correction.

The key to dealing with large programs is to limit the number of variables that must be controlled. Testing and debugging only a few modules at a time limits variables. By testing each module thoroughly, the programmer gains confidence in the reliability of the modules tested earlier. This approach limits the number of variables that will demand attention in later tests.

How Testing Works

Generally, good testing practices are based on one of three basic test strategies: top-down, bottom-up, or critical-path.

The partial structure chart shown in figure 2.1 describes a "generic" file processing application. During processing, two large data structures are used: a two-dimensional table and a linked list (to manage dynamic storage, perhaps).

The modules setup(), buildtable(), and linklist() are responsible for initializing these structures. Modules doinput(), readrec(), and storerec() read records from a file and reorganize those records into the table (perhaps sorting or condensing them). Function doinput() returns a count of the number of records read to main() so that modules executed later will know how much of the table to process. Function process() works through the loaded table, calculating an adjustment to each row. Then process() totals a column out of the table, which creates a new summary line at the end of the table. Finally, dooutput() writes a new file from each of the table's updated rows and writes the summary line to a separate summary file.

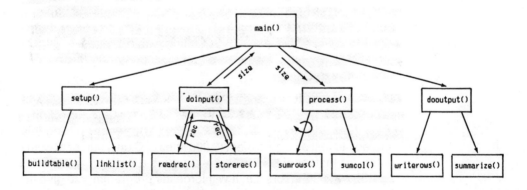

Fig. 2.1. Structure chart for sample file-processing application.

Top-Down Testing

The top-down strategy first tests top-level control modules, sub-
stituting *stub modules* (empty or nearly empty functions that serve
as "place holders") for each untested lower-level module. Figures
2.2 through 2.7 illustrate how top-down testing might progress in
the sample application.

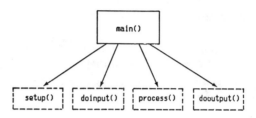

Fig. 2.2. Top-down approach: first test configuration.

The modules in dotted boxes represent stubs. Stubs do not have
to be complex. If we assume, in figure 2.2, that setup() receives a
file name as input, that process() receives only size as an input,
and that none of the other modules have inputs, the stubs might
look like this:

```
void setup(fname)
char *fname;

{
fprintf(stderr, "setup called with /%s/ as fname\n", fname);
}

int doinput()
{
fprintf(stderr, "doinput called\n");
return 9;
}

void process(size)
int size;
```

```
{
fprintf(stderr,"process called with %d for size\n",size);
}

void dooutput()
{
fprintf(stderr,"dooutput called\n");
}
```

Stubs for modules with a return value, like that for doinput(), (see fig. 2.3) should return a value known to be "good" (one that will generate correct behavior in all modules called later). Every stub should echo all its input values and announce its invocation. Finally, sending all test output to a channel other than standard output is helpful, especially when working on an interactive, display-oriented application.

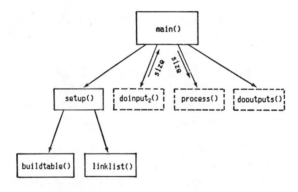

Fig. 2.3. Top-down approach: second test configuration.

Although the purist might insist that only one module should be added during each new testing phase, using a "complexity test" is perfectly reasonable. Testing a few simple, related, easily managed modules (such as setup(), buildtable(), and linklist(), shown in fig. 2.3) all at once is reasonable also. The goal is

- to keep the testing process manageable
- to restrict the number of variables
- to test each module exhaustively

Whenever a module is added, ask, "Am I keeping the change in complexity between this test and the last test small enough to guarantee a manageable test?"

Figure 2.3 illustrates a heuristic for top-down program expansion.

- Test output modules before input modules when the input is simple and the input-output path spans only one or two levels in the hierarchy (readrec(), doinput() to storerec(), in this case).

The tested output modules are available to be used as tools during the test of the input modules. If the input-output path spans several levels of the hierarchy, develop input modules before output modules using a mixed strategy (explained later).

In figure 2.4, doinput() and storerec() have been added as a pair because they are relatively simple. Because function storerec() needs input to process, the readrec() stub must return fake records. Depending on the needs of storerec() testing, readrec() could act in one of several ways. It might

- return the same record whenever called

- return the same record 99 times and then return an end-of-file marker

- use an internal counter to return slightly different records each time

- read records from a simply structured file

- prompt for input from the keyboard

In this example, the fourth method is roughly equivalent to writing readrec(). In other applications, such as lexical scanners for a compiler, the fourth method might be a feasible simplification.

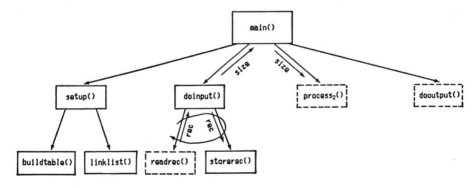

Fig. 2.4. Top-down approach: third test configuration.

In figure 2.4, the stub for process() is subscripted to indicate that it is different from the stub used in figure 2.3. In figure 2.3, a table had not been created when the process() stub was invoked. In figures 2.4 and 2.5, however, a table already exists when process() is reached. The process() stub becomes a convenient home for code that dumps the contents of the table, verifying that all the earlier modules have completed their work correctly.

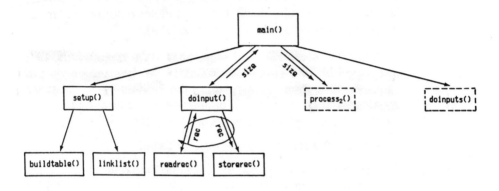

Fig. 2.5. Top-down approach: fourth test configuration.

In figure 2.6, two modules are added at once. process() and dooutputs() are control modules that don't directly change any values in the table. Because they are independent of each other (until sumrows() is installed), process() and dooutputs() can be tested in parallel.

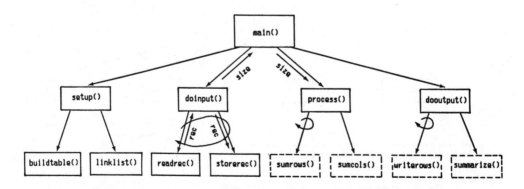

Fig. 2.6. Top-down approach: fifth test configuration.

In figure 2.7, the table modifying modules has been added. The
writerows() stub has been replaced with a version that dumps
the modified table. (This version is similar to the one used for
process() in fig. 2.4.)

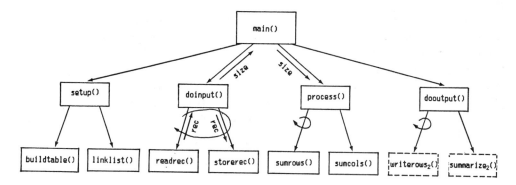

Fig. 2.7. Top-down approach: sixth test configuration.

Bottom-Up Testing

Bottom-up strategies test bottom-level modules first. Short main
functions, called *drivers*, are written to exercise each low-level
module. The tested modules are gathered into progressively more
complete subsystems. Figures 2.8 through 2.11 illustrate a reasonable bottom-up testing sequence for the application shown in figure 2.1.

Again, a purist might insist that only one new module should be
added at each testing phase. Figure 2.8 tests all the modules to
initialize data structures. These modules, if tested first, can be used
by drivers in later tests.

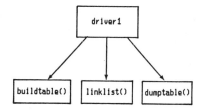

Fig. 2.8. Bottom-up approach: early test configuration.

Notice the test function `dumptable()`. This function copies the entire data structure to a printer or file, in an easily generated form, thereby minimizing the need to debug the debugging support. If the function is tested early, it is available to support later module testing and simplifies the difficulty of writing drivers for those tests.

In figure 2.9, a common driver is used to test modules collected from different parts of the program. These modules are tested jointly because they manipulate similar data structures. In fact, they would probably be tested individually using trivially modified versions of the same driver. In this case, the number of separate drivers needed may be reduced by repeatedly expanding the driver to call additional modules. Figure 2.9 could represent the final test in a series of "subtests."

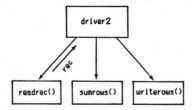

Fig. 2.9. Bottom-up approach: early test configuration.

Figure 2.10 tests functions `setup()`, and `storerec()` and a new driver in the presence of several previously tested functions. In the example, a "working set" of low-level modules is being selected. That set, which includes one or two untested modules, minimizes the driver's complexity. The set also completes data structures of low-level tasks requisite to their operation and simplifies later testing of other modules.

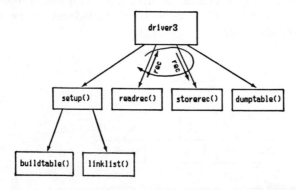

Fig. 2.10. Bottom-up approach: intermediate test configuration.

In figure 2.11, three untested modules and the driver are added. If this much code cannot be added in a single step, the same configuration can be achieved after a sequence of two or three trivial expansions of driver 4. Note the repeated use of dumptable() in this design. The driver is, in effect, conducting two relatively independent tests: doinput() and process().

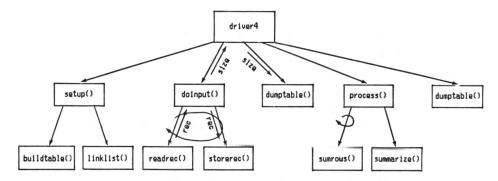

Fig. 2.11. Bottom-up approach: late test configuration.

Notice that the drivers in figures 2.10 and 2.11 bear a strong resemblance to the modules doinput() and main(). These drivers can be generated by modifying the code for doinput() and main(). Alternatively, the program can be coded incrementally. Code is developed by writing drivers and, when they are no longer needed for testing, converted to the next level of untested functions.

To support exhaustive testing with many different input values, drivers are usually structured as endless loops. Each pass through the loop invokes the module under test with a different value. These values may be generated

- from the loop counter
- by reading from an input file
- by reading from standard keyboard input

A Mixed Strategy

Top-down and bottom-up strategies can be used effectively on small projects. Neither testing strategy in its pure form is altogether adequate for large projects.

With bottom-up testing, it's likely that subtle communications problems between major subsystems won't be discovered until almost all the modules have been coded and tested. If the mismatch requires recoding specific low-level modules, major portions of the coding and testing effort must be repeated. Furthermore, drivers capable of generating realistic data for complex output-oriented subsystems are frequently complex enough to constitute a serious testing problem.

Top-down testing avoids these problems, but requires complex stubs if they must return realistic input values to support the testing of superordinate modules.

The best test strategy (especially for larger programs) is a compromise that tests modules incrementally, working in top-down fashion, except in one or two critical input-oriented parts of the program hierarchy.

This mixed strategy approach minimizes the opportunity for nasty, last-minute surprises. And because this approach completes critical input paths early in the testing process, the paths can be used to provide realistic input when other parts of the program are tested.

In many respects the most important issue (especially for single-person projects) isn't whether testing proceeds top-down and bottom-up, or bottom-up and top-down. What is more significant is that the testing proceeds in carefully controlled increments.

The object of testing is to disclose bugs, hopefully one or two at a time. Bugs discovered singly are the easiest to recognize, stabilize, and locate. While locating and correcting a bug, the careful programmer will consider the test that first disclosed the error. If any given test discloses more than one or two bugs, an examination of the code added during testing is warranted. A good programmer will study the size and complexity of the block, perhaps noting that the entire increment is too large to test.

Selecting Test Data

It is good practice in each test increment to divide the test activities into

- testing the most important "normal" behavior of a module or partial system

- testing special cases or less frequently used portions of the system.

Using normal, "middle-of-the-road" data, test the major paths to verify that the basic design is correct. If names with a maximum of 20 characters are being tested, use a 9- or 10-character name for the initial test. If the system is supposed to sort names, use names with different initial characters for the first test of the sort algorithm.

With these "usual" cases under control, begin more stressful tests using *exceptional* values and *boundary* values in the test data. Exceptional values are values that are never expected in normal operation, but should not cause the module under test to crash. ZZZZZZZZZZZZZZZZZZZZ and ZZZZZZZZZZZZZZZZZZZY are exceptional values if you are sorting 20-character names. Although no one actually has these names, the sort program should handle them correctly.

It is reasonable to expect to encounter boundary values from time to time. Boundary values are special because they can trigger a program-control structure, exceed the bounds of a data structure, or generate an arithmetic fault.

To determine the first class of boundary values, examine the control structures in the modules under test. In loops, values that cause the loop to execute zero times and one time are boundary values. Values that cause a loop to exit abnormally through a return, break, or goto are also boundary values. In branch and case statements, boundary values are those that "just separate" two cases.

In the following listing, 1 and 2 (which cause the while loop to execute zero and one time, respectively) are boundary values. 7, which causes an exit from the function, is a boundary value also. Because they are near the critical control value, 7, 6, and 8 also may be considered boundary values.

```
while (k > 1){
   switch (k){
      case 7: return ERROR;
      case 2:
      case 3:
      case 4:
      case 5:
      case 6: k -= 1;
              break;
      default: k = 6;
               break;
   }
}
```

Values that can trigger arithmetic errors are also boundary values. Zero, 1, -1, and large positive and negative numbers make good test data. Including odd, even, and prime numbers in the test data is a good idea.

If modular arithmetic is involved, numbers near the modulus become important. For example, use 7, 8, and 9 in test data for mod 8 arithmetic. When using bit wise operators, powers of two are important boundary values. In floating-point arithmetic, values with large positive and negative exponents (values near the precision limits of the representation) make stressful test data.

Many boundary values are related to data structures. In a module that manipulates lists, for example, the boundary values are the empty list, a list with only one item, and a large list. If the list's size bound is small (20 elements, perhaps), lists of 19 and 20 become boundary values.

Once the module works correctly with all relevant boundary values, consider testing it with exceptional or *abusive* values (data values that shouldn't be encountered). Test with abusive values because:

- the module must handle input from an end user

- module design should be "bullet proof." It should behave reasonably, regardless of what the system it is attached to does

- it is wise to preview the possible symptoms that the module may exhibit if it is called incorrectly

Every module that handles user input should be bullet proof, even if no one other than the programmer is expected to use the program. Anyone can lean against the keyboard at the wrong time!

Functions that will be part of a general-purpose library should be bullet proof unless, for efficiency's sake, input checks must be sacrificed. Library modules tend to be, and should be, taken for granted. A major advantage is lost if it's necessary to test a library module whenever it's used in a progam. Unfortunately, unless a library module "puts us on notice" when it receives invalid input, there's little choice but to include it in the testing.

If the next increment to be tested is a complex piece of code that promises to generate several subtle bugs, deliberately feed exceptional data to that code's subordinate modules as they are tested. The results of the subordinate module testing may suggest which interface to study if similar symptoms crop up when testing the complex module.

Keeping Adequate Records

The programmer should keep a detailed lab notebook just as conscientious laboratory scientists maintain thorough records of their work. A useful notebook will describe each code change and test run and will record all observations in a sequential time-stamped framework such as that shown in this example:

VER/TIME	TEST	RESULT
10/24/87		
10:00	Reversed pointer references	Traverses Links correctly, but
1:04	in getnode function	prints garbage from head node.
	tested with *a* and *b* data.	Something funny is happening
	Data sets *a* and *b*.	also in the sorting routine. Typo "zAndroid" was placed before "Android".
10:15	Adding more detailed trace	Nothing on *a* test, but
1:05	of list during getnode	*b* test shows head pointer changed value unexpectedly.

VER/TIME	TEST	RESULT
10:25	Repeating test of list initialization routine with maximum detail enabled.	Verified list is initialized correctly.
10:40	Not satisfied test data is adequate. Added two more items at positions three and four in set B. Again test with maximum detail.	No visible change.
10/25/87		
8:40	Added list dump functions to append function.	Second and third values in B data set are being added to wrong spot in list.
1:06		

The notebook helps the programmer track *all* bug symptoms, not just those associated with the immediate problem. The run-time stamps give the programmer objective feedback about his or her progress. Sometimes, reading the most recent entries helps one "get back into it" after a weekend or even after a coffee break.

A detailed record of all experiments can be essential if the programmer needs to replicate certain environmentally sensitive bugs. Being obligated to write something in the observations column will compel the programmer to take a least a few seconds to evaluate each set of test results. After the project is finished, reviewing the lab notebook will often help a programmer spot fundamental errors of method and provide some objective measure of error cost. The evaluation and feedback exercise is a valuable resource for the programmer interested in self-improvement.

Although a good notebook can be kept manually, it seems natural to automate the process. When test runs and new compilations are invoked from a batch file, that batch file can be expanded to include a call to the editor. With some editors, the batch file can even position the cursor at the end of the file on each invocation. Co-resident programs (such as TopView™) also provide immediate access to the notebook. Some multitasking systems permit two edit sessions to be open simultaneously. And there are editors that allow two files to be edited in the session (through separate windows).

In addition to the lab notebook, the programmer should keep copies of all code revisions and all input and output test data. A revision manager such as UNIX's SCCS (Source Code Control System) offers the most efficient and convenient means of keeping all code revisions. Source created by SCCS is maintained as a base file and a set of incremental revision records. Any desired version may be re-created by applying the appropriate revisions to the base record. This method has the advantage of conserving disk space by "packing" many versions of a program into a single source file. SCCS's comment-collecting features also make a convenient mechanism for maintaining a lab notebook.

Test data can be captured by redirecting input and output to a disk file or by echoing all console transactions and debugging output to a printor. MS-DOS® <control-P> and printscreen features facilitate hard-copy records. On UNIX systems, test data can be captured in a file if the program input and output both are fitted to tees (tee is a UNIX utility that splits an I/O stream into duplicate tributaries).

Hunting versus Verifying

Testing can focus on exposing bugs or verifying correctness. Of the two testing approaches, verifying correctness produces more thorough results, and is faster for large programs with complex input-output relationships.

The first approach can be characterized as "bug hunting." As a bug hunter, the programmer feeds a program various input combinations until some combination produces erroneous output. Unless bug hunters are looking for the telltale tracks of a specific bug, they usually won't look "inside" the program (by tracing variable values or execution flow). A bug hunter expects all bugs to surface initially as wrong output.

Using the second approach, the program verifier begins testing by observing what is happening "inside" the program. As a program verifier, the programmer demands that the module be correct internally, regardless of external effect. The program verifier must have a more complete set of initial expectations about program workings, and learn more from each set of test data.

In smaller programs, verification takes more time than bug hunting. Both approaches are probably equally reliable. In larger programs, program verifying can substantially reduce debugging time when the relationship between output and the actions causing that output are complex.

Verification tends to ensure that debugging time is spent productively. The programmer progresses through program modules one by one, declaring each to be bug free before moving on. Bug hunters, on the other hand, can waste time going in circles because they have no clear idea of which modules are reliable and which modules are not.

Verification challenges the programmer to examine the module's primary effects as well as its desired and undesired side effects. Primary effects and intended side-effects usually can be verified with conventional debugging tools. C's unrestrained pointers, however, occasionally create undesired side-effects which can only be spotted with special functions and breakpointer debuggers. These tools are necessary because they can monitor not only the memory that the programmer meant to change but also the memory that the programmer meant to leave unchanged. These special debugging tools are discussed in Chapters 8, 9, and 10.

RETURN

Bugs differ in two important ways. First, they differ in how soon they can be identified in the testing process. Second, they differ in how difficult they are to stabilize.

Testing for bugs must proceed methodically and incrementally. To fully exercise all modules and decision structures, input data must be selected carefully. Test data should test normal execution, should include boundary values chosen to activate all arms of branch structures, and perform single cycles of each loop structure. Comprehensive data sets will include also exceptional and abusive values.

Record-keeping should include frequent listings (or independent backups) of the source code, a lab notebook, and printed or captured images of test input and output. Archival utilities such as UNIX's Source Code Control System can facilitate source code version control and even allow some parts of the lab notebook to be kept on-line. Unix's tee or MS-DOS's printscreen or <control-P> capabilities can facilitate the capture of test input and output.

Although initially demanding, program verification consistently yields useful information and guarantees steady, reliable progress through the testing process. Moreover, because verification examines the program internally, the verification approach thoroughly exposes existing bugs.

3
Localizing
Compile-Time Errors

Compile-time errors are relatively easy to localize because the compiler provides information about the line containing the error. Lexical errors, although they may not be easy to recognize, are always pinpointed. Occasionally, the compiler accepts hundreds of lines following an error before it realizes that an error has been generated. This chapter looks at the tools and techniques programmers use to locate such errors.

Compiling: Process and Components

Unlike interpreters, which integrate editing, translation, execution, and debugging into a single environment, conventional compilers consist of several separate programs. Each of the programs accomplishes only part of the translation process. These programs are conceptually strung together as a sequence of filters. The programmer who understands how compiler parts function is in a good position to guess about the real meaning of an error message. Knowing which part of the compiler produced the error message can make the programmer's debugging efforts more efficient.

The preprocessor recognizes #statements and all symbols defined by #define statements. Preprocessors are relatively unintelligent so the C symbols to be processed must be easy to identify. For example, parameterized macro invocations cannot have a space be-

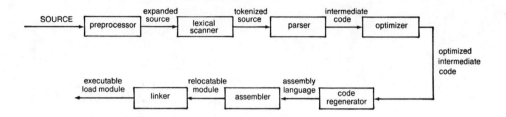

Fig. 3.1. The compiler's translation process.

tween the macro name and the first parenthesis, and some compilers force #statements to begin in the first column. The pre-processor performs simple textual deletions (#ifdef) and textual substitutions (macro invocations) and writes the resulting text back to disk. In figure 3.1, this file is called *expanded source*. Expanded source is simply a legal C program, unenhanced by pre-processor symbols and macro definitions.

Think of the lexical scanner as a "word recognizer" running through the program, replacing human-oriented keywords and symbols with more compact, machine-oriented numeric values. In many respects, the lexical scanner is a large lookup table. When-ever it recognizes a keyword (while, for example), the scanner finds that keyword in a symbol table and replaces the textual sym-bol with a number known as a *token*. Although this process, like preprocessing, is largely one of substitution, the lexical scanner often has more intelligence and more C-specific knowledge than the preprocessor. The lexical scanner, which must be somewhat context-sensitive, is usually responsible for capturing (in the sym-bol table) information about the type of all declared variables.

The parser is the compiler's C expert. It knows the syntax and most of the semantics of the language. It reads the tokenized source, trying to recognize legal syntactic structures. Whenever it recog-nizes a structure, the parser generates what can be thought of as a statement of the structure's semantic content. Unlike the earlier steps in the translation process, the compiler doesn't preserve any sort of simple, one-to-one mapping from its input to its output. The parser outputs a form of idealized assembly language called *in-termediate code*.

The parser has primary responsiblity for contextual analysis. An error that is recognized only after two or three statements (or even three or four symbols) have been analyzed will be discovered (if it *is* discovered) by the parser. Solely responsible for semantic interpretation, only the parser has the intelligence to detect a statement that asks for an impossible act (such as division by a constant zero).

Subtle semantic errors and syntax errors involving relationships between various parts of a program are difficult to analyze and frequently cause the parser to become thoroughly confused. From the human point of view, the confused parser generates inaccurate error messages, messages which point to a segment of the program that is actually correct.

After the parser completes its job, the real work of translation is finished. The remaining steps delete redundant (optional) code and replace the intermediate code with code specific to the target processor and run-time environment (in other words, with code that's compatible with the operating system and linker/loader).

As you try to relate all this information to your own compiler, please keep in mind that figure 3.1 shows a generalized, conceptual partitioning of the translation process. Actual compilers may combine more than one phase of the process into a single process. For example, the lexical scanner and parser are frequently combined into a single module.

Moreover, information frequently passes between modules through other than intermediate files. Tables, particularly the symbol table constructed by the lexical scanner, can remain in memory. Occasionally, entire intermediate files remain in memory instead of being written to disk. For instance, the BDS C compiler (for CP/M) combines phases in a minimum of memory-resident activities. Compilation speed increases significantly when disk activity is reduced.

Virtually all C compiler systems include a system (usually a program or batch file called *cc*) that automates the chain of processes by coordinating the invocation of the various compiler components. Occasionally, bypassing *cc* and invoking a component directly can be useful.

For example, if the preprocessor is suspected of not expanding a macro as originally supposed, the programmer can invoke the preprocessor directly (as a stand-alone program) and examine the expanded source that it writes to disk. Similarly, to write certain functions in assembly language or to optimize certain low-level functions manually, the programmer must have access to the assembly language file produced by the code generator.

Knowing how responsibilities are allocated in the compiler and which pass generated the error permits better error message interpretation.

Error-generating pass	Probable cause
preprocessor	seriously malformed #statement (Example: #defind JOE 13)
lexical scanner	seriously malformed symbol, illegal punctuation, or bad (possibly nonprinting) character in file (Example: 4our = 2 + 2;)
parser	possibly subtle error in order of symbols; not likely to be clear without considering surrounding symbols (Example: foo(), when foo is declared as having an input argument)
optimizer, code generator	a disk read/write error or a compiler error

Later passes should not generate error messages. The parser should accept only legal programs and generate acceptable output. A problem during the code-generation phase is always a compiler error, perhaps triggered by an error in your program.

The code generator becomes the resource of choice if the compiler fails to recognize a syntax error and blithely generates impossible code. This kind of error requires a search for the portion of the program that triggered it. Narrowing the stimulus often enables the programmer to replace the offending code with something equivalent but acceptable to the compiler (something, in other words, that gets the program running). Narrowing the stimulus also permits the programmer to more succinctly communicate the nature of the error to the compiler vendor.

Syntax Errors:
Some All-Purpose Advice

Don't read and reread the code. In fact, until the line containing the syntax error is identified and proven inaccurate, code should be read only once to spot obvious flaws. If all errors vanish when the suspect line is deleted or if (using a few fragments from the original program) a tiny test program duplicating the error can be built, the programmer has proven that he or she has located the error.

However, if errors remain after deleting the suspect line, the bug remains at large. If the same error crops up in another place or if a new error appears on an adjacent line, the user should seriously doubt the compiler's specificity and test further (before reading more code).

All compiler messages should be taken with a grain of salt. Only the first one or two are warranted to be the bug's fault; subsequent messages probably result from compiler confusion. Many personal computer compilers generate a single error message (or messages describing a single syntax error) on each compilation.

Error messages generated after the compiler attempts to "recover" from an error should not be ignored. Instead, try to get a feeling for the reliability of the messages. Experienced programmers recognize that certain messages are reliable, even when those messages aren't among the first in the report. The message `undeclared variable` often fits in this class. Compilation will be more productive if, before recompiling, a check of all `undeclared variable` messages and the first one or two messages is made.

Don't make random changes to the code. Before changing and recompiling the code, form expectations for and conclusions about the intended changes. In other words, guessing about how to correct the error is inappropriate, at least until the error is located.

Try to make only one change (or clearly unrelated changes) between compilations. If recompilation of multiple changes produces unexpected results, undo the changes and work through them one at a time. (A source-code control system—or iron-willed discipline—is a prerequisite to this advice.) Remember that the object is to control the process by limiting the number of variables at every step.

When all else fails, delete the suspect line and retype it. This procedure should eliminate any nonprinting character corrupting the file. Verify that such a character is the problem by writing a simple filter that searches a file for nonprinting characters and prints their coordinates. The output might look like this:

```
***Warning nonprinting character 04 in line 43, position 27****
```

Accept the compiler's authority. The goal is to produce a working program. Although having the compiler work as expected would be nice, the user and the compiler author may interpret the language's semantics differently. In terms of the project, investing time and energy in proving that a particular interpretation is "right" is not productive; time might be better invested in understanding the idiosyncrasies of the tool and in doing the job reasonably.

Sometimes compilers have bugs. These bugs very infrequently may be serious enough to warrant getting a different (better) compiler. However, before indicting the compiler writer, carefully read Chapter 6. In six years of coding C on four different C compilers, I have never encountered such a compiler bug. In fact, I've encountered only one behavior that I consider a compiler bug, as opposed to a legitimate difference of opinion about how the compiler should work. Although the new ANSI C standard should significantly reduce variation in compiler semantics, my advice stands. Invest time in making programs work with the compiler. Don't "waste" time testing and challenging the compiler.

Forcing More Useful Error Messages

Programs consist of nested and sequenced syntactic entities: statements, expressions, function definitions, functions, invocations, and many others. By carefully deleting entire entities, large or small chunks of a program can be eliminated without affecting its syntactic legality. Although the hacked-up program may not work, the immediate concern is to get the program to compile.

Although the compiler can't define precisely where the bug *is*, it can reveal precisely where the bug *isn't*. The programmer's technique, when searching manually for compile-time bugs, should rely on this property.

"Chop" out a large chunk of code that corresponds to a complete syntactic entity and recompile. If the error remains, it isn't in the code removed. If the error goes away, it isn't in the code that remains.

Whatever the "after-surgery results" may be, more information about the bug's location has been gathered. Repeating this operation reduces the portion of code that can contain the error. Eventually, the single line or at least some small syntactic structure causing the error message becomes evident.

All this drastic hacking should be done on a copy of the program. Once the bug's location is identified, return to the complete source and make the necessary correction. This technique is most efficient if each deleted chunk contains about half of the suspect code, in other words if a binary search is performed.

To illustrate this technique, a subtle error has been introduced into the following program (part of a public domain letter-formatting system by Jon Simkins of SoftFocus). The error confuses the compiler, causing it to generate a completely misleading error message.

Program 3.1.

```
/*
 *  address      Address a standard letter using the file 'address' (created
 *               by the letter program).
 */
#include <stdio.h>

#define HEAD 4
#define LENGTH 24
#define PO 5;

#define WIDTH 95

#define ERROR -1
/*
 *  read address into this array
 */
#define MAXLINES 10
char *lines[MAXLINES];
```

```
FILE *fd, *printer;

main()
{
    char buff[80];
    int max, j, offset, len, count;
    char *malloc();

    /*
     *  open the address file
     */
    if ( (fd = fopen("address", "r")) == 0) {
        /*give the user some help... * /
        printf("address file does not exist.\n");
        exit(ERROR);
    }
    printer = fopen("LPT1", "w");

    for(count=0, max=0; count<MAXLINES; count++) {
        if ( fgets(buff, 80, fd) == 0)
            break;
        else {
            len = strlen(buff);
            lines[count] = malloc(80);
            if (len > max)
                max = len;
            strcpy(lines[count], buff);
        }
    }
    offset = ( (WIDTH - max) / 2) + PO
    for(j=0; j<offset; j++)
        buff[j]=' ';
    buff[j] = '\0';

    offset = ( LENGTH - count ) / 2 - HEAD;

    for(j=0; j<offset; j++)
        fputs("\n", printer);

    for(j=0; j<count; j++) {
        fprintf(printer, "%s%s", buff, lines[j]);
    }
```

```
/* now clean house before exiting */
fputs("\Ø14", printer);
fclose(fd);
fclose(printer);
}
```

When compiled under Eco-C88™, this program produces an error message. In fact, Eco-C88 is so "picky" that it normally produces an error message that takes all the challenge out of the problem. To make Eco-C88 behave more like the typical ineffective compiler, it has been invoked with a certain option switch set. The following error message results

```
CC (Hard Disk) Version 3.Ø1
Eco-C Pre-Processor Pass. Version 3.Ø1
Copyright © 1985 by Ecosoft, Inc. All rights reserved.
Source File: demo1.c
Including file: \headers\stdio.h
Eco-C Parser Pass. Version 3.Ø1
Eco-C Error Pass. Version 3.Ø1
Error in File: demo1.c   Line: 68   Char: Ø   Error: 8   Token:
Warning!! A closing brace (assumed) was expected instead of
```

The message indicates that a closing brace (}) was expected at the end of the program (line 68 is that last brace), but instead, nothing was found. (The space before the period isn't a typesetting error. It indicates a null symbol.) Unfortunately, if the braces are counted ({ }), they all obviously match. The problem then lies elsewhere. The compiler hits the end of the file before it figures out that something is wrong.

The main body of this program is about 30 lines long. Eliminate about 15 lines in the first test. Begin by removing the central for loop and the three statements that follow it. They are easy to delete. (In other words, delete from for (count = ... to buff[j] = '\Ø';) Notice that complete syntactic entities (in this case, four statements: a large for statement, an assignment, a small for statement, and another assignment) are being deleted. After the hatchet job, the test file will look like this:

Program 3.2.

```
/*
 * address       Address a standard letter using the file 'address' (created
 *               by the letter program).
 */
#include <stdio.h>

#define HEAD 4
#define LENGTH 24
#define PO 5;

#define WIDTH 95

#define ERROR -1
/*
 * read address into this array
 */
#define MAXLINES 10
char *lines[MAXLINES];

FILE *fd, *printer;

main()
{
    char buff[80];
    int max, j, offset, len, count;
    char *malloc();

    /*
     * open the address file
     */
    if ( (fd = fopen("address", "r")) == 0) {
        /*give the user some help... */
        printf("address file does not exist.\n");
        exit(ERROR);
    }
    printer = fopen("LPT1", "w");


    offset = ( LENGTH - count ) / 2 - HEAD;
```

```
for(j=0; j<offset; j++)
    fputs("\n", printer);

for(j=0; j<count; j++) {
    fprintf(printer, "%s%s", buff, lines[j]);
}

/* now clean house before exiting */
fputs("\014", printer);
fclose(fd);
fclose(printer);
}
```

Compiling results in the same error message, again at the last line of the file

Error in File: demo2.c   Line: 53   Char: 0   Error: 8   Token: Warning!! A closing brace (assumed) was expected instead of

Evidently, the error isn't in the deleted lines. Because there are still several suspect lines, it's possible to chop out a little more code and try again. This time, about seven lines are removed, including the first if statement. The new test program is:

Program 3.3.

```
/*
 * address     Address a standard letter using the file 'address' (created
 *             by the letter program).
 */
#include <stdio.h>

#define HEAD 4
#define LENGTH 24
#define PO 5;

#define WIDTH 95
```

```
#define ERROR -1
/*
 *  read address into this array
 */
#define MAXLINES 10
char *lines[MAXLINES];

FILE *fd, *printer;

main()
{
    char buff[80];
    int max, j, offset, len, count;
    char *malloc();


    for(j=0; j<offset; j++)
        fputs("\n", printer);

    for(j=0; j<count; j++) {
        fprintf(printer, "%s%s", buff, lines[j]);
    }

    /* now clean house before exiting */
    fputs("\014", printer);
    fclose(fd);
    fclose(printer);
}
```

A different error message is generated. In fact, it's not an error message at all; it's a warning. This time the compiler has progressed to the code-generation stage instead of aborting after the parsing stage.

```
CC (Hard Disk) Version 3.01
Eco-C Pre-Processor Pass. Version 3.01
Copyright © 1985 by Ecosoft, Inc. All rights reserved.
Source File: demo3.c
Including file: \headers\stdio.h
Eco-C Parser Pass. Version 3.01
Eco-C Error Pass. Version 3.01
```

```
Error in File: demo3.c   Line: 29   Char: 22   Error: 500   Token: offset
WARNING - Variable offset was used before a value was assigned to it.

Error in File: demo3.c   Line: 32   Char: 21   Error: 500   Token: count
WARNING - Variable count was used before a value was assigned to it.

Eco-C Optimizer Pass. Version 3.01
Eco-C Code Generation Pass. Version 3.01
Eco-C Assembler Pass. Version 3.01
Compilation Complete for: demo3.obj
```

These warnings are just a product of chopping. The variables offset and count don't have values because, as part of the test, the lines that initialized offset and count were removed.

The real error (the one involving a brace) has disappeared, which means that it must be in the deleted code. In the next step, the user creates a test file including part of the code removed when the last test was made. In that test, an if and two assignment statements were removed. For this test, use a main that consists only of the if.

Program 3.4.

```
/*
 *  address       Address a standard letter using the file 'address' (created
 *                by the letter program).
 */
#include <stdio.h>

#define HEAD 4
#define LENGTH 24
#define PO 5;

#define WIDTH 95

#define ERROR -1
/*
 *  read address into this array
 */
#define MAXLINES 10
char *lines[MAXLINES];
```

```
FILE *fd, *printer;

main()
{
    char buff[80];
    int max, j, offset, len, count;
    char *malloc();

    /*
     * open the address file
     */
    if ( (fd = fopen("address", "r")) == 0) {
        /*give the user some help... * /
        printf("address file does not exist. \n");
        exit(ERROR);
    }
}
```

The compiler generates this error report:

```
CC (Hard Disk) Version 3.01
Eco-C Pre-Processor Pass. Version 3.01
Copyright © 1985 by Ecosoft, Inc. All rights reserved.
Source File: demo4.c
Including file: \headers\stdio.h

Error in File: demo4.c   Line: 32   Char: 11   Error: 8   Token: /*
        Error - end of file before end of comment.
```

This is a real error. The compiler aborts long before the code-generation pass. The conclusion is that the error is in one of the lines left in the program. The possibilities have been narrowed to two lines. And this error message is different from the message chased originally. Good news!

Had the original error message been reasonably helpful, the error could have been spotted and corrected without this search. Because the message applies to a very small section of code, it's time to read the code carefully. The error message mentions a comment. There is only one comment in the suspect block. It contains the error. Carefully examine the comment.

```
/*give the user some help... * /
```

Notice that the closing comment delimiter is improperly formed.

Many programmers will consider this bug unworthy of special techniques. Some will spot the problem immediately, especially if they understand how compilers work and what error messages really mean. Admittedly, this bug is fairly easy to spot in such a short program. But its behavior is typical of many subtler bugs. Finding even this simple an error in a program of hundreds or thousands of lines can be very time consuming.

The point is not that this bug is difficult, but that the technique is reliable and always productive. Whenever a test is compiled, more is learned about the bug's location. Reading the code is never as reliable or productive as testing. What if the space had been a non-printing character? (I have used at least one editor that habitually, and without warning, dropped Control S (XOFF) into the file.) Could *that* error be found by simply reading the code?

If the compiler allows nested comments, avoid creating multiple copies of a file by simply commenting out the code to be deleted. (Or, use #ifdef JUNK ... #endif—where JUNK is undefined—to bracket the code to be left out.) For floppy-based systems, the savings in disk space can be important.

Using the "commenting-out" technique demands that the boundaries of syntactic entities be accurately identified. Anything that passes for a statement or, more generally, an expression will do. However, identifying these boundaries may be difficult for programmers who are struggling to master the syntax. When drafting code, those whose understanding of syntax is still imprecise have trouble deciding where to put semicolons. Hand parsing exercises such as those described later in this chapter can help these programmers, forcing them to analyze the language as the compiler does.

Using Curly Brace Checkers

Trivial problems in delimiter matching (the comment problem in the preceding section, for example) are as confusing to the compiler as any error a programmer can make. Such problems are by far the most common source of misleading and time-consuming error messages. A curly brace checker offers easy and inexpensive aid. Writing one is a good exercise for beginning C programmers. Alternatively, several nice public domain versions are available.

To illustrate the usefulness of these programs, I include the output produced by running a public-domain brace checker on listing 3.1. The brace checker, written by T. Jennings and David Smith, can be found on Volume 152 of the C Users' Group Library.

```
 0: {0} (0) /*0*/       |/*
 1: {0} (0) /*1*/       | *  address    Address a standard letter using the
     file 'address' (created by the letter program).
 2: {0} (0) /*1*/       | *
 3: {0} (0) /*1*/       | */
 4: {0} (0) /*0*/       |#include <stdio.h>
 5: {0} (0) /*0*/       |
 6: {0} (0) /*0*/       |#define HEAD 4
 7: {0} (0) /*0*/       |#define LENGTH 24
 8: {0} (0) /*0*/       |#define PO 5;
 9: {0} (0) /*0*/       |
10: {0} (0) /*0*/       |#define WIDTH 95
11: {0} (0) /*0*/       |
12: {0} (0) /*0*/       |#define ERROR -1
13: {0} (0) /*0*/       |/*
14: {0} (0) /*1*/       | *  read address into this array
15: {0} (0) /*1*/       | */
16: {0} (0) /*0*/       |#define MAXLINES 10
17: {0} (0) /*0*/       |char *lines[MAXLINES];
18: {0} (0) /*0*/       |
19: {0} (0) /*0*/       |FILE *fd, *printer;
20: {0} (0) /*0*/       |
21: {0} (0) /*0*/       |main()
22: {0} (0) /*0*/       |{
23: {1} (0) /*0*/       |    char buff[80];
24: {1} (0) /*0*/       |    int max, j, offset, len, count;
25: {1} (0) /*0*/       |    char *malloc();
26: {1} (0) /*0*/       |
27: {1} (0) /*0*/       |    /*
28: {1} (0) /*1*/       |     *  open the address file
29: {1} (0) /*1*/       |     */
30: {1} (0) /*0*/       |    if ( (fd = fopen("address", "r")) == 0) {
```

```
31: {2} (0) /*0*/    |        /*give the user some help... * /
32: {2} (0) /*1*/    |        printf("address file does not exist.\n");
33: {2} (0) /*1*/    |        exit(ERROR);
34: {2} (0) /*1*/    |    }
35: {2} (0) /*1*/    |    printer = fopen("LPT1", "w");
36: {2} (0) /*1*/    |
37: {2} (0) /*1*/    |    for(count=0, max=0; count<MAXLINES; count++) {
38: {2} (0) /*1*/    |        if ( fgets(buff, 80, fd) == 0)
39: {2} (0) /*1*/    |            break;
40: {2} (0) /*1*/    |        else {
41: {2} (0) /*1*/    |            len = strlen(buff);
42: {2} (0) /*1*/    |            lines[count] = malloc(80);
43: {2} (0) /*1*/    |            if (len > max)
44: {2} (0) /*1*/    |                max = len;
45: {2} (0) /*1*/    |            strcpy(lines[count], buff);
46: {2} (0) /*1*/    |        }
47: {2} (0) /*1*/    |    }
48: {2} (0) /*1*/    |    offset = ( (WIDTH - max) / 2) + PO;
49: {2} (0) /*1*/    |    for(j=0; j<offset; j++)
50: {2} (0) /*1*/    |        buff[j]=' ';
51: {2} (0) /*1*/    |    buff[j] = '\0';
52: {2} (0) /*1*/    |
53: {2} (0) /*1*/    |    offset = ( LENGTH - count ) / 2
- HEAD;
54: {2} (0) /*1*/    |
55: {2} (0) /*1*/    |    for(j=0; j<offset; j++)
56: {2} (0) /*1*/    |        fputs("\n", printer);
57: {2} (0) /*1*/    |
58: {2} (0) /*1*/    |    for(j=0; j<count; j++) {
59: {2} (0) /*1*/    |        fprintf(printer, "%s%s", buff, lines[j]);
60: {2} (0) /*1*/    |    }
61: {2} (0) /*1*/    |
62: {2} (0) /*1*/    |    /* now clean house before exiting */
63: {2} (0) /*1*/    |    fputs("\014", printer);
64: {2} (0) /*1*/    |    fclose(fd);
65: {2} (0) /*1*/    |    fclose(printer);
66: {2} (0) /*1*/    |}
```

Unbalanced brackets
Unbalanced comments

Listing 3.1.

This curly brace checker actually checks braces, parentheses, and comment delimiters. It tells for each line how deeply each kind of delimiter is nested.

In lines 27–28 of this listing, for example, the beginning of the short comment causes the comment nesting to increase from level Ø to level 1. After the comment is closed (at lines 28–29), the nesting returns to level Ø.

It is easy to identify the line containing the problem, using this record of nesting depth. In lines 31 and 32, the comment nesting increases to 1 and remains there. The report clearly warns that the closing comment delimiter hasn't been recognized. To understand why, the user need only examine the comment.

Using Lint To Analyze Syntax

C compilers are not nearly as picky as, for example, Pascal compilers. Traditionally, UNIX™ programmers have used a sophisticated syntax analyzer known as *lint* to compensate for the general simple-mindedness of C compilers. Lint is picky enough to satisfy the most persnickety user. It identifies technically erroneous usage and it flags technically correct usage that is considered "poor style." Poor style creates problems when transporting the code to another environment. Lint even flags usages that are legal but a frequent source of inadvertent mistakes. For example, lint will flag with an "informational" warning an assignment operator without a relational operator in a test:

```
while (c = getchar()){...
```

Similarly, lint will flag variables that are not used and code that is unreachable.

Lint is a good teaching tool for advanced beginners who want to build a thorough, detailed understanding of type nuances and learn to write highly portable code. Lint produces a torrent of analytic information. It's wise to use it once early on to identify uninitialized variables and other blatant problems, and again during a "code polishing" stage.

A tool like *grep* (global regular expression pattern matcher) can help manage lint's diagnostic output. If lint's voluminous output can be redirected to a disk file, grep can be used to select only the error messages of most interest (those involving uninitialized and unused variables, for example).

To illustrate the picky nature of lint, use Gimpel Software's PC-Lint™ (a version for IBM compatibles) to examine a file that compiled without so much as a warning:

```
PC-Lint lines



---- Module ged3.c
File ged3.c, Line 113
            if ( (c=_os(DIRIO,0xff))) inbuf[inbufp++]=c & ~PARBIT;
                                      ^

     Warning 534: function _os -- return mode inconsistent
          with module ged3.c, file ged3.c, line no. 94


File ged3.c, Line 153
     for (i=8-i-uspr(cursorx+1,0L); i > 0; i--) _os(DIRIO,' ');
                                                               ^

     Warning 534: function _os -- return mode inconsistent
          with module ged3.c, file ged3.c, line no. 113


File ged3.c, Line 249
     if (dim) enddim();
              ^

     Warning 534: function enddim -- return mode inconsistent
          with module ged3.c, file ged3.c, line no. 242


File ged3.c, Line 262
            begdim();
            ^

     Warning 534: function begdim -- return mode inconsistent
          with module ged3.c, file ged3.c, line no. 242


File ged3.c, Line 274
                 if ( (cc=_os(DIRIO,0xff)))
inbuf[inbufp++]=cc & ~PARBIT;
                                  ^

     Warning 534: function _os --d return mode inconsistent
          with module ged3.c, file ged3.c, line no. 269
```

```
File ged3.c, Line 285
{
^
```

    Warning 532: function calcoffset -- return mode inconsistent
            with module ged3.c, file ged3.c, line no. 258

```
File ged3.c, Line 286
    for (offset=0; cursorx >= SWIDTH+offset-(offset>0); offset+=OFFWIDTH);
                                                   ^
```

    Warning 514: Unusual use of a Boolean

```
File ged3.c, Line 287
    return offset;
                ^
```

    Warning 533: function calcoffset -- return mode inconsistent
            with module ged3.c, file ged3.c, line no. 285

```
File ged3.c, Line 303
    gotoxy(cursorx-offset+(offset>0), cursory);
                              ^
```

    Warning 514: Unusual use of a Boolean

```
File ged3.c, Line 320
                    strcpy(defext, np);
                              ^
```

    Warning 534: function strcpy -- return mode inconsistent
            with module ged3.c, file ged.h, line no. 278

```
Warning 526, _move not defined
Warning 526, _os not defined
Warning 526, adjustc not defined
Warning 526, begdim not defined
Warning 526, deleteline not defined
Warning 526, delpage not defined
Warning 526, dispch not defined
Warning 526, enddim not defined
Warning 526, getline not defined
Warning 526, gotoxy not defined
Warning 526, insertline not defined
Warning 526, loc not defined
Warning 526, makebright not defined
Warning 526, makedim not defined
Warning 526, putch not defined
Warning 526, strcpy not defined
Warning 526, uspr not defined
```

All the Warning 526 messages merely indicate that there were no external definitions for functions referenced but "not defined" in this source file. In fact, those functions are defined—but in other source modules.

Some systems, especially large word-size systems, insist on the external definitions to determine what type to assign to the function's return value. Smaller systems usually assume a 16-bit return value. The failure to include external type definitions for these functions constitutes poor style because the portability of the source code is limited.

The 534 error messages are a warning that the return value for a function wasn't used. In each instance, the original programmer deliberately ignored the return value—not an uncommon practice. Assume, for example, that a programmer reading input from the keyboard has just read the last character in a fixed-field record. He or she knows that an unimportant space follows that character and simply writes

    getc(file);

to step over the unwanted character. Such usage would generate the 534 error message because the declared int return from getc hasn't been assigned to anything. This particular message isn't related to portability problems; it's an effort to warn the programmer about code that seems inconsistent. Such little inconsistencies are frequently associated with real mistakes.

The 534 error message can become overwhelming during linting of a large body of code. Programmers have two options. They can select a grep-like tool to remove all 534 messages from the lint output (ignoring all of them), or they can inform lint of their intention so that some differentiation between error and intentional use is made. In PC-Lint, the programmer can declare his or her deliberate intention by applying a void typecast (adapted directly from the ANSI C standard) to the function

    (void) getc(file);

Using boolean values in an arithmetic statement triggers message 514. This message warns you that 5 + true has no predictable answer unless you know something special about the bit pattern representing true. Although machine true should be equal to one, it may not be with older compilers. At any rate, because adding true is not a common usage, lint warns the user to double-check it.

Lint is useful for producing carefully polished, highly portable code. However, with the more precise language definition now available in the ANSI standard, compilers already are incorporating many of the tests traditionally delegated to lint. For example, by adjusting the "picky" flag, you can force Eco-C88 to check:

- type matching across assignment statements
- type and count matching between formal and actual parameters
- use of nonpointers as pointers
- unused return values
- mismatched return types

The overlap between these compiler-generated warnings and the traditional lint analysis is sizable.

Isolating Bugs with Tiny Test Programs

Occasionally, users will narrow a problem to a single line and still not be able to identify the cause of the error. In such a case, placing the offending line in a tiny program is helpful. The program can be compiled and edited easily and quickly, and the programmer is assured that the balance of the code isn't influencing the compiler.

Once, for example, as I was transporting an editor (written originally for CP/M) to a new UNIX system, an error message that meant absolutely nothing to me was consistently generated by a line similar to this

```
k=-(joe(14)+12*BYTES);
```

I hadn't a clue to what was wrong, but because I was certain that the problem was in this line, I wrote the following test program:

```
#define BYTES 2

main()

{
int k;
```

```
k=-1;
k=-1+12;
k=-1+12*BYTES;
k=-joe(14)+12*BYTES;
k=(-1);
k=(-(1+12));
k=(-(joe(14)+12*BYTES);
}

int joe(inval)
int inval;

{return 1; }
```

I used two heuristics to generate this test program:

- change only one thing between each line
- fully parenthesize all expressions

Parentheses force the compiler to see things the way the user sees them. Frequently, an error can't be identified because the compiler and author "see" the intent very differently.

When this program compiled, the first four lines generated exactly the same error as the original program, but the last three lines compiled correctly. This information provided a point of reference; simply adding parentheses to the original lines erased the problem. To understand the cause, select the two smallest instances

```
k=-1;
```

and

```
k=(-1);
```

and ask how they might look to the compiler. The obvious difference is that there is a delimiting symbol between the = and –. Add the statement

```
k= -1;
```

to the test program and recompile. The line compiles without error. The fact that C apparently accepted =- as a near synonym for -= was unknown until the old fashioned assignment op message generated by this statement was encountered. The message provided an easy fix for this error. Using search-and-replace, replace every instance of =- with -=.

These are but two guidelines used for constructing little test programs. Here are others that will be helpful:

- focus on one or two lines
- make each variation differ from another by only one feature
- fully parenthesize everything
- whenever possible, reduce complex expressions to several simple expressions
- to test type mismatches, replace complex expressions with simple constants of a known type
- put all variations in one file and compile them on one pass

Tiny test programs are a better alternative to changing and recompiling the original program because the test programs

- *save time.* The programmer compiles fewer times because a dozen different tests can be compiled in a single pass. Each compilation is fast because the program is tiny.
- *provide better control.* The programmer doesn't have to worry about the influence of the rest of the program.
- *simplify tracking results.* All the results from an entire set of experiments are available in a single error report. The test program is so small that the whole program can be listed at the printer.
- *verify the location of the bad line.* Duplicating an error in the tiny test program verifies the error's location.

Using the Preprocessor as a Stand-Alone Program

Programmers may be dealing with a problem caused by the misuse of a macro if, even after the compile-time problem has been reduced to a few lines involving one or more preprocessor macros, the trouble cannot be located.

In this case, it's necessary to know how the preprocessor expands user-written macros. In effect, the preprocessor writes some of the code, and it's difficult to find the bugs if the code isn't visible.

Usually, the compiler can be forced to generate a listing of the preprocessor's expanded source. Each system employs its own method. If the preprocessor is a truly separate program, all the programmer must do is discover its name and command syntax. If the preprocessor isn't separate, there's probably a "switch" to request preprocessor output. Typically, this switch is either an optional argument (specified as part of the compiler invocation) or a special comment embedded in the source file.

It is possible to have a problem involving a macro and not be aware of it. Many compilers define low-level functions such as `getc` and `strcpy` as macros. If a preprocessor-related problem is suspected, read the manual. Find out which standard functions are used as macros and how to get preprocessor output.

Realistically, the nastiest preprocessor-related errors will not generate compile-time errors. Nevertheless, before the programmer can identify an error, he or she has to be able to define what a macro is and how that macro is being expanded.

Understanding C Syntax

If you have found Chapter 3 easy to understand and helpful, you are probably comfortable with C syntax and can almost always spot an error after locating the offending line of code. If you are finding the reading difficult or if you have no clear idea of *why* you encounter `misplaced semicolon` or `missing semicolon`, you need to improve your understanding of the syntax.

The less practical of two suggestions (but the one with best long term results) is that you study formal grammar. Get a major textbook on compiler design and study the chapter on BNF. After you've become familiar with BNF, try to hand parse some of the statements that give you trouble. You'll need scrap paper and a good set of syntax rules. (See Appendix A for a list of resources.)

Using Hand Parsing

Hand parsing means applying the BNF rules manually until you've reduced a piece of code to a top-level structure (such as function, statement, or program). If the following simplified BNF rules

```
compound-statement ::= '{' statement '}'
statement ::= expression-statement
expression-statement ::= expression ';'
expression ::= no-comma-expression
no-comma-expression ::= name
```

are read to specify that the right part may be replaced by the left part, a simple statement parses like this:

```
{foo; } --> {name; }
         --> {no-comma-expression; }
         --> {expression; }
         --> {expression-statement}
         --> {statement}
         --> compound-statement
```

This is the kind of analysis that a compiler performs. To explore the role of the semicolon in this example, attempt to hand parse a statement without one.

```
{foo} --> {name}
       --> {no-comma-expression}
       -->
```

Without the semicolon, the rules don't apply. Applying BNF rules isn't complex once the extended grammar is understood. Hand parsing nontrivial code segments can foster surprisingly useful insights into compiler operations.

Understanding BNF provides more than just a deeper understanding of syntax. Because many manuals use a simplified form of BNF to specify command syntax and other application program options, the programmer familiar with BNF will be a better-prepared reader.

Using a Syntax-Directed Editor

The syntax-directed editor is a program editor that checks syntax and refuses incorrect symbols as the programmer enters the program. Poor typists find the better syntax-directed editors very helpful. The best editor not only displays the legal options for the symbol needed next but also allows the programmer to select that symbol (perhaps a long function name) with one or two characters. A word of warning: good typists find the editor irritatingly slow.

Don't assume that because its short-term impact is good, a syntax-directed editor is the ultimate solution to syntax problems. For example, before it will accept the code contained in each syntactic structure, one public domain editor requires that the name of each syntactic structure be selected.

In other words, to write a compound statement, the programmer must first select *compound statement* from a menu; the editor then supplies the opening brace and a menu of statement types. Although one might expect a better interface in a good commercial product, in many respects the syntax-directed editor will demand that the user's understanding of syntax be more (not less) formal.

The syntax-directed editor forces the user to a higher level understanding of syntax after writing a few programs. In that role, the editor becomes an effective learning tool.

RETURN

Conceptually, syntax errors are the simplest type of bug; they stand still and ordinarily can be recognized (even if not isolated) by the compiler. They are most efficiently isolated, however, with such deliberate testing methods as "commenting out" blocks of code.

In a compiled environment, syntax testing is supported by a suite of tools and compiler options. Portions of the compiler can be used separately to examine partial results. Auxiliary tools range from the simple brace checker to lint.

Syntax debugging relies on the programmer's—as well as the compiler's—understanding of syntax, an understanding built by exposure to formal notational systems (BNF). Deliberate testing with tiny test programs and a disciplined insistence on "understanding" bugs as opposed to just fixing them will not only isolate syntax bugs but also build an increasingly precise understanding of the language's nuances.

4
Conventional Trace Methods

The lexical and syntactic errors have been exposed, and it's time to begin run-time debugging. Run-time debugging relies on both temporal and referential proximity, which unlike the static lexical proximity are dynamic and exist only at run-time. Temporal and referential proximity aren't explicitly visible; you can't measure them by simply laying a ruler on the listing. Instead, instrumentation must be created to function as a "window" that opens upon the internal workings of a running program.

The window can be created by instrumenting a program with trace statements. In an "instrumented" program, extra printf statements (trace statements) allow the program's internal behavior to be monitored.

"Instrumented" is a particularly accurate description for a program with built-in trace. The trace statements aren't added randomly throughout a program any more than windows are scattered arbitrarily throughout a house. (Of what use is a window in the basement floor?) Moreover, not just any printf statement will do. Useful trace statements must be suitably placed, as windows must be appropriate to the wall and room they illuminate. Furthermore, (and again like windows) trace statements that are always "open" are as much a liability as they are an asset.

Effective trace statements must be designed specifically, placed judiciously, and enabled selectively. The first two objectives are interdependent; usually, the decision about where to put a statement is based on the purpose that statement will serve.

Selectively enabling various statements is a more independent process. Because run-time debugging relies on temporal and referential proximity, the purpose in tracing must always be to expose temporal relations (*control-flow tracing*) or referential relations (*data-flow tracing*).

This chapter begins with a discussion of control-flow tracing and data-flow tracing that explains "where" to put "what" for both. The chapter goes on to suggest several ways to selectively enable trace statements.

Control-Flow Tracing

Control-flow tracing identifies the order in which program components execute. Each control-flow trace statement need announce only the component of the program it belongs to, as in

```
printf("\nfirst branch of loop");
```

and

```
printf("\nentering getrecord()");
```

For the sake of clarity, control-flow tracing and data-flow tracing are discussed separately. In practice, combining the two is convenient. Assuming that getrecord() has a single argument index, the previous example would be more informative if it had been written

```
printf("\nentering getrecord() with index = %d", index);
```

Later sections of this chapter offer other examples of integrated control-flow traces and data-flow traces.

Similar trace statements should be used to "bracket" every statement that changes the order of execution. In C these statements are: if, switch (case), do, while, break, continue, and function calls. Programmers often trace intermediate points in long runs of purely sequential code as well.

"Bracketing" means that trace statements should appear on "both sides" of the control statements. Execution must be monitored *before* the control structure to be certain it was reached, and *after* the control structure to find out if the program followed the anticipated path. Because each bracket ordinarily shares a trace statement with an adjacent bracket, the tracing isn't as onerous as you might expect.

Instrumenting If Statements

Listing 4.1 shows how to instrument an if branch. Line 1 is the leading side of a bracket around the major if clause. Lines 3, 7, and 11 are the closing sides of the same bracket. Note that lines 3, 7, and 11 are also the opening sides of brackets around the function calls in lines 4, 8, and 12. These function brackets are closed by line 14.

```
1:      printf("\nApproaching age branch, person.age = %d",person.age);
2:      if (person.age < 5) {
3:            printf("\nCalling addtopreschool");
4:            addtopreschool(person);
5:            }
6:      else if (person.age < 14){
7:            printf("\nCalling addtogrades");
8:            addtogrades(person);
9:            }
10:     else {
11:           printf("\nCalling addtohigh");
12:           addtohigh(person);
13:           }
14:     printf("\nreturned from call in age branch");
```

Listing 4.1.

Tracing Control Values

When tracing control flow, always print *control values* (as in line 1). Control values are variables or complete expressions that govern the operation of control structures. This testing is complicated by C's tendency to encourage side effects in expressions. Consider the following example:

```
if (getchar() == 'B') .....
```

If a trace before the if calls getchar to list the control value, getchar will return the following value when the if is executed. A similar problem occurs if the programmer tries to trace after the if. One solution is to do and undo the side effect in the trace statement. For example:

```
printf("getchar returns %c",  c=getchar());
unget(c);
if (getchar() == 'B' ) .....
```

Unfortunately, not all actions are so neatly reversible. Undoing a side effect may be so complex that it becomes a testing issue in itself. An alternative is to capture the test value for later printing.

```
if ((cval = getchar()) == 'B' ) ....
printf(" In if branch, getchar() returned %c", cval);
```

Parameterized defines can be used to insert and remove the assignment to cval, providing a more attractive alternative.

Instrumenting Loops

A properly instrumented loop notifies the programmer

- as soon as the loop is begun

- each time the loop is repeated

- as soon as the loop is exited

Additionally, the control value used in each decision about whether or not the loop is repeated will be presented. For example, in the following nine-line do loop

```
1:   printf("\napproaching four part loop");
2:   do {
3:       part1();
4:       part2();
5:       part3();
6:       k = part4();
7:       printf("\nIn four part loop, after part4, k = %d",k);
8:       } while (k < 15);
9:   printf("\past four part loop");
```

line 1 notifies the user that the loop is about to be entered. Ordinarily, the indication that the loop is about to be entered indicates also that the loop was entered. The compiler-generated code should always execute the body of the loop at least once.

In certain cases, however, the code generated by the compiler is not the code that executes at run time. (Such cases are discussed thoroughly in Chapter 6.) To guard against misinterpreting trace results in those cases, some programmers prefer a "beginning loop" marker immediately after the do.

Line 9 notifies you that the loop has terminated. Line 7 serves a dual role: it marks each iteration of the loop and publishes the control value used in deciding whether to perform another iteration.

The following while loop is similar to the do loop. Line 21 reports that the loop is imminent and echoes the governing control value. Line 28 advises that the loop has terminated. Because a while can execute zero times, these two traces may be the only ones printed. Whenever the loop is entered, however, line 26 should print (once for each iteration) and echo the governing control value.

Instrumenting Breaks and Continues

C's break and continue statements create special, easily over-looked control points that require monitoring. These statements normally are embedded in an if, except when break appears in a case statement as discussed later in this chapter. Except when break appears in a case statement, instrumenting the enclosing if implicitly instruments the break.

```
21:  printf("\napproaching checkit loop, k = %d",k);
22:  while(k-- > 7){
23:      checka();
24:      if ((stat = checkb()) == 13){
25:          printf("\nbreaking, stat = 13");
26:          break;
27:          }
28:      else if (stat > 25) {
29:          printf("\ncontinuing, stat = %d, k = %d",stat,k);
30:          continue;
31:          }
32:      checkc();
33:      printf("\nat end of checks, k = %d",k);
34:      }
35:  printf("\nnow past checkit loop");
```

Because the continue statement (line 30) abruptly terminates an iteration, line 29 must echo the control value.

Instrumenting Case Statements

case statements are like branches, except that overlooking some of the paths is easier in a case. Good debugging practice requires every case statement to include a default clause even if an explicit switch for each possible control example is provided.

This fragment contains a bug. Whenever this segment of code is executed, line 1 prints, then the program hangs forever.

```
1:   printf("\nApproaching while");
2:   while (c = getchar() != 'X') {
3:       switch (c) {
4:         case 'R' :
5:                     printf("\nIn R case");
6:                     dorwork();
7:                     break;
8:         case 'L' :
9:                     printf("\nIn L case");
10:                    dolwork();
11:                    break;
12:        case 'Z' :
                       printf("\nIn Z case");
13:                    dozwork();
14:                    break;
15:      } /*end of case */
16:      }    /*end of while */
17:  printf("\nExiting while");
```

The bug is simple, but so subtle that it is particularly easy to read over. If you see the bug now, don't feel too smug. Someday you'll read past one that is just as simple. This is a nice example, not only because it is typical of the kinds of bugs that frustrate C newcomers, but also because it can be exposed completely by fully instrumenting the code.

In this example, the programmer thought that the code had been fully instrumented. Markers were inserted at every branch of the case, as well as before and after the while. However, the control value wasn't printed. When the program didn't work, the programmer changed the code so that the getchar was separate and printed out the value it returned.

```
1:   printf("\napproaching while");
2:   ch = getchar();
3:   printf("\ngetchar returns %c", ch);
4:   while (c = ch != 'X'){
         .
         .
         .
```

The modification verified that getchar was returning a legal value (R, to be precise). Nevertheless, the fragment never reached the trace statement in the R case.

Although this test and the traces in the program are well chosen, the instrumentation is incomplete. This fragment has two major control structures: the while loop and the case.

There should be trace statements that echo the control value for each of these structures, mark the iteration of the loop, and mark the default branch in the case statement. A fully instrumented fragment (with the getchar modification) looks like this:

```
1:   printf("\nApproaching while");
2:   ch = getchar();
3:   printf("\ngetchar returns %c", ch);
4:   while (c = ch != 'X') {
5:      printf("\nLoop entered, selecting on %c %d", c, c);
6:      switch (c) {
7:         case 'R' :  printf("\nIn R case");
8:                     dorwork();
9:                     break; X
10:        case 'L' :  printf("\nIn L case");
11:                    dolwork();
12:                    break;
13:        case 'Z' :  printf("\nIn Z case");
14:                    dozwork();
15:                    break;
16:        default:    printf("\nERROR 19!!!! default entered unexpectedly");
17:                    exit();
18:                    }
19:      }
20:   }
21:   printf("\nExiting while");
```

With the same test input, this version generates the following trace:

```
Approaching while
getchar returns R
Loop entered, selecting on 1
Error 19!!!! default entered unexpectedly
```

Then the program aborts. Given this information, it is immediately obvious that something is wrong with the value assigned to c. The third line of the trace should have been

```
Loop entered, selecting on R 52
```

ch is ′R′. It has been traced. But when the assignment is made as a side effect in the while test, something goes wrong.

Curiously, the trace statement in line 5, which is supposed to print two values, prints only one—the hexadecimal representation of the nonprinting ASCII character known as *SOH*. Now, it is probably easier to understand (given this example) why two different print representations in line 5 were used.

Had

```
printf("\nLoop entered, selecting on %c", c);
```

been used, the result would have been

```
Loop entered, selecting on
```

And there still wouldn't have been specific information about which value was controlling the case. The example illustrates an important heuristic:

- Always print character data in two formats so that you learn about nonprinting characters as well as printing characters.

The character assigned to c isn't really meant to represent a character. Rather, it is the "true" generated by the relation on the right. C assignment operators have lower precedence than C relational operators and are performed last. The test must be fully parenthesized to work as intended:

```
while ((c = ch) != ′X′){
```

Methodical Instrumentation, Not Mystical Insight

The previous example is not particularly inspiring unless you've spent hours looking for a similar bug. "Where's the magic? Where's the mystical insight?" Frequently, the disappointing truth is that effective debugging is less a matter of mystical insight and inspiration than one of methodical instrumentation and information gathering. The debugger's challenge is:

- to stabilize the bug (which, in this example, is not an issue)

- to instrument the program adequately, following the guidelines given here

- to form explicit, specific expectations about what the instrumentation should indicate with the test data

None of these steps requires inspiration. First, for every run-time environment, specific facilities are available for stabilizing the bug (as discussed in Chapter 7). Second, trace mechanisms are always adequate if they meet the minimal standards set out in this chapter and in Chapter 7. Finally, forming expectations about the desired result is a mechanistic application of the program language's semantics.

An experienced "guru" will usually, but not always, spot bugs like this without complete instrumentation. After hunting for this bug in 40, 50, or 100 different situations, users begin checking every control expression for proper grouping before investing time implementing full instrumentation.

The "insight" that the new user may envy in others is less insight than it is a collection of heuristics about where to look first. Every one can build a set of heuristics by taking the time to evaluate his or her own performance. Whenever a bug takes what seems to be an inordinate amount of time, take a few minutes to examine why. These little studies are the foundation for a library of time-saving heuristics.

Building heuristic knowledge creates a sensitivity to heuristic limits. Heuristics require information. Before you are able to "leap" to a solution, there must be some instrumentation in the program, and the bug must be stabilized. Remember that until a bug is stabilized, you have no reliable information about its location.

Instrumenting Functions

Each function call causes two changes in execution order. At invocation, control is transferred to the function, and at return, control is transferred back to the calling routine. Each of these execution discontinuities should be bracketed with trace statements. This may seem particularly futile to programmers accustomed to languages such as BASIC and Pascal in which one can always trust the subroutine linkages. It can be very important in C, however, for reasons given in the next chapter. In other words, bracketing the function call

```
k = n + j;
   printf("\nready to call foobar");
m = foobar(k);
   printf("\nreturned from foobar");
k = m + j;
```

isn't adequate unless such bracketing is coupled with trace statements at the entrance and exits of foobar. (Note that *exits* is plural.)

C allows, and certain applications benefit from, functions that have several exits. Each potential exit must be instrumented so that the programmer "knows" exactly how the function actually exited. Just as control values are essential to loop and branch traces, parameter and return values are essential to function traces.

The same (as yet undiscussed) reasons that require function linkages to be bracketed require parameters and return values to be echoed on both sides of their respective control linkage. Formal and actual parameters, and transmitted and received return values should be traced. Listing 4.2 illustrates all of these points.

```
k = n + j;
printf("\nready to call foobar with %d", k);
m = foobar(k);
printf("\nreturned %d from foobar", m);
k = m + j;
   .
   .
   .
```

```
int foobar(parm)
int parm;

{
int result;

printf("\nentered foobar with %d", parm);
result = table[parm];
if (result > 0) {
   printf("\npositive exit, result=%d", result);
   return;
   }
printf("\nneg result, returning %d", parm);
return parm;
}
```

Listing 4.2.

Data-Flow Tracing

Data-flow tracing collects information that is useful to the programmer who is trying to locate a bug referentially. Because data references are structurally less complex than cases or loops, the body of rules describing placement of data-oriented traces is not large. Simply put, trace variables before they are used and after they are assigned.

To illustrate, k is fully traced in the following sequence of code:

```
1:   k = process(m);
2:   printf("\nafter process k = %d", k);

        .
        .      /* no references to k in missing code */
        .

10:  printf("\nbefore proc2 k = %d", k);
11:  proc2(k);

        .
        .      /* no references to k in missing code */
        .

34:  printf("\nin addition, k = %d", k);
35:  j = k + m;
36:  k = 2 * process(n);
37:  printf("\nafter 2*process, k = %d", k);
```

In this example, the traces in lines 10 and 35 will seem superfluous to the C initiate. In Pascal and BASIC, variables can be trusted to remain unchanged if no one assigns to them. In C, however, an aberrant pointer can affect almost anything. Before using this code, verify that the value k hasn't been changed unintentionally. (For further information, see Chapters 6 and 8.)

Data traces should include enough information to clearly place the reference in time. To be effective, a data-flow trace must be an effective control-flow trace. Skimping on time-identifying information will confuse the program verification process.

Selecting Variables

In most programs, tracing every reference to every variable is not practical. The trace burden can be reduced by fully instrumenting only the important variables in specific parts of the program. This "lack of thoroughness" is offset by the occasional sampling of a broad selection of variables. For this approach to be effective, the programmer must choose carefully the "important" variables and have a simple mechanism for dumping the broad sample.

Variables that influence control structures directly are always important in the temporal vicinity of such control structures. The programmer who "knows" his or her program will be able to select other key variables such as major data structures and other globally significant variables. Each modification of these central structures should be verified with a small local trace.

Using Snapshots

Debugging functions known as *snapshots* dump the values of a large number of variables. Unfortunately, a snapshot is limited to variables that are known to the current context. A large matrix that is to be dumped from modules at several different levels of the programming hierarchy must be known to each level. Global data structures most easily satisfy this constraint, but local data structures also can be "snapped" by means of an explicitly passed or globally known pointer. If a global table is declared as

```
int map[ROWS][COLS];
```

the programmer can get a complete image of it by using this function:

```
void snaptable()

{
int i, j;

for (i = 0; i < ROWS; i++){
    for (j = 0; j < COLS; j++){
        printf("%2.2d ", map[i][j]);
        }
    printf("\n");
    }
}
```

This works only because map is globally declared. If map were local to a function, a similar effect could be achieved in functions below map's home by having snaptable() access the table through a pointer. This pointer could be passed down from function to function, but the extra function argument necessary to this mechanism cannot easily be removed from the finished code.

A more convenient approach is to deposit a pointer to map into a global debugging variable (say map_pnt). Snaptable() can then reference the table by way of the pointer

```
printf("%2.2d ", (*map_pnt)[i][j]);
```

Listing 4.3 illustrates this method in the context of a complete (although trivial) program.

```
#include <stdio.h>

#define ROWS 3
#define COLS 4

int (*map_pnt)[ROWS][COLS];    /* the global debugging pointer */

main()
{
junk();
}
```

```
junk()
{
int map[ROWS][COLS];
int i, j;
void snaptable();

/* fill the array with a multiplication table */
for (i = 0;  i < ROWS;  i++){
    for (j = 0;  j < COLS;  j++){
        map[i][j] = i * j;
        }
    }
map_pnt = &map;
snaptable();
}

void snaptable()
{
int i,  j;

for (i = 0;  i < ROWS;  i++){
    for (j = 0;  j < COLS;  j++){
        printf("%2.2d ",  (*map_pnt)[i][j]);
        }
    printf("\n");
    }
}
```

Listing 4.3.

Snapshots can capture more than a single data structure. With a single snapshot, the programmer can dump a tree, a matrix, and 25 modal parameters (global variables that affect the behavior of several = functions). In large programs, programmers probably will want several different snapshot functions: some that are specialized for specific data structures, some specialized for certain portions of the program, and some that are as general as is reasonable.

Tracing Local Variables

By understanding how the compiler uses the stack and by building on that knowledge, the programmer can create a general-purpose snapshot facility for local variables. Although not pretty, such a snapshot is useful because it's easy to call. Unfortunately, this technique is extremely implementation-dependent. It won't port across machines or across compilers. It may not port even from an interpreter to a compatible compiler.

Modern compilers keep all local variables on the run-time stack. If variables are declared in this order

```
int j;
int k, l, m;
char str[15];
char *buf;
```

they will be allocated stack space in either the same or reverse order (see figs. 4.1 and 4.2). Knowing the starting address of the stack space occupied by these variables would permit the programmer to dump the entire block by "pretending" that it is a character array. In fact, the address is known: it's identical to the address of one of the end variables. The programmer only needs to determine which end.

Assume, for a minute, that &j is the address needed and that on this machine ints and pointers are each two bytes. The local snapshot facility can be called in this way:

```
dumploc( (char *) &j, 32);
```

Function dumploc can then print out the value of all 32 bytes following the starting address.

The difficulty with this approach is that dumploc does not know what kind of information it is printing. It doesn't understand the differences between bytes that are parts of an integer, bytes that are characters, and bytes that are parts of a pointer. As a partial solution to this problem, the information can be printed in more than one format, as is common in machine-level debuggers.

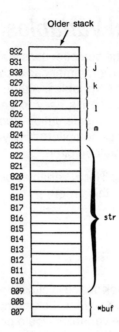

Fig. 4.1. Stack: Local variables allocated in order declared.

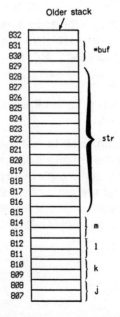

Fig. 4.2. Stack: Local variables allocated in "reverse" order.

The dump functions in listing 4.4, which mimic the dump format used by DEBUG, dump a block of memory in both hexadecimal and ASCII format.

```
void foo_bar(), dumpnloc(), dumpploc();

main()

{
foo_bar();
}

void foo_bar()

{
int j, k, l, m;
char str[16], *buf;

j = 5;
k = 1;
l = 25;
m = 14;
strcpy(str, "A DEMONSTRATION");
buf = (char *) 513;
printf("Version with increment\n");
dumpnloc( (char *)(&j) + 1, 32);
printf("Version with decrement\n");
dumpploc( &buf, 32);
}


void dumpnloc(start, len)
char *start;
int len;

{
char locbuf[17];
int i, j;
char *pnt;
```

```
        pnt = start;
        for (i = 0,  j = 0;  i < len;  j++,  i++){
            printf("%02.2x ", (unsigned char)(locbuf[j] = *pnt--));
            if ((locbuf[j] < ' ') || (locbuf[j] > 126)) locbuf[j] = '.';
            if (j == 15){
                locbuf[16] = 0;
                printf("   %16.16s\n", locbuf);
                j -= 16;
                }
            }
        if (j > 0){
            locbuf[j+1] = 0;
            printf("   %16s\n", locbuf);
            }
        printf("\n");
        }


        void dumpploc(start, len)
        char *start;
        int len;


        {
        char locbuf[17];
        int i, j;
        char *pnt;


        pnt = start;
        for (i = 0,  j = 0;  i < len;  j++,  i++){
            printf("%02.2x ", (unsigned char)(locbuf[j] = *pnt++));
            if ((locbuf[j] < ' ') || (locbuf[j] > 126)) locbuf[j] = '.';
            if (j == 15){
                locbuf[16] = 0;
                printf("   %16.16s\n", locbuf);
                j -= 16;
                }
            }
        if (j > 0) {
            locbuf[j+1] = 0;
            printf("   %16s\n", locbuf);
            }
        printf("\n");
        }
```

Listing 4.4.

Listing 4.4 is a complete although trivial program that calls two slightly different versions of the local variable dump: function. dumpploc() works through memory in ascending order, and dumpnloc(), in descending order. This program, when compiled under Eco-C88 and executed on a PC clone, produces this output

```
Version with increment
00 05 00 01 00 19 00 0e 00 4e 4f 49 54 41 52 54    ........NOITART
53 4e 4f 4d 45 44 20 41 02 01 00 20 ff f9 00 4d    SNOMED A.. ...M

Version with decrement
01 02 41 20 44 45 4d 4f 4e 53 54 52 41 54 49 4f    ..A DEMONSTRATIO
4e 00 0e 00 19 00 01 00 05 00 00 00 03 00 5c 02    N............\
```

Clearly, this kind of debugging trace can't be used effectively unless the programmer has learned to think in hexadecimal. The trace isn't pretty, but it's easy to get and gives a comprehensive view of what is happening or not happening to local variables. For reasons discussed in Chapter 6, this machine-level view of what's happening is exactly where the programmer needs to spot bad subscripts or pointers.

The "+ 1" adjustment in listing 4.4's call to dumpnloc() extends the end of the block to include the last byte of the two-byte integer. A similar adjustment frequently will be necessary (depending on how multibyte values are ordered in memory) when the "end" variable is a multibyte value. In a 32-bit system, for example, integers might require a "+ 3" adjustment.

Function dumpnloc() works quite naturally with the storage mechanism detailed in figure 4.1. On some systems, however, dumpploc() may give more usable results. If both versions produce garbage, reverse the parameters in the two calls to the dump functions and try again. The change to foo_bar() is:

```
printf("Version with increment\n");
dumpnloc( &buf , 32);
printf("Version with decrement\n");
dumpploc( (char *) (&j) + 1 , 32);
```

If you don't know how the compiler allocates local storage (it's usually not documented), running a few experiments with variations on dumploc will provide experience and insight.

Easy-to-spot values should be assigned to several local variables. dumploc is then called twice—once with the first declared variable and a second time with the last declared variable. One of these calls should dump a portion of the stack that contains the variables. If it doesn't, the increment of pnt should be changed and the test repeated.

This trick won't work if the compiler isn't storing local variables on the stack. Sophisticated optimizing compilers try to keep certain frequently used local variables in registers.

dumploc can't be used if the compiler optimizes in this manner; there is no way to predict which variables will be in the stack, or how they will be ordered. In this situation, it is advisable to carefully search the compiler manual for a switch to disable optimization, at least while debugging. Running under UNIX, the Green Hills compiler (marketed by Oasys Corporation) optimizes in this way and, fortunately, has such a switch.

RETURN

Various forms of trace statement are the programmer's "window" into the executing program. To efficiently exploit both referential and temporal proximity, programmers usually combine data-flow and control-flow traces into common statements. Full "instrumentation" requires traces that bracket all control discontinuities and that frequently report the state of all control variables and major data structures.

Data structures and local variables are more conveniently traced with special-purpose functions as opposed to simple trace statements. C's unique ability to "peek through" to the underlying hardware facilitates the creation of general-purpose memory dump routines that can be used to trace contiguous data structures (such as large arrays) and segments of the stack. Although this machine-oriented display of the state of a program runs counter to the philosophy of other high-level languages, it is often exactly what the C programmer needs.

5
Managing Trace Facilities

As a programmer works to instrument a large program, he or she may add literally hundreds of trace statements. Those trace statements create two problems.

First, if all the trace statements are always activated, output from a single test run can require hours of printer time and boxes of paper.

Second, if trace statements are left in the production version of the program, they degrade performance and significantly increase code size.

This chapter addresses both problems beginning with several ideas for limiting the volume of trace-generated output. Later sections describe coding techniques that allow trace facilities to remain in the source but absent from the compiled code.

In this book, it is assumed that the user never removes trace statements from the source. Program design, coding, and instrumentation represent a significant amount of work. Why waste the effort by removing the statements from the source? Another bug will show up, and when it does, all those statements have to be reentered.

Some programmers try to save debugging efforts by keeping two copies of a program: a production copy without trace statements, and a debugging copy with trace statements. This arrangement simply replaces the problem of unattractive source code with a different and potentially more difficult problem: how to ensure that both copies of the program remain updated.

Where is it written that proper program instrumentation is unattractive? Why be so anxious about letting someone see that the program has been debugged? If quality design and quality coding are pleasing, why isn't quality program instrumentation pleasing?

Instead of removing all program instrumentation before showing the program to someone else, learn to understand instrumentation as a natural program ingredient. Instead of hiding instrumentation under the rug, learn to integrate it in a coherent and unobtrusive way.

Controlling Trace Output

The crudest output control the programmer can build is a simple switch that disables or enables all program instrumentation. A global variable records the current value of the switch, and each trace statement is embedded in an if that tests the value of the switch. Adding a simple debug switch to listing 4.1 (in Chapter 4) produces this result:

```
 1:     if (debug) printf("\nApproaching age branch, person.age = %d",person.age);
 2:     if (person.age < 5) {
 3:          if (debug) printf("\nCalling addtopreschool");
 4:          addtopreschool(person);
 5:          }
 6:     else if (person.age < 14){
 7:          if (debug) printf("\nCalling addtogrades");
 8:          addtogrades(person);
 9:          }
10:     else {
11:          if (debug) printf("\nCalling addtohigh");
12:          addtohigh(person);
13:          }
14:     if (debug) printf("\nreturned from call in age branch");
```

When the global variable debug is nonzero, all the trace statements are activated. When it is zero, all the trace statements are deactivated.

Stepping from a simple switch to a multilevel switch is natural. A multilevel switch works like a faucet: the more "on" you make it, the more output you get. With a multilevel switch, the code might look like this:

```
 1:     if (debug > 1) printf("\nApproaching age branch, person.age = %d", person.age);
 2:     if (person.age < 5) {
 3:             if (debug > 2) printf("\nCalling addtopreschool");
 4:             addtopreschool(person);
 5:             }
 6:     else if (person.age < 14){
 7:             if (debug > 2) printf("\nCalling addtogrades");
 8:             addtogrades(person);
 9:             }
10:     else {
11:             if (debug > 2) printf("\nCalling addtohigh");
12:             addtohigh(person);
13:             }
14:     if (debug > 1) printf("\nreturned from call in age branch");
```

And, in function addtohigh(), the programmer might find this:

```
void addtohigh(who)
structure body *who;

{
if (debug > 3) printf( "\ncalled addtohigh with %04.4x", who);
        .
        .
        .
if (debug > 3) printf( "\nexiting addtohigh");
}
```

When debug is zero, no trace statements are printed. When debug is one, only top-level (main-line) traces are activated. Each increase in the value of debug activates traces that correspond to a deeper level of the program hierarchy.

Making Control More Convenient

By building a debugging function, the programmer can avoid constantly retyping

```
    if (debug...) printf...
```

A truly useful function must allow, as printf does, a variable number of arguments, making it a nontrivial project. (Look in Appendix B for source for such a debugging function.) A convenient form is:

```
    dbg(level, format string, arg, arg, arg.....)
```

In this call, level is the minimum debug switch value necessary to enable output from this debugging statement. Function dbg assumes responsibility for referencing the global debugging switch and calling printf or other appropriate output routines.

Setting the Control Variable

The value assigned to debug can be determined at compile time by changing a manifest global or at run time by inputting a value from the command line or keyboard. Selecting the latter option allows several tests of varying detail to be run without recompiling the program. If the debug switch value comes from the command line

```
myprogram -d3
```

-d is a debug flag and 3 is the chosen debug level. If debug is initialized to zero before command line options are processed, the debug input will be invisible to users who aren't aware of the debug option.

If input from the keyboard is explicitly requested, the input line must be removed from the production code and replaced with an explicit assignment. A conditional compile directive can be used instead of actually deleting the input line.

Temporal Switches

A multilevel switch controls trace output more effectively than a simple switch. The multilevel switch is, however, inadequate for large systems. If the programmer needs to trace (at a low level of detail), a section of code that executes at the end of a long, complex run, a multilevel switch will enable full trace detail through the entire run. Because the switch setting is constant throughout the run, the effect is no control at all.

Temporal switches and multilevel switches use the same level-sensitive tests to enable or disable code. Temporal switches include, however, an additional mechanism for varying the switch setting during the run. Three such mechanisms are: hard-wired changes, mile-post counting, and function-by-function reconfiguration.

Hard-Wired Changes

An assignment statement, placed anywhere within the code, can change the setting of the debug level as the program runs. The programmer initializes the debug variable so that it selects only very high-level trace statements. Then, immediately before the section of code to be examined more carefully, he or she uses either an explicit assignment statement to change to a lower level or prompts the keyboard for a new level.

This mechanism is reversible. In other words, by adding appropriate assignments, it is possible to move (several times) between high-level trace mode and low-level trace mode. Programmers use this method for a detailed trace on more than one segment of code (to inspect references to a specific variable, for example). Because a new edit-compile-link cycle is required whenever the change point is modified, examining large blocks of code (one segment at a time) may become time consuming.

Counting Mile Posts

A more dynamic (but sometimes less flexible) method counts "mile posts" as the program runs. After the program has passed a specified number of mile posts, the debug routines change the debug level. Almost any programming event can be used as a mile post. The critical mile post count can be selected from the keyboard or specified as a command-line argument allowing the count to be changed dynamically without recompiling the program.

The mile post count is kept in a global variable and incremented whenever a mile post is passed. In simple variations, only the highest level trace statements generate output until the mile post is reached, after which *all* trace statements generate output.

The process can be enhanced by specifying the two trace levels at the beginning of each run. It can be enhanced also by creating start and stop mile posts.

The critical parts of a debug system, with two start and stop mile posts and run-time selected trace levels for each, are illustrated in the following code segment:

```
/* The trace routine */

dbg(level, fmt, ...)    /* variable number of args !*/
int level;
char *fmt;

{
if ((miles < onmark1) && (level > initlevel)) return;
if ((miles >= onmark1) && (miles < offmark1)
   && (level > onlevel1)) return;
if ((miles >= offmark1) && (miles < onmark2)
   && (level > initlevel)) return;
if ((miles >= onmark2) && (miles < offmark2)
   && (level > onlevel2)) return;
if ((miles  >= offmark2) && (level > initlevel)) return;

    .
    .
       code to print the trace
    .
    .
}
```

A mile post may be placed anywhere in the program. Select a location in the program and increment the global miles variable with

```
miles += 1;
```

Function boundaries are natural spots for mile posts. If a trace call already exists at each function boundary (a good practice), make a one-line change in the trace routine.

```
/* The trace routine with embedded mile post */

dbg(level, fmt, ...)    /* variable number of args !*/
int level;
char *fmt;

{
if (level == 0) miles += 1;
if ((miles < onmark1) && (level > initlevel)) return;
if ((miles >= onmark1) && (miles < offmark1)
   && (level > onlevel1)) return;
if ((miles >= offmark1) && (miles < onmark2)
   && (level > initlevel)) return;
```

```
if ((miles >= onmark2) && (miles < offmark2)
   && (level > onlevel2)) return;
if ((miles  >= offmark2) && (level > initlevel)) return;
      .
      .
   code to print the trace
      .
      .
}
```

Because of the change, every top-level trace statement will double as a mile post. Embedding the mile post in the debugging function produces a more dynamic and maintainable system. It isn't necessary to choose only top-level trace statements. In fact, the top three levels can be treated as mile posts. Try using two trace routines, one with and one without mile posts.

Function-by-Function

Mile posts are an awkward mechanism for selectively tracing functions that are called throughout a program. To get detail trace from a specific function (whenever the function is called), use a simple multilevel switch and hard-wire changes at the boundaries of the function.

```
#define MAXDETAIL 99999
      .
      .
      .


void foo()

{
int oldlevel;

oldlevel = debug;
debug = MAXDETAIL;

      .
   function code including normal trace statements
      .
debug = oldlevel;
}
```

Because this example restores the original trace level at exit, it is more elaborate than necessary. Even in simpler form the program is awkward. The code must be modified each time the programmer chooses to trace a specific function in detail, thereby incurring the overhead of edit-compile-link cost.

Including a function identifier in each call to the debug routine creates a dynamic mechanism for selecting specific functions. The function prompt asks the user for numeric input by printing its single string argument. It validates the console input and returns the value as an integer. Such a debugging tool should be used in combination with the mile-post mechanism. The enhancements are shown in the following code fragment:

```
/* debug system initialization
   including function select */

miles = Ø;
initlevel = prompt("background debug level");
onmark1 = prompt("first on mile post");
onlevel1 = prompt("and its debug level");
offmark1 = prompt("first off mile post");
onmark2 = prompt("second on mile post");
onlevel2 = prompt("and its debug level");
offmark2 = prompt("second off mile post");
f1 = prompt("first function");
f1lev= prompt("and its debug level");
f2 = prompt("second function");
f2lev = prompt("and its debug level");
f3 = prompt("third function");
f3lev = prompt("and its debug level");
   .
   .
   .
```

Thus, the programmer would respond to the prompt

```
first function
```

to turn on tracing in function 27.

```
/* The trace routine with embedded mile post
   and function select */
```

```
dbg(level, funct, fmt, ...)      /* variable number of args !*/
int level, funct;
char *fmt;


{
if (level == 0) miles += 1;

/*process functions first...they override mile post */

if ((funct == f1) && (level <= f1lev)) goto prtrace;
if ((funct == f2) && (level <= f2lev)) goto prtrace;
if ((funct == f3) && (level <= f3lev)) goto prtrace;

/* now look for normal traces */

if ((miles < onmark1) && (level > initlevel)) return;
if ((miles >= onmark1) && (miles < offmark1)
   && (level > onlevel1)) return;
if ((miles >= offmark1) && (miles < onmark2)
   && (level > initlevel)) return;
if ((miles >= onmark2) && (miles < offmark2)
   && (level > onlevel2)) return;
if ((miles  >= offmark2) && (level > initlevel)) return;
   .
   .
   .
prtrace:  /* code to print the trace */
   .
   .
   .
}
```

The assumption is that every function has been assigned an integer identifier. A third-level trace appearing in function 27 would now look like this

```
dbg(3, 27, "%s", joe);
```

The trace becomes more readable by giving to 27 a global name that suggests the function's name. Alternatively, the function's name can be captured as a string (during the debug system initialization) and pass the function name as a string at each dbg invocation. Although it complicates the coding, the latter is the preferred arrangement. (See Appendix B for a set of debugging routines with these features.)

Granularity

Mile posts are an effective trace control when the bug can be placed in execution time—that is, when the programmer suspects that the bug occurs in a specified function or segment of code.

Sometimes, though, the programmer knows only that a bug involves a certain variable. The variable ends up with a wrong value, but the programmer is uncertain where or when the variable acquired that value.

In such a case, the programmer may decide to examine every 1,000th reference to the suspect variable. Then, within the 1,000 references that surround the error, he or she examines every 100th reference. Finally, within the 100 references that surround the error, every reference is examined. This kind of adjustment is referred to as an adjustment in *granularity*. Granularity controls the frequency of the trace (without reference to trace locations in the program hierarchy).

A granularity control is implemented with a modulus operator and a global counter. Whenever a trace function is called, the granularity counter is stepped. Each 7th, 10th, or 1,000th call can be detected by testing the counter with modulus arithmetic.

Because granularity controls are most useful when searching for the location at which a variable was changed, they are best used when combined with a snapshot. This approach should be blended with techniques discussed earlier in the chapter.

```
/* debug system initialization
   including function select and granularity
   control over snapshots
   */

miles = Ø;
calls = Ø;
initlevel = prompt("background debug level");
onmark1 = prompt("first on mile post");
onlevel1 = prompt("and its debug level");
offmark1 = prompt("first off mile post");
onmark2 = prompt("second on mile post");
onlevel2 = prompt("and its debug level");
offmark2 = prompt("second off mile post");
f1 = prompt("first function");
```

```
f1lev= prompt("and its debug level");
f2 = prompt("second function");
f2lev = prompt("and its debug level");
f3 = prompt("third function");
f3lev = prompt("and its debug level");
gran = prompt("granularity for snapshots");
strtsnp = prompt("starting call for snapshots");
endsnp = prompt("ending call for snapshots");
    .
    .
    .



/* The trace routine with embedded mile post,
   function select, and granularity control */

dbg(level, funct, fmt, ...)     /* variable number of args !*/
int level, funct;
char *fmt;

{
calls += 1;
if (level == 0) miles += 1;

/*process functions first...they override mile post */

if ((funct == f1) && (level <= f1lev)) goto prtrace;
if ((funct == f2) && (level <= f2lev)) goto prtrace;
if ((funct == f3) && (level <= f3lev)) goto prtrace;

/* now look for normal traces */

if ((miles < onmark1) && (level > initlevel)) goto snap;
if ((miles >= onmark1) && (miles < offmark1)
   && (level > onlevel1)) goto snap;
if ((miles >= offmark1) && (miles < onmark2)
   && (level > initlevel)) goto snap;
if ((miles >= onmark2) && (miles < offmark2)
   && (level > onlevel2)) goto snap;
if ((miles  >= offmark2) && (level > initlevel)) goto snap;
```

```
prtrace:   /* code to print the trace */


snap:   if ((calls > strtsnp) && (calls < endsnp) &&
            (!(calls % gran))) snapshot();
}
```

Practical Variations

The programmer has created an extremely flexible debugging tool that requires answers to 16 questions at the start of each debugging run. In the preceding example, all the questions are answered with numbers.

A perceptive programmer, however, will question the practicality of all this. The debugging tool poses two potential problems:

- it seems to require a lot of code.

- it has an ugly, time-consuming user interface.

The code isn't a real problem because with the exception of the snapshot function, which is unique to each program, all of the code is general purpose. It can be written once, put in a library, and never again considered. In fact, the code written for each trace call—this line, for example—

```
dbg(3, "thisfunct", "%s %d", buffer, count);
```

is no more awkward than the traditional printf.

The real problem is the debugging system's user interface. It can be improved by adding defaults for all questions and by using strings for function names. Of course, by the time the programmer adds all these "user-friendly" features, the underlying ideas are difficult to see. This chapter presents trace facilities in stripped-down form. Appendix B contains full-featured versions with some explanation.

To the Reader

Study the trace routine in Appendix B to explore how general-purpose, easy-to-use trace facilities can be implemented. Try to adapt the routine to your compiler. Begin with the stripped-down versions in this chapter; when they work, add from the expanded versions in Appendix B.

If your compiler includes source code for printf and sprintf, study those functions. You may find hints that can help you with what is probably the hardest part of the function: passing a variable-length list of parameters.

If you can't determine which function printf and sprintf call, you probably should settle for printing a single parameter in one or two formats (like dumploc()) on each dbg call.

When you understand how the trace routine works in your environment, throw it away (or at least make several variations that respond to specific needs). The version in Appendix B is not meant to be the "ultimate" debugging tool. It is simply one example of how you can dynamically control the tracing process.

Managing Source Code

As program instrumentation becomes more powerful and complete, the program must support an ever larger burden of ancillary trace code. This code is undesirable in production versions of an application program, because it doesn't contribute directly to the application task. If the programmer observes a specific set of coding practices, the C preprocessor will remove all debug facilities automatically.

Bracketing all trace facilities with #ifdef and #endif directives is the least sophisticated (and least satisfactory) approach. This technique and the trace routine to fully instrument the program fragment shown in the "Instrumenting Case Statements" section of Chapter 4 result in this monstrosity:

```
1: #ifdef TESTING
2: dbg(3, "foo", "\nApproaching while");
3: #endif
4: ch = getchar();
5: #ifdef TESTING
6: dbg(3, "foo", "\ngetchar returns %c", ch);
7: #endif
8: while (c = ch != 'X') {  /* the error, remember? */
9: #ifdef TESTING
```

```
10:    dbg(4, "foo", "Loop entered, selecting on %c %d", c, c);
11: #endif
12:    switch (c){
13:       case 'R' :
14: #ifdef TESTING
15:                 dbg(5, "foo", "\nIn R case");
16: #endif
17:                 dorwork();
18:                 break;
19:       case 'L' :
20: #ifdef TESTING
21:                 dbg(5, "foo",  "\nIn L case");
            .
            .
            .
```

No wonder programmers don't want others to see their debugging, if it looks like this. Six lines of productive code occupy 21 lines of source. The original program's indentation has been thoroughly obscured by placement restrictions for preprocessor directives. In short, it's hard to find the program!

The problem is that the programmer is manually typing #ifdef... #endif pairs. The process can be automated by using another "level" of preprocessor substitution. Instead of calling dbg directly, call a preprocessor macro that (if TESTING is defined) will call dbg. If testing is not defined, the macro call will be replaced by an empty line. The macro definition is:

```
#ifdef TESTING
#define TRACE(args) dbg args
#else
#define TRACE(args)
#endif
```

The code that uses this new macro is:

```
1:    TRACE((3, "foo", "\nApproaching while"));
2:    ch = getchar();
3:    TRACE((3, "foo", "\ngetchar returns %c", ch));
4:    while (c = ch != 'X' ) { /* still an error */
5:       TRACE((4, "foo", "\nLoop entered, selecting on %c %d", c, c));
6:       switch (c){
7:          case 'R' :  TRACE((5, "foo", "\nIn R case"));
8:                      dorwork();
9:                      break;
```

```
10:          case 'L' :   TRACE((5, "foo", "\nIn L case"));
11:                       dowork();

            .
            .
            .
```

The double parentheses in the trace calls aren't a stutter. The macro TRACE() has a single argument: the list of all arguments to be passed to dbg. Unfortunately, many preprocessors will stop copying the trace argument list as soon as they reach the first comma.

The problem is avoided by packaging the entire list with parentheses. The preprocessor will now pass the entire list (including parentheses) to dbg. Because the parentheses move with the list, the usual parentheses around args in the substitution string aren't needed.

These removable trace statements don't obscure the structure of the program. They are easy to use and so consistent in form that the programmer can learn easily to "read over" them. There shouldn't be objections to leaving these trace statements in the source. However, if it does become necessary to remove them, a program editor or grep-like tool can be used to identify and remove all lines with trace calls.

RETURN

The trace statements added during the debugging process represent knowledge about the problem and the program. This knowledge should not be discarded just because the program has been placed in production but should remain an integral part of the program source.

Permanent debugging structures, however, aren't practical tools unless they include suitable output control mechanisms and preserve the readability of the code. Trace output should be selectable in the separate dimensions of time, detail, and program hierarchy.

To protect the source, as much of the trace mechanism as possible should be embedded in lexically uniform functions. Uniform trace statements are easily "read over" and easily removed with preprocessor mechanisms or grep-like pattern-matching utilities.

6
Why Is Debugging C
Difficult?

Most of today's programmers have "grown up" in the protected environment of Pascal and BASIC. Many know that usually C is compiled and that C has no run-time type and bounds checking. Some may have read that C is descended from the typeless language, B.

To the newcomer, these matters seem small and academic—matters that are clearly overshadowed by C's promise of portability, flexibility, modularity, and speed. The unspoken assumption is that the process of debugging C will be much like that of debugging Pascal or any other small, well-structured language. And once the new syntax has been mastered, programming in the new language has been mastered.

It simply isn't so.

Programmers who take up C acquire

- the ubiquitous and treacherous pointer
- easy access to machine-level operations (such as bitwise shifts)
- the expressive power of a highly orthogonal language

What these programmers seldom realize is that they give up the reliability of all the conventional debugging techniques they ever learned. These C differences (the lack of protection and the inclusion of unusual mechanisms) combine to make debugging difficult in two ways:

- C compilers can't be as helpful as Pascal compilers or BASIC interpreters.

- C doesn't guarantee the integrity of the virtual machine.

This chapter begins by explaining why C compilers can't be as helpful as other translators. An explanation of virtual machines follows. The chapter ends with a general discussion of how C's peculiarities affect the debugging process.

Strong Types and Error Detection

C is not strongly typed; Pascal is. In a strongly typed language, the compiler can identify all type mismatches at compile time. In Pascal, naming the parameters of a procedure in the wrong order will probably cause the compiler to detect the error as a type clash. Using the wrong variable name in an expression will signal the compiler to flag the error.

C compilers rarely detect such problems. Instead of flagging the error, the typical C compiler blindly generates the unintentionally requested code, creating a program that is guaranteed to "crash and burn."

To understand the differences more clearly, compare these examples:

```
/* A Pascal program with trivial errors that, thanks to
   strong type-checking, are easily spotted */

Program example;

Var
   str: string;
   k, stp: integer;
```

```
Function joe(a:string; b:integer):integer;
    .
    .
      .
Begin
   k:=7; str:='demo string';
   k:=joe(k,str);                    {oops, should be str,k}
   str:=k                            {a typo, I meant stp}
end.
```

```
/* An equally wrong C equivalent that would compile correctly
   under many microcomputer compilers */

main()

{
char *str;
int k, stp;

k = 7; str = "demo string";
k = joe(k,str);                     /* the same errors */
str = k;
}

int joe(a,b)
char *a;
int b;
{
   .
   .
      .
}
```

Understanding why arguments are not tightly checked requires an examination of C's intended use. C was designed to support the convenient use of separately compiled modules, a feature that allows C to successfully exploit "canned function libraries."

Because the definition of a function may be unavailable at compile time (indeed, it may be the closely-guarded secret of the function library's vendor), the compiler may not be able to identify the parameter types. Historically, C compilers have responded uniformly to this possibility: because the compiler can't check some types at function boundaries, the compiler doesn't check any.

Because their types are never checked, the misordered parameters aren't detected. The new ANSI C standard addresses this issue by allowing a "function template," which specifies parameter and return types, to appear in a file. Certainly the template represents a significant improvement, but the opportunity for undetected errors still exists; what if the template doesn't agree with the actual definition?

Early C implementations ran on 16-bit minicomputers in which a pointer was almost always exactly the same size as an integer. Consider as well the fact that C was designed as an "implementation language" (a language with which to build languages), and it is easier to understand why assigning an integer to a string pointer is reasonable (although not what was intended in the sample program).

If pointers and integers are the same size, enforcing type distinctions between them only serves to complicate certain tasks. For example, a compiler might need to initialize a pointer with a specific memory address, perhaps to set up a stack or data area. If types are ignored, the code representation is much more convenient; otherwise, explicit type coercions must be included. Operations that involve arithmetic on pointers (those necessary in subscript computation, for example) become especially awkward when types are enforced.

Examples of such operations are:

```
Code to Initialize a Pointer
    pointer = 0x400000;              /*ignoring types  */
    pointer = (adrtype) 0x400000;   /*enforcing types */

Code to Compute the Address of Element(5, 7)
                                    /*ignoring types  */
    pointer = element + 5 * rowsize + 7;
                                    /*enforcing types */
    pointer = (adrtype)((int) element + 5 * rowsize + 7);
```

On many machines, C merely adapted the attitude of its typeless predecessor, allowing certain types (usually pointers and characters) to be treated as integers. In such an environment, the compiler can't distinguish between an intentional type coercion and an accidental one.

For good reasons, modern practice and modern compilers are moving away from this earlier practice. Integers that are treated as pointers and characters that are treated as integers must be found and corrected when transporting C programs from one environment (a machine with 16-bit integers and 16-bit addresses, for example) to a dissimilar environment (a machine with 16-bit integers and 24-bit memory addresses).

This change in practice is reflected in the preliminary results of the ANSI X3J11 Standards Committee. The committee's most significant contribution (aside from resolving technical details) are language extensions that support portable coding practices and better static error analysis (better compiler error detection). These extensions allow (but do not require) the programmer to supply more complete information about his or her intent. The most significant of these extensions takes the form of additional type information, including new keywords, such as *void, const*, and *violate*, and new syntactic structures, such as *prototypes*.

(As a consequence of this stronger typing information, compilers that fully exploit the new X3J11 language features will probably absorb many of lint's major functions.)

Although interpreted languages are seldom described as strongly typed, most provide error detection equivalent to strongly typed languages as a by-product of the interpretation process.

In the example

```
100 K=7: ST$ = "demo string"
105 A$=K: B=ST$
110 GOSUB 300
120 ST$ = K
    .
    .
    .
300 K = .....
400 RET
```

the obvious misordering of the parameters in line 105 is not a natural mistake in BASIC. But that is not the issue. Again, unlike the C compiler, the BASIC interpreter would spot both errors immediately.

Orthogonality and Error Detection

In orthogonal languages, each language structure can be combined with virtually every other structure to produce a meaningful and legal statement. C is less orthogonal than APL but more so than BASIC or Pascal. C's orthogonality is derived from its treatment of almost everything as a value-carrying expression. Many of C's pithy optimizations, such as

```
            /* using orthogonality property */
  foo( (a = 7), (k = (b > 7) ? 6 : 2));

  a = 7;          /* conventional sequence */
  k = (b > 7 > ? 6 : 2;
  foo(a , k);
```

are a by-product of orthogonality.

Although the first form may appear unnecessarily terse, it can be viewed also as cheap code optimization. To capture information about the future utility of variables a and k, the assignments have been embedded in the parameter references.

Now, the compiler can generate code with two fewer references, a significant economy in a sequence with only five variable references. However, everything has its price. The fewer the restrictions on how constructs can be put together, the greater the probability that a mistake in construction will appear legal.

On most C compilers, for example, this mistake

```
  k = (a , b);        /* I meant k = foo(a , b); */
```

will not generate an error. Instead, it will generate code that references a (but does nothing with the value), and then references b, assigning the value to k. Note that this construct is legal not only at compile time but also at run time. A program containing this kind of mistake may terminate normally and frequently generates correct results.

Opportunities for subtle bugs abound when orthogonality is combined with overloaded or confusing operators. (An *overloaded* operator is one that is used to mean several different things in different contexts.)

C combines symbols to produce unique operators for most operations. Accusing C of operator overloading then is not really fair.

The ampersand (&) and asterisk (*) are the only truly overloaded operators in C. The ampersand functions as the *address of operator* and the *bitwise and*. The asterisk functions as the *dereferencing operator* (pointer) and *multiply*. The other combinations, although unique, are themselves a source of subtle errors, such as

Typo	*Intended*
if (a = b)	if (a == b)...
if (a & b)	if (a && b)...

The compiler can't detect such errors because in certain circumstances the expressions in the left column might be exactly what was intended; those in the right column might be the error.

General Impact of Structural Differences

The compiler's inability to find trivial typos can be attributed to C's lax approach to information typing and the language's willingness to treat anything and everything as an expression. Therefore, typing errors are discovered more frequently during run-time testing in C than in other languages. Pascal and BASIC programmers expect to stop looking for minor typos and concentrate on logic errors after a program has compiled correctly.

Most of the typos presented in this section will generate symptoms similar to logic errors. The preceding example might cause a test to be always false, always true, or (even worse) sometimes true and sometimes false in a seemingly impossible pattern. Because humans often see exactly what we expect to see, typos in programs that have compiled and run to execution tend to become invisible.

C's powerful and elegant language structures have the undesirable side effect of forcing run-time debugging of many relatively trivial errors. Because run-time debugging is always more difficult and time-consuming than compile-time debugging, C is harder and more time-consuming to debug than other compiled languages. And, as if this weren't enough, there are other, more challenging issues involved.

The Virtual Machine and Our Expectations

Assembly language (real machine programming) horrifies some programmers. High-level languages, created to hide the real machine's uglier features, reflect the capabilities of an idealized "virtual" machine. Arrays, strings, user-defined types, and floating-point arithmetic are all services of the virtual machine, services that usually don't exist on the real machine.

The virtual machine isn't tangible. Its capabilities are generated by a collection of software and data structures. In a compiled environment, the virtual machine might be built of a run-time package, a stack, a heap, a global data area, and the compiler-generated application code. In an interpreted environment, the interpreter is the virtual machine.

Programmers who write in a high-level language perceive themselves as writing machine instructions for this virtual machine. As they write and test instructions, programmers assume that the virtual machine is always in working order. Because Pascal and BASIC take great care to protect the integrity of the virtual machine from the programmer's mistakes, in those environments the assumption is reasonable. C, however, offers no such protection.

A faulty C pointer or an array subscript that has traveled out of bounds can violate the virtual machine in several ways. It should be emphasized that faulty pointers and out-of-bounds subscripts are really the same in C. Pointer arithmetic and array subscripts are considered equivalent (see Kernighan and Ritchie's *The C Programming Language*, page 93).

Faulty pointers write on arbitrary spots in memory. If they write on the run-time stack, the function linkages or local variables are destroyed. If they write on the run-time package (or a standard library module), the semantics of an operator or function can change while the program is running. If they write on the operating system, I/O devices can disappear, or for no apparent reason stop functioning. If they write on data or program code, the program will develop strange symptoms that change magically from run to run.

Bugs generated by these failure mechanisms aren't just time-consuming; they are often untraceable. Finding them with conventional debugging techniques isn't difficult; it's impossible.

Conventional debugging techniques (various forms of source-based tracing, stubbing, and module testing) are based on assumptions derived from an expectation that the virtual machine will work correctly.

The virtual machine is reliable. This assumption is really "the granddaddy of 'em all." Programmers expect addition and assignment to work properly in spite of errors made in code; they also expect sequential statements to execute sequentially. These expectations are reasonable only if the programmer believes that the virtual machine is "invulnerable."

The application code is lexically static. Programmers expect code to remain the way it was written. If the print module works once but fails later in the run, the programmer may deduce that the application passed it correct data the first time but not the next. This conclusion is reasonable only if the programmer assumes that the print module code doesn't suffer from random changes during the run.

Cause and effect are closely related. Programmers expect the principles of lexical, referential, and chronological proximity to hold. But these expectations are based on the assumption that the virtual machine sequences instructions correctly and performs only references and assignments that were requested in the code.

Time starts anew with each invocation. In other words, programmers expect the machine to behave deterministically. They expect that runs which process identical input will generate identical results.

Users' expectations about how systems should operate become so ingrained that instead of challenging their expectations and assumptions (even when faced with bugs that obviously violate the assumptions), they turn to sources of error they would seldom consider in another environment.

C newcomers question either the integrity of the compiler vendor or their own talent for programming, and neither is usually at issue. What is at issue is whether traditional debugging methods can be suitably adapted or augmented to function reliably, even when the virtual machine doesn't.

Bugs that Attack the Virtual Machine

In preparation for the specialized C debugging techniques of Chapters 7 and 8, the balance of this chapter examines how different bugs attack the virtual machine.

Pointer Bugs and the Stack

In any C environment, the run-time stack is one of the virtual machine's most vulnerable components. Modern compilers use a single run-time stack to maintain a "sense of history" (information about what has been completed, and what needs to be done after the current task is finished). The run-time stack also manages allocated memory dynamically; it makes space for variables that "come and go." It is not practical for the hardware to distinguish between valid and invalid stack references because of the way the stack is used.

Almost any locally declared pointer or array can be misused to damage the stack. Symptoms that result from stack damage are interesting: programs crash "between" lines of code or between functions, variables change without being referenced, and in rare cases, functions execute and return smoothly (but to the wrong part of the program). It is important to learn the intended use of the stack and to study how simple errors can cause impossible symptoms.

Local variables are dynamic objects; they are created and destroyed dynamically as functions are entered and exited. At the beginning of each function, the compiler must generate code to "make space" for these variables; at exit, similar code must reclaim this space for later use.

Modern compilers "make" this space on the stack by generating code at the beginning of every function that "skips" the stack pointer over a block of stack space large enough to hold all the declared local variables. This block together with other information is called a *stack frame*. The process of allocating local variables generates a special pointer, called the *frame pointer*, which points to one end of the local variables. By keeping this pointer in a suitable register, the compiler can reference any of the active local variables by adding an offset to the frame pointer.

Figures 6.1 through 6.5 illustrate this process for a hypothetical machine in which every memory location is large enough to hold an integer. Figure 6.1 shows the stack as it appears while line x1 is executing. Figure 6.2 presents the stack after all the parameters of line call1 have been evaluated but before function foo has received control.

In figure 6.3 the parent function has called foo, causing a return address to be pushed onto the stack. This return address is part of the "other information" mentioned earlier. foo must save not only the parent's return address but also the parent's frame pointer.

In figure 6.4 the frame pointer has been saved, and in figure 6.5 local variable space and a new frame pointer have been generated. Symbolic labels for each of foo's local variables have been included in figure 6.5.

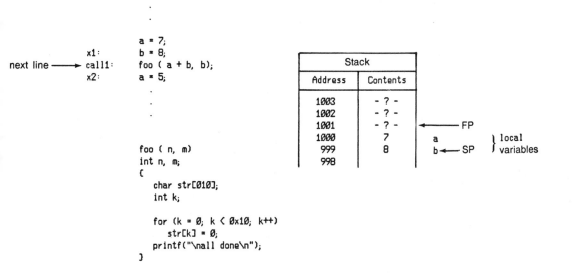

Fig. 6.1. Stack for hypothetical machine with integer (not byte) memory. Stack structure after line x1 has executed. a and b are local to code fragment containing x1.

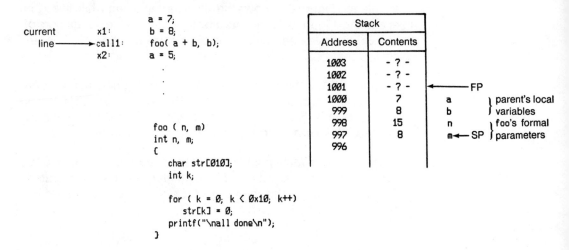

Fig. 6.2. Stack after evaluating foo's formal parameters but before transfering control to foo.

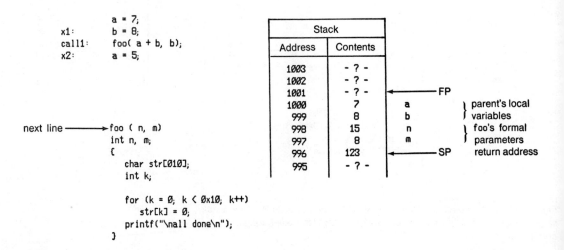

Fig. 6.3. Stack after call to foo but before allocation of foo locals. 123 is address of code generated for line x2.

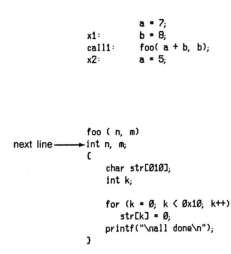

```
                a = 7;
x1:             b = 8;
call1:          foo( a + b, b);
x2:             a = 5;




            foo ( n, m)
next line ──→ int n, m;
            {
                char str[010];
                int k;

                for (k = 0; k < 0x10; k++)
                    str[k] = 0;
                printf("\nall done\n");
            }
```

Stack	
Address	Contents
1003	- ? -
1002	- ? -
1001	- ? -
1000	7
999	8
998	15
997	8
996	123
995	1000

a
b   } parent's local variables
n   } foo's formal
m   } parameters
} return address
←SP←FP } parent's frame pointer

Fig. 6.4. Stack after saving parent's frame pointer.

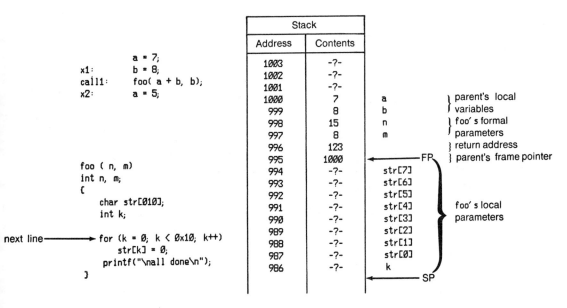

```
                a = 7;
x1:             b = 8;
call1:          foo( a + b, b);
x2:             a = 5;




            foo ( n, m)
            int n, m;
            {
                char str[010];
                int k;

next line ──→ for (k = 0; k < 0x10; k++)
                    str[k] = 0;
                printf("\nall done\n");
            }
```

Stack	
Address	Contents
1003	-?-
1002	-?-
1001	-?-
1000	7
999	8
998	15
997	8
996	123
995	1000
994	-?-
993	-?-
992	-?-
991	-?-
990	-?-
989	-?-
988	-?-
987	-?-
986	-?-

a
b   } parent's local variables
n   } foo's formal
m   } parameters
} return address
←FP   } parent's frame pointer
str[7]
str[6]
str[5]
str[4]   foo's local parameters
str[3]
str[2]
str[1]
str[0]
k
←SP

Fig. 6.5. Stack after allocation of foo locals. Next action will be to execute for loop in foo.

Notice that the stack grows downward, as it would with the Z80®, 8086, 8080, 6800, and 68000 families of processors. Notice also that the stack has been somewhat simplified. Addresses, integers, and characters all occupy one location in these figures, because each item stored on the stack is assumed to be the same size. (Because most personal computers use byte-addressed memories, characters ordinarily will fill a single location, and all other objects will require multiple locations.) The concept of a stack frame hasn't changed. From time to time, the addresses simply increment by more than one between adjacent objects. Given this background information, here are bugs unique to C.

Out-of-Range Subscripts

In figure 6.2 function foo contains a simple typo: str was supposed to be declared as having 0x10 elements to match the loop limit in the following for statement. In standard C, 010 is the octal representation for 8; thus in figure 6.5 the compiler has set aside eight locations for str.

The for loop, however, is going to attempt to zero sixteen elements. In a language with run-time range checks, the program would be aborted as soon as k reached 8. However, because C doesn't test for out-of-range subscripts, it can't know that anything is wrong. C blithely makes sixteen assignments to locations where the array "should have been." Unfortunately, these assignments destroy important historical information.

When the stack grows downward and arrays grow upward, the programmer accesses a particular element of a local array by creating a pointer to the "zero-th" element and adding, as a displacement, the index of the desired element.

To access str[1], for example, the compiler generates a pointer to str[0] by adding an offset to the frame pointer. Then the compiler selects the element by adding the index (1) to the result.

```
frame pointer        995
offset             -  8
index                 1
------------------------
location of str[1]   988
```

If this computation is performed blindly (as it is in compiled C code), str[8] = 0 will wipe out location 995, and str[9] will replace the return address with a 0.

frame pointer	995	frame pointer	995
offset	- 8	offset	- 8
index	8	index	9
------------------------		------------------------	
location of str[8]	995	location of str[9]	996

Note that foo, "thinking" that all is well, succeeds in making the 16 assignments as required and prints out an "all done" message.

But the return linkage, which allows the program to resume at line x2 when foo completes, has been damaged. As foo exits, it will unallocate its declared local variables by backing the stack pointer to match the frame pointer (location 995). It will then pop the top of the stack (what should be the old frame pointer but is instead a bogus zero) into the frame pointer (implicitly backing the stack pointer to 996).

With the stack pointer now pointing at what is supposed to be the return address, foo will execute a return and take up execution at the location specified in location 996 (zero). Under many operating systems, jumps to location zero cause a boot.

To a programmer who is trying to trace this gem, the program seems to have failed between lines. The last line of foo executed correctly, but line x2 is never reached. Moreover, if additional trace statements are added, one can easily verify that exactly 16 locations in str have been initialized and that foo was called with legitimate (but unused) arguments.

Conventional source-level tracing will never identify the cause of this bug. The programmer can only read and reread the code, hoping someday to spot the dimensioning error.

Variations

Writing zero into every element of an improperly dimensioned array isn't the programmer's only alternative. Writing *123* or *456* is appropriate, as is writing *123* when foo is called with certain arguments, and *456* when it is called with others. If foo sometimes writes *123* only into location 996, foo will occasionally return correctly although for the wrong reason. Changing only location 996 may cause the entire program to execute correctly.

foo will return correctly if it changes only location 995, but when foo gets to line x2, all of the local variables will seem to have changed because the frame pointer has been damaged. A source-level trace will reveal: correct values before foo is called, correct manipulations throughout foo, and wrong values after foo has returned. Another impossible bug!

If it manipulates only certain large indexes in str, foo may damage only certain variables in its parent's local variable space. If the mismatch between declared and accessed array size is great enough, foo may leave intact the parent stack frame but damage a frame higher in the stack (allowing foo, its parent, and several other functions to return before the damage becomes problematic). Frequently, the symptoms in this special case are similar to those created by uninitialized pointers.

Uninitialized Pointers

C, unlike Pascal and BASIC, doesn't give an initial value to local variables when it creates them. As each function is entered, the stack pointer and frame pointer are adjusted. The space set aside for local variables remains unchanged.

In figures 6.6, 6.7, and 6.8, the effect of a function entry in Pascal is compared to the effect of a function entry in C. Note that in C, the "garbage" in the local variable storage remains after the stack frame has been created. In Pascal (most Pascals, anyway), the local variable section is marked as invalid before the function begins. (Certain other languages clear the area to zero.)

Both languages manipulate the frame pointer as in figure 6.6. When the Pascal program (see fig. 6.7) attempts to print c, the print routine (recognizing that nil is not a valid value) will cause an abort. In the C version, shown in figure 6.8, the printf call will print 12.

Bugs that result from reading an uninitialized value are easy to locate with conventional tracing. Bugs (like the strcpy call in figure 6.9) that write to a memory location selected by an uninitialized pointer are more difficult.

Figure 6.9 shows what happens when strcpy is executed. The frame pointer of joe's parent is overwritten. When joe exits, the local values of its parent will be "lost."

A special feature of uninitialized pointer bugs is that the symptoms can change radically from one run to the next. If the uninitialized pointer occurs in a function that uses stack space not yet used by any other part of the program, the value acquired by the uninitialized pointer will be garbage left by the preceding program.

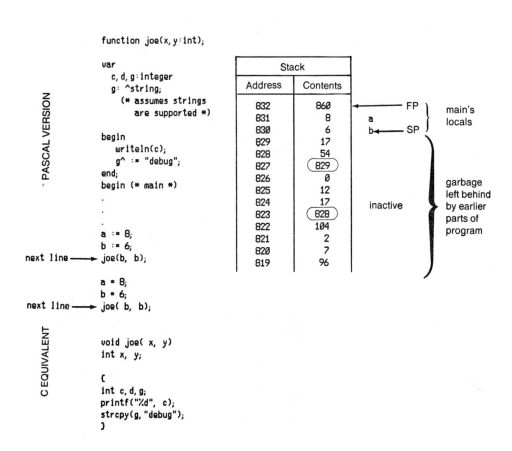

Fig. 6.6. Hypothetical integer machine's stack prior to invoking joe. The circled values are old frame pointers left behind by other parts of the program.

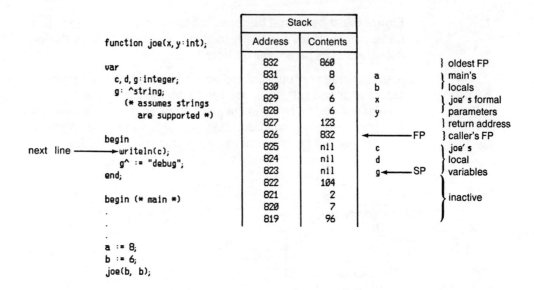

```
function joe(x, y:int);

var
    c, d, g:integer;
    g: ^string;
        (* assumes strings
           are supported *)

begin
next line ────► writeln(c);
    g^ := "debug";
end;

begin (* main *)
    .
    .
    .
a := 8;
b := 6;
joe(b, b);
```

Stack	
Address	Contents
832	860
831	8
830	6
829	6
828	6
827	123
826	832
825	nil
824	nil
823	nil
822	104
821	2
820	7
819	96

- 860 } oldest FP
- a } main's
- b } locals
- x } joe's formal
- y } parameters
- 123 } return address
- 832 ◄──── FP } caller's FP
- nil c } joe's
- nil d } local
- nil g ◄── SP } variables
- inactive

Fig. 6.7. Stack after Pascal function has allocated storage for local variables. Notice that joe's locals are initialized with special nil values.

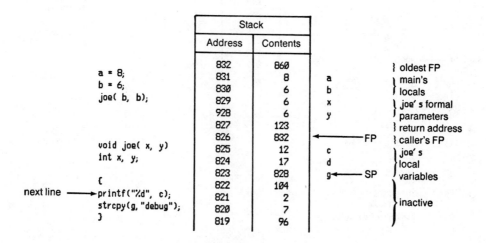

```
a = 8;
b = 6;
joe( b, b);

void joe( x, y)
int x, y;

{
next line ────► printf("%d", c);
    strcpy(g, "debug");
}
```

Stack	
Address	Contents
832	860
831	8
830	6
829	6
928	6
827	123
826	832
825	12
824	17
823	828
822	104
821	2
820	7
819	96

- 860 } oldest FP
- a } main's
- b } locals
- x } joe's formal
- y } parameters
- } return address
- 832 ◄──── FP } caller's FP
- 12 c } joe's
- 17 d } local
- 828 g ◄── SP } variables
- inactive

Fig. 6.8. Stack after C function has allocated storage for local variables. Notice that joe's locals assume the "left-behind" garbage as their initial values.

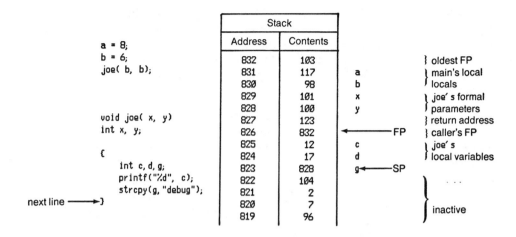

Fig. 6.9. Stack after joe has attempted to copy a string to g. The stored frame pointer at 832, all of main's locals, and joe's parameters have been overwritten in the process.

Therefore, if the linker and the file-dump utility are loaded into the memory segment occupied by the program (as commonly happens with single-tasking personal computers), these command sequences

```
link myprog          link myprog
myprog               dump myprog
                     myprog
```

will generate different results, if link and dump use location 823 differently.

If the uninitialized pointer happens to point to a segment of unused memory, the program will run perfectly! (I have created three or four such programs which, if linked before each run, run quite reliably; the linker happens to leave a "safe" value. These programs crash and burn, however, if preceded by any other task—even by the linking of another program.) It is clear that C's behavior is different from that of Pascal or BASIC!

While on the subject of garbage, the programmer may wonder what kinds of garbage he or she can expect to find in the stack. Will the garbage always be random or will it favor certain values? The answer is "yes and no."

If the stack space used by the current stack frame hasn't been used by any other part of the program under test, you can assume that it is pure garbage, dependent only on the task that preceded this test run. On the other hand, if the currently executing stack frame occupies a portion of the stack used during the run (perhaps because the current function is higher in the calling hierarchy than a function executed earlier in the run), the garbage will tend to favor certain values.

Most stack frames are relatively small (less than 20 bytes) but every stack frame has a *frame pointer* (an address higher in the stack) and a *return address* (an address in the code area). Because uninitialized pointers will use these obsolete addresses which occur frequently in reused areas of the stack, the programmer can expect 10 to 30 percent of the uninitialized pointers to reference code or areas of the stack.

Ordinarily, uninitialized pointers are more insidious than out-of-bound arrays. An out-of-bound array reference usually attacks a stack frame adjacent to the frame in which the array is located. An uninitialized pointer can attack *anywhere*.

In the strcpy example shown in figure 6.8, g could have contained literally any number. Had the number been an address much higher in memory, the stack frame of a function several calling levels removed from joe would have been damaged. Before the damaged stack frame was needed and the symptoms of the bug became visible, joe would have completed correctly. joe's parent (and possibly dozens of other routines) also might have completed correctly.

Had the number been lower, joe might have actually overwritten portions of the program. (This special problem is discussed in greater detail in the next section.) The same random mechanism might instead write on global data or on a dynamic memory structure (perhaps a heap).

Pointers that Write on Code

In multiuser systems, the memory management hardware usually catches pointers that write on code. That hardware generates a *memory fault* or *bus error* message at the point at which the faulty pointer was used.

Multiuser systems need the memory-protection hardware to protect users from one another. Single-user personal computers seldom use memory protection hardware. Some architectures, such as the 8086, allow stack, data, and code to reside in separate "segments"; a feature that potentially could be exploited to implement a form of memory protection.

Unfortunately, many C compilers designed for these machines avoid the complexity of managing references to separate segments by forcing code, stack, and data to share the same segment. On single-user machines, the programmer is likely to encounter bugs, particularly uninitialized pointer bugs, that write on code.

Ordinarily, when code (overwritten through a faulty pointer reference) executes, a catastrophic crash occurs.

The results will depend on which of the following was targeted by the faulty pointer:

- the library code
- parts of the run-time package
- application code or in-line constants that will not be used after the damage is inflicted
- application code or in-line constants that will be used later

If the damaged code is part of the standard library, a function that is *known to be bug-free* will stop working. The most vulnerable function is printf. Because printf is used frequently and calls several subordinate functions, return addresses that correspond to points within the printf code body frequently will appear in the stack. When an uninitialized pointer assumes one of these values, printf will be damaged. The next time it is called, even though the call is perfectly correct, printf blows up.

If the damaged code is part of the run-time package (a group of subroutines used frequently by the compiled code), the program may seem to blow up between lines. This happens because the compiler has generated an "invisible" call to a function in the run-time package, perhaps to add two floating point numbers. That function, which has been damaged by a faulty pointer, blows up.

The run-time function may have been only slightly damaged, in which case it will return; but the result will be wrong. Such cases are usually the result of a short string of zeros (no-operation code, on many machines) that has been written in the center of a subroutine's code. Although the linkages to and from the subroutine are intact, the gutted subroutine will not perform a complete computation. To the programmer, addition, assignment, or another primitive operation will seem to have stopped working.

If the damaged code is part of a function that is not needed by the program section immediately executed after the damaged code, the program will seem to work correctly until the functions are linked in a slightly different order. Because linking modules in a different order rearranges their relative position in memory, the faulty pointer (harmless until now) becomes ruinous. The program will crash if the new target is code.

The correlation between the code's physical position in memory and the symptoms of the crash serves to explain bugs that "disappear" during debugging. An uninitialized pointer that picks up a constant value (an earlier function's return address, perhaps) from the stack garbage will always point at the same physical address. When the program contains trace statements, this location might hold code that is never used, but without the trace statements the location might hold critical code.

Certain compilers place string literals within the code segment. If the faulty pointer targets one of these literals, some calls to printf may seem to be using the wrong format string. These calls are, in fact, using the correct string, but the string has been changed by a faulty pointer operation.

If the damaged code is part of a function that will be used later, it will crash even though it worked perfectly during an earlier call. This mechanism explains the mysterious cases in which functions that work perfectly when called from one point in a program blow up when called from another. Similarly, if the target is a string constant, a printf call that works perfectly once may (although called with the same argument values) die. This happens not because printf has been damaged but because it has been called with an endless or otherwise malformed format string.

RETURN

C's strengths—loose typing, strong orthogonality, and pointers—easily become C's weaknesses when on the one hand, those strengths permit the disciplined, experienced systems programmer to sculpt efficient, readable, and reasonably portable solutions to challenges ranging from the bit-picky device driver to the elegantly abstracted theorem prover; and on the other hand, those strengths allow beginner and expert alike to destroy the virtual machine by contriving errors that the compiler can't anticipate and that conventional debugging tools can't correct.

This is a price many programmers won't and shouldn't pay. Not everyone needs C's wide-ranging expressiveness. And those who are convinced that they can afford the price needn't always pay in blood and sweat. Chapters 7 and 8 explain how the programmer can manage the C-debugging process by controlling machine-level variations in the experimental environment and by monitoring the virtual machine's health.

7
Stabilizing Pointer Bugs

Uninitialized pointers create the most erratic C bugs—bugs so errant that they not only exhibit extreme sensitivity to their environment (radically changing with each test run) but also refuse to hold still long enough to be localized.

The environmental sensitivity that these bugs demonstrate reflects simply the initial contents of memory. Stabilizing the behavior of such bugs is a matter of controlling the initial contents of global variables, local variables, and unallocated data memory.

Globals don't demand special attention because C language specifications require that globals be initialized to zero (except under pre-1.5 versions of BDS C). This chapter, then, focuses on techniques that programmers can use to initialize local variables and unallocated data memory.

All the techniques presented in the chapter are machine- and compiler-specific. To illustrate how they are adapted to divergent environments, each technique is discussed in the context of both CP/M and MS-DOS. Some (using a debug tool, for example) are inordinately machine-oriented and require that the programmer understand the hardware thoroughly. Other techniques (running an initialization program, for instance) are machine-dependent but sport much higher-level interfaces.

The Importance of Unallocated Memory

In high-level programming environments other than C, unallocated memory isn't an issue; the program can reference only allocated memory. In BASIC (because all simple variables usually are preallocated), the user can reference the wrong variable unintentionally but cannot reference an unallocated variable.

C pointers, however, can reference any portion of accessible memory. In multiuser environments this capability doesn't create special problems because hardware mechanisms detect references to unallocated memory and abort the guilty task.

Single-user microcomputers, however, seldom have hardware memory-protect mechanisms with which to confine stray pointers. A misformed pointer reference can easily access garbage in an unallocated portion of data memory. The bug symptoms generated by such a reference have the potential to change dramatically whenever the garbage in unallocated memory changes.

The Benefits of Initialized Memory

Users who choose the right value when initializing memory enjoy these benefits:

- stabilized pointer bugs
- improved temporal proximity between bug and symptom
- easier detection of uninitialized pointers

First, the programmer stabilizes bugs produced by mechanisms equivalent to uninitialized pointers. The bugs stabilize because each run encounters identical garbage in memory causing the uninitialized pointer to either reference (always) the same bogus location or to reference the same meaningless value.

Second, by carefully choosing the initialization pattern the user can increase the probability that a program will crash immediately after a faulty-pointer reference. The most troublesome consequence of violating the virtual machine is that the proximity properties so important to localizing the error are destroyed. If a crash can be forced immediately after each pointer error, temporal proximity will be preserved.

Third, if the user chooses an unusual pattern, uninitialized pointers will be easier to recognize in a trace statement. This, in part, is why the C language specification requires that externals be default-initialized to zero; zero is always the *null* pointer. This property enables programmers to check pointers at run-time with a simple function such as

```
chkptr((unsigned)pointer, "call7");
```

when chkptr is defined as

```
(void) chkptr(inval, idstring)
unsigned inval;
char *idstring;

{
if ( inval == 0 )
  printf("\nUninitialized pointer at %s", idstring);
}
```

Alternatively, this function can be replaced with a macro that enables the preprocessor to remove it (look back at the trace routine in Chapter 5), or the user can perform an automatic check on global pointers by embedding this test in a snapshot function.

Because global memory is static, it needs to be initialized only once—at the beginning of each program run. Local variables, however, are allocated dynamically on the stack. Stack space is continuously reused as the program runs. To initialize all local variables, a small segment of stack space must be initialized whenever a function is called. Because this process represents substantial and usually redundant overhead, the initialization of local variables remains the programmer's responsibility.

Initializing Unallocated Memory with a Debug Tool

Under single-user, single-tasking operating systems (those that, like CP/M, run only one program at a time for only one user at a time), programs are always loaded into the same memory location.

Because the programmer can predict exactly which memory will be unused, initializing unallocated memory is easy. On more sophisticated operating systems, predicting where globals will reside is more difficult. The load address may vary in such systems depending on how the operating system is configured, how much memory is available, or how many programs are resident (held in memory although they may not be executing).

To illustrate how dynamic debuggers can be used to initialize memory, the following section describes the process under CP/M and MS-DOS.

Initializing Memory Using DDT

On CP/M systems, programs always load beginning at 100 hex. Usually, memory is allocated to the globals immediately after the code. The stack begins high in memory (just below the bottom of the operating system) and works down, as shown in figure 7.1.

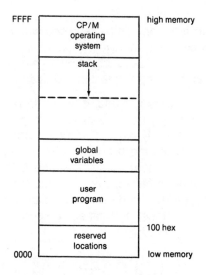

Fig. 7.1. Typical CP/M memory map.

Like most operating systems, CP/M is designed to tell the program where the "top" of usable memory is. The top of CP/M user space is also the bottom of the operating system. CP/M maintains this address in locations 6 and 7. User memory extends from 0x100 through the address in locations 6 and 7. Because this range includes every possible location for global or unallocated memory, initializing the entire range also initializes all globals and unallocated memory space.

The programmer can use the breakpoint debugger, DDT™, to accomplish this initialization and then run program foo with

```
A>DDT
-d6, 7
0006 00 d0
-f100, CFFF 00
-^C
A>foo
```

In this sequence DDT is invoked, contents of locations 6 and 7 are dumped, and all the memory between 100 and d000 is filled with zero.

(Actually, the initialization stops just before 0xd000, at 0xcfff. Location 0xd000 cannot be changed because it is the first byte of the operating system or, in this case, of its temporary surrogate, DDT.)

Z80 addresses are stored low-byte first; thus 00 d0 is address 0xd000. Program foo is invoked after DDT has been exited with control-C. The programmer doesn't set the high memory occupied by DDT to zero but does initialize it with the code pattern of DDT.

Initializing Memory Using MS-DOS's DEBUG

Under MS-DOS, programs aren't always loaded into the same spot in memory. The user can't be certain that all available unallocated memory has been initialized by simply wiping clean a particular 64K segment of memory.

To overcome the problem, the program is initialized *and started* under DEBUG. It is a process that can be quite difficult with large, complex programs (those that require "large model" compilation). The process described in this chapter is used for programs small enough to compile in the "small model."

Frankly, initialization with DEBUG is inconvenient at best. However, by attempting it a few times, you can expand your under-

standing of program loading. Moreover, these DEBUG examples
are an instructive prelude to the more complex DEBUG applications in Chapter 8. With DEBUG, initialization proceeds in three
steps:

1. Generate a load map.

2. Locate the globals.

3. Fill the balance of the data segment with zeros.

Generating a Load Map

The *load map* is a report (a by-product of the linking process) that
shows where, relative to the actual load spot, the various pieces of
the program and the data areas are located. Locating the globals
requries a load map.

The user may be able to direct the compiler to request a load map
as it requests the linking operation. If not, it is possible to get one
by forcing the link operation. Assuming that the file *foo.c* has already been compiled to produce a relocatable image *foo.obj, foo*
can be linked to produce an executable image (foo.exe) and a load
map (foo.map) with this MS-DOS command

   link foo,,foo.map,mylibrary /MAP

(The item *mylibrary* represents the library of standard functions
provided with the compiler. Under Eco-C88 on a hard disk, this library is \bin\ecoc.lib.) On some compilers, it is necessary also to
link a small root program. Early Lattice™ compilers, for example,
require

   link c+foo,foo,foo.map,lc /MAP

In this case, *c+foo* indicates that *c.obj* and *foo.obj* should be loaded
in that order. The file *c.obj* contains the linkage between the operating system and the program's main function. The second parameter, *foo*, is required to keep the resultant executable module
from being named *c.exe.* The name of the Lattice standard function
library is lc.

When the link command is correct, the linker will generate a large
text file named *foo.map*. This file is the load map. It reveals where
all the functions and variables in the program will reside (all relative to the beginning of the appropriate MS-DOS load module).

MS-DOS allows a program to be loaded in separate segments: the code segment, data segment, stack segment, and extra segment.

The file *foo.map* will contain many names not declared in the program. These are names that the compiler uses to reference routines in the run-time package.

Furthermore, because an underscore or two typically is appended (or "pre-pended") to each function name, the programmer may actually need to find _count() if he or she is searching for the function count() or count_. The file won't include entries for local variables, which are allocated dynamically on the run-time stack.

The process can be illustrated by "walking through" it in the following C program. This tiny segment of code has global variables, easy-to-recognize constants and string literals, and a few function calls—everything that a real program has but in a smaller package.

```
/*
This short program makes it easy to identify
date areas in memory, even when you look at memory
with debug.
*/

char ststr[15];
char endstr[15];

main()
{
    strcpy(ststr,"marks start");
    strcpy(endstr,"last data is15");
    step1("literal string", 0x123456L);
}

void step1(str,num)
char *str;
long num;

{
    printf("received what I wanted");
}
```

Ordinarily, the Eco-C88 compiler automatically invokes the linker but won't pass a request for the load map. To get a load map, the linker is invoked separately. The command sequence is

cc –nl demo.c
link demo,,,\bin\ecoc.lib /map

The *–nl* option keeps the compiler from automatically invoking the linker. The second line directs *link* to load *demo*, generate default output files named *demo.exe* and *demo.map* (the load map), and search the library *\bin\ecoc.lib* for standard functions. The load map is quite long. For this example, the significant portions are

```
Start   Stop    Length   Name                Class
00000H  00000H  0000H    $a$chain            code
00000H  01E6FH  1E70H    $b$prog             code
01E70H  01E7FH  0010H    $c$strtseg          data1
01E80H  02127H  02A8H    $d$dataseg          data2
02128H  02128H  0000H    $e$usdseg           data3
02128H  02163H  003CH    $f$udseg            data4
02164H  02164H  0000H    $g$uedseg           data5
02170H  021D3H  0064H    $h$stkseg           data6
021D4H  021D4H  0000H    $i$endseg           data7


Origin    Group
01E7:0    DGROUP
0000:0    PGROUP


Address         Publics by Name

0000:012C       $8087c
01E7:018A       $append
0000:12D4       $bal
          .
          .

01E7:02B4       __topmem
```

```
Address              Publics by Value

0000:0000            _main
0000:0032            _step1
0000:0042            $start
0000:0098            _strcpy
        .
        .
        .
01E7:02B4            __topmem
01E7:02B8            _ststr
01E7:02C7            _endstr
01E7:02F2            __allocp
01E7:0364            $last
```

Program entry point at 0000:0042

The last portion of this map (publics by value) lists each function and global variable next to the physical address it would occupy if the program were loaded at location zero. (PGROUP 0000:0 means: the program group loads at segment zero, offset zero. DGROUP refers to the data group that includes the globals that are of interest to the programmer. The data group begins at 01E7:0.)

The order of symbols in the publics by value list reflects their eventual order in memory. The code appears first, followed by the global variables. This map is a convenient source of information about a compiler's placement policy. When this map is compared to the previous code listing, it is evident that externals are placed into memory in order of their declaration.

8086 Address Notation

Load-map addresses are provided in *segment:offset* format. The four-digit hexadecimal number to the left of the colon represents a sixteen-byte paragraph. Paragraph zero corresponds to physical byte zero in memory. Paragraph 0x10 corresponds to physical byte 0x100.

Every paragraph boundary can be converted to a byte address by suffixing it (in hexadecimal notation) with another zero. The number to the right of the colon is an *offset* from the named paragraph boundary. `ststr`'s segment:offset address can be converted into a byte address in this manner:

extend the paragraph number to create a byte address	01E70
add the offset (in hex)	+ 02B4
byte address of `ststr`	2124

Byte addresses are unique. Segment:offset addresses aren't. That is, two different byte addresses refer to different locations in memory. Two different segment:offset addresses can refer to the same location in memory. The segment:offset addresses 0174:02E3 and 0178:2A3 both refer to byte address 1A23.

To further complicate matters, the addresses given in the load map are relative addresses; that is, they would be the physical addresses of the named locations if the program loaded at physical byte zero. In fact, programs can't load at physical byte zero because important interrupt vectors and the resident portion of the MS-DOS command interpreter have already been loaded in low memory (see fig. 7.2).

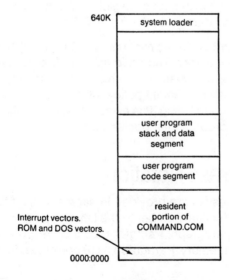

Fig. 7.2. Typical MS-DOS memory map.

Identifying Globals

Using the information in the load map, the beginning and ending locations relative to the actual load address of the global-variable area can be determined. The first byte of global storage is identical to the first byte of ststr at address Ø1E7:Ø2B8. The last byte of global storage coincides with the last byte of endstr at Ø1E7:Ø2D5 or, 2C7 + ØF. . ., the length of endstr minus 1.

Figure 7.3 illustrates how several important locations, including global variables and function entry points, are placed in memory. Each entry's address is given as a relative and absolute byte address as well as in several segment:offset forms.

Segment offset Relative to DS with DS = DDD	Segment offset Relative to CS with CS = BF6	Segment offset Relative to Load Point	Absolute Physical Address	Symbol or Program Resource
	inaccessible from CS	BE6:0000	0BE60	PSP
inaccessible from DS	BF6:0000	BE6:0100	0BF60	code segment (main)
	BF6:0032	BE6:0132	0BF92	step1
	BF6:0042	BE6:0142	0BFA2	$start
	BF6:0098	BE6:0198	0BFF8	strcpy
DDD:0010	BF6:1E80	BE6:1F80	0DDE0	literals
DDD:02B4	BF6:2124	BE6:2224	0E084	_topmem
DDD:02B8	BF6:2128	BE6:2228	0E088	ststr
DDD:02C7	BF6:2137	BE6:2237	0E097	endstr
DDD:02D6	BF6:2146	BE6:2246	0E0A6	
DDD:0364	BF6:21D4	BE6:22D4	0E134	$last
			1DDCE	stack space
DDD:FFFE	inaccessible from CS			
inaccessible from DS				

Fig. 7.3. Equivalent segment:offset addresses for various parts of MS-DOS program.

These forms are far more convenient to use than they seem to be. The segment part of each entry (usually held in one of the segment registers) can be referenced easily from DEBUG. The absolute address is found by adding the actual load address to the relative byte address.

For this figure, the load address is BF60. The address was determined by using DEBUG to look at the contents of specific registers. This application of DEBUG is described in the following section.

Using DEBUG

DEBUG is invoked on the sample program (demo) by entering

debug demo.exe.

DEBUG will load the program into the lowest available memory, relocating memory references as necessary and leaving 100H bytes preceding the program for a block of memory called the *program segment prefix* (PSP).

Next, DEBUG will

- initialize the PSP with information that the operating system needs

- load the CX register with the program size

- load the CS register with the actual load address

- load the DS and ES registers with the paragraph number of the first byte of the PSP. Having completed these tasks, DEBUG will indicate its readiness with a hyphen prompt.

Responding *r* to the hyphen will prompt a list of registers. It gives the programmer a chance to see the load address and size in DS and CX. A test run gave the following display:

```
AX=0000  BX=0000  CX=2128  DX=0000  SP=0064  BP=0000  SI=0000  DI=0000
DS=0BE6  ES=0BE6  SS=0E0D  CS=0BF6  IP=0042   NU UP DI PL NZ NA PO NC
0BF6:0042 B8DD0D          MOV     AX, 0DDD
```

Any small difference in the configuration of the operating system will change both the size of the operating system and the address of the lowest available memory location.

Therefore, each time this test is conducted, a completely different set of numbers may appear in the listing. In this report, DS, ES, SS, and CS are mnemonics for *data segment*, *extra segment*, *stack segment*, and *code segment*, respectively. The number initially given in CS is the beginning address of the code segment—in other words, the load address. To adjust for the linker's assumption that this address is zero, this load address is added to the previously computed byte address. The computations for the beginning and ending addresses of global storage are:

BEGINNING ADDRESS		ENDING ADDRESS	
load address	BF60	load address	BF60
segment address	+ 1E70	segment address	+ 1E70
phys. data segment	DDD0	phys. data segment	DDD0
offset	+ 02B8	offset	+ 02D5
physical address	E088	physical address	E0A5

The contents of this (or any) portion of memory can be examined by using the DEBUG D (display) command. The following commands are equivalent because both reference the same physical location:

D 0:E088,E0A5
D DDD:2B8,2D5

The second form is more convenient because it allows the programmer to use offsets directly off the load map. The first form gives this listing:

```
0000:E088  46 32 89 5E 30 0B C3 75                        F2. ^0. Cu
0000:E090  9F 83 7E 2E 00 74 10 8B-46 2A 48 8E 46 2C 8B F0   ..~..t..F*H.F,.p
0000:E0A0  26 C6 04 2D 89 46                              &F. -. F
```

The pairs of hex digits in the center of the listing are byte-by-byte images of memory; each pair represents one byte. The "junk" on the right side is also the contents of this memory (interpreted as ASCII character codes in which periods represent nonprinting codes).

If this listing proves difficult to interpret, it's because the listing isn't supposed to make sense; it contains the garbage left behind by the previous program.

Each time DEBUG is started, the listing will be different. In fact, if large programs have not run since the machine was booted, a listing of all zeros may be generated. This special case is a side-effect of MS-DOS's power-up memory test. The memory allocated to globals, unless it has been used by a program that ran earlier, will hold that initialization.

Discovering garbage in the area allocated to global variables seems contradictory because the default initialization for externals is supposed to be all zeros. At this point, however, the program hasn't begun running. It is simply loaded and ready to run. The globals, in fact, are initialized during program start-up. If the programmer sets a breakpoint at main() and begins execution (break points are discussed in Chapter 8), this area will contain all zeros by the time main() is reached.

After the globals have been located, memory can be initialized by writing zeros from the end of the globals to the top of the data segment. The *fill* command writes a byte to memory

  F 0:E0A6,FFFF 00

At first glance, it may seem logical that the programmer could start at the beginning of the globals instead of the end, without disturbing anything—after all, the start-up code will reinitialize globals. Such brutish technique is safe only if the externals haven't been explicitly initialized. If explicitly initialized externals, which are loaded with the program, are overwritten by a DEBUG command, they won't be corrected by the start-up code.

Exploring with DEBUG

DEBUG and this little program can be used to learn a great deal about the structure of a C program. The S command can be used to search for a literal string (to discover where the compiler places literals). To search for the string *marks...* in the code portion of program demo, use

  S CS:0,2128 "marks"

CS is shorthand for "the current contents of the code segment register," and *2128* is the code length (the number in the CX register when DEBUG begins). Debug responds with

  ØBF6:1E8Ø

Dumping memory at this location with *D CS:1E80* will generate

```
ØBF6:1E8Ø  6D 61 72 6B 73 20 73 74-61 72 74 ØØ 6C 61 73 74   marks start.last
ØBF6:1E9Ø  20 64 61 74 61 20 69 73-31 35 ØØ 6C 69 74 65 72    data is15.liter
ØBF6:1EAØ  61 6C 20 73 74 72 69 6E-67 ØØ 72 65 63 65 69 76   al string.receiv
ØBF6:1EBØ  65 64 20 77 68 61 74 20-49 20 77 61 6E 74 65 64   ed what I wanted
```

followed by more garbage. Here, string constants from two functions (`main` and `step1`) are brought together. Furthermore, because the address ØBF6:1E8Ø is close to the end of the program (ØBF6:2127), it seems reasonable to conclude that Eco-C88 places all constants at the end of the code segment.

In fact, the constants are at the very end of the code space as well as at the very beginning of the data space. Examine the address representations given for the literals in figure 7.3.

Words of Caution

On multiuser systems, it is difficult to determine where (in physical memory) a program resides. And on a virtual-memory system, the program's location actually can change during a run. That's not a big problem, however, because the breakpoint debuggers on these systems usually allow the programmer to pretend that he or she "owns" all of memory, the program begins at zero, and the data begins at another predictable "logical" address.

Unallocated memory isn't a problem in these systems because it isn't physically accessible. One exception is dynamically-allocated memory acquired through a call to `malloc()`. That is why `calloc()`, which always initializes the allocated block, is safer than `malloc()`.

Building a Memory-Initialization Function

Fortunately, memory usually can be initialized without the low-level tinkering described in the preceding section. Under CP/M and MS-DOS, unallocated memory lies between the end of the globals and the bottom of the application stack.

Knowing just a little about how the compiler places global variables will help (using the address of operator) in defining the ending address of the global area and the bottom address of the stack at run time.

This is an implementation-dependent technique coded at a high level. But because all of the nonportable code is confined to a single function, only one small function must be modified to make the initialization transport to a new environment. The technique works without modification under both CP/M and MS-DOS (as long as the globals fit in one 64k segment) because the technique requires only that the compiler allocate globals in a coherent block.

Compilers usually allocate global storage in the order in which it is declared. Thus the address of the first declared global variable is usually the beginning of the global data area.

Similarly, the last declared global variable is close to the ending address of the global data area. (If the variable is char type on a byte-organized machine, its address is the ending address of the global data area.)

Under CP/M and MS-DOS, the stack is placed high in memory and grows downward. The most recently declared local variable is always at the stack's lower active addresses. If this variable is character type, its address is the lowest active address in the stack.

These addresses mark the bounds of user memory. The initialization program treats all of the intervening memory as a large character array, assigning zero to each element. This is the code:

```
/* global variable declarations */

    .
    .                    /* other declarations */
    .
char endglobal;    /* just to mark end of area .... */

main()

{
    initmem();
    .
    .                        /* application program */
    .
}


void initmem()
    {
    char *pnt, *end;
    char endmark;        /* to mark the bottom of the stack */
```

```
        pnt = &endglobal;
        end = &endmark;

        while (pnt != end) *pnt++ = '\0';
}
```
Listing 7.1.

It is wise to invoke the function in a macro so that it can be deleted easily from the production code or to observe a naming convention that will allow grep to remove the initialization calls as it removes other debugging code. This kind of initialization can generate a noticeable startup delay if a large unallocated data area exists.

Adding a Special Initialization Program to the Invocation Sequence

Programmers working in a single-user environment can initialize memory without adding special code to the program by writing a separate program that zeros all available memory and exits. Running the special program before every test run of the "main" program will guarantee that all of the memory has the same initial value for every test.

Listing 7.1 is such a program for CP/M, if no code other than the call to initmem() appears in main().

MS-DOS Initialization Programs

Although MS-DOS and the 8086 are supposedly "upwardly compatible" with CP/M and the 8080, the simple CP/M initialization technique can not be used under MS-DOS. Even the programmer working with a "small model" compiler (one that limits code to 64K, and data and stack to 64K) will find that the CP/M technique won't work reliably because with programs of different sizes, the 64K data segment will reside in different places.

This happens because the data segment always starts on the first paragraph (16-byte) boundary following the end of the code. And the application code will not be the same size as the code for the initialization program.

The initialization program must zero memory that lies outside its natural 64K data segment. Because most MS-DOS C compilers implement pointers as 16-bit values, no pointer can address more than 64K unless certain normally invisible machine registers are changed. Therefore, the programmer can't use the simple pointer tricks relied on so far.

To address all of memory, the registers must be modified directly, causing pointers to reference a different segment of memory. Because C has no knowledge of segments or segment registers, segment registers must be changed by special (assembly language) system functions. The functions needed are

```
void intdos(inreg, outreg)
char inreg[8], outreg[8];
```
is a direct interface to the MS-DOS assembly language interface. It first loads the values in inreg into registers AH, AL, BH, BL ... etc., respectively, and then performs an INT 21H. On return, it copies the values of all registers into outreg.

```
unsigned getseg()
```
returns the present value of the data segment. This value corresponds to the upper 16 bits of the actual physical address of the first memory location currently available to the program.

```
fillmem(segment, count, val)
unsigned segment, count;
char val;
```
fills count bytes, beginning at paragraph segment, with val.

(See Appendix C for assembly language versions of these functions for Eco-C88. For other compilers, the appropriate function may be sysint21(). Check the compiler documentation for additional information.)

The following program initializes memory (using fillmem) beyond the program's normal data segment and then uses the CP/M technique to clear all memory in the program's normal data segment (except a small portion of stack).

```
#define AH 0
#define AL 1
#define BH 2
#define BL 3
#define CH 4
#define CL 5
#define DH 6
#define DL 7

char startinit;    /* to mark the low end of memory */

main()

{
    char *pnt, *end;

    char inregs[8], outregs[8];
    unsigned graphs;
    unsigned baseseg;

/* find out how many paragraphs are available by requesting
   all of RAM from DOS (function 48H). It will return the
   number of available paragraphs in BX */

    inregs[AH] = 0x48;
    inregs[BH] = 0x7f;
    inregs[BL] = 0xff;
    intdos(inregs,outregs);
    graphs = (outregs[BH] << 8) + outregs[BL];

/* now allocate all of them, to get the first segment address */
    inregs[BH] = outregs[BH];
    inregs[BL] = outregs[BL];
    intdos(inregs,outregs);
    baseseg = (outregs[AH] << 8) + outregs[AL];

/* now wipe it out in 16K chunks */

    while (graphs > 1024) {
      fillmem(baseseg, 1024*16, 0);
       graphs -= 1024;
       baseseg += 1024;
       }
    if (graphs > 0) fillmem(baseseg, graphs*16, 0);
```

```
/* now wipe out the normal segment, using the CP/M method. We
   wait till last to do this to avoid leaving more
   uninitialized stack than absolutely necessary. */

pnt = &startinit;
end = &basereg;
end -= 6;
while (pnt != end) *pnt++ = '\0';
}
```

This program doesn't really fill all available memory with zeros. It skips the program's code space and a small part of the stack space. Although these small parts of memory aren't set to zero, they are initialized. They are always forced to a predictable value each time the program is run. Most of memory is forced to zero, some is forced to code values, and some is forced to appropriate stack values, but everything is forced to a repeatable value.

Users need to know less about the machine to use the initialization function than they need to know to use an initialization program. The initialization program, however, does not require any change in the program under test. This is an asset when the production code is tested to identify an extremely elusive bug. Running the initialization program before each test provides for a repeatable, controlled testing environment.

Using a batch file that first invokes the initialization program and then invokes the test program is a good idea; testing is more convenient, and initialization is guaranteed.

Special Loaders

The *loader* is a piece of system software (invisible to the typical user) that is responsible for loading programs from disk or another secondary store into memory in preparation for execution.

On MS-DOS, the loader lives high in user memory. Under CP/M, the loader is an integral part of the BDOS. A loader that is separate from the operating system can be replaced by a custom loader which initializes available memory and then loads the next program.

A loader that is part of the operating system can't be replaced but can be circumvented with a user-written loader. These special loaders can be particularly useful on multiuser systems when the programmer needs to stabilize the environment to test for a bug that appears only in production code.

To create a loader, the programmer writes a program that does nothing but requests (from the operating system) a chunk of memory large enough to hold the application under test, initializes the allocated memory, loads the program into that memory, and transfers execution to the test program.

The trick to writing the program is figuring out how to transfer execution to the test program without confusing the operating system, a process that usually involves tricky manipulation of "slave areas" or "process control blocks." Under MS-DOS, for example, the loader would have to construct a correct PSP and somehow convince the operating system to transfer control to the process that it describes.

Initializing Local Variables

For most users, the direct initialization of local variables is more complex conceptually than the initialization of unallocated memory. Because it is normally "hidden" from the programmer's view, the stack is a somewhat mysterious resource. Moreover, local variables aren't statically positioned; potentially, each invocation of foo() could store its locals at a unique position in the stack. Therefore, the challenges are

- to find a way to access the stack resource
- to define a rule that always describes where a given function's local variables reside

Accessing the Stack

Because all local variables are allocated in the stack, any pointer to a local variable is also a pointer into a portion of the stack.

Because the local variables for a given function are always placed in a single contiguous block of the stack, the function's locals can be initialized with only two pointers: a pointer to the first allocated local and a pointer to the last allocated local. (For convenience's sake, assume that both locals are character variables.)

Given these two pointers, all that is needed is to zero everything between them. The following fragments of code illustrate one such technique:

```
int foo()
{
    char ch;
    int i, j, k, l;
    char *m;
    char ex;

    initloc(&ch, &ex);

    dosomework(ch, i, &l);
    .

    .


    void initloc(start, stop)
    char *start, *stop;

{
    while (start >= stop) *start-- = 0;
}
```

The code is similar to the dumploc() function in Chapter 4. Like dumploc(), this function assumes that locals are allocated in the order they are declared with the first local declared in high memory (see fig. 7.4).

These assumptions are reasonable; all modern compilers (except certain optimizing compilers) allocate variables in the order they are declared, and stacks that grow downward (later allocations receive lower addresses) are common.

The exact behavior of the machine and compiler can be determined by dumping pointers for an entire set of local variables and drawing a "custom" version of figure 7.4.

For the preceding example, this printf statement can be used:

```
printf("\n%04.4x %04.4x %04.4x %04.4x %04.4x %04.4x\n",
        &ch, &i, &j, &k, &l, &m, &ex);
```

The values that print are the stack addresses (in hexadecimal) where the respective local variables reside.

C Expression Yielding Stack Address	Stack	
	Address	Variable
&ch	ØxEEEF	CH
&i	ØxEEED	i
&j	ØxEEEB	j
&k	ØxEEE9	k
&l	ØxEEE7	l
&m	ØxEEE5	m
&ex	ØxEEE4	ex

Fig. 7.4. Detail of local variable allocation for text's sample function foo and a downward-growing stack (on hypothetical byte-oriented machine).

Automating Local Traces

The method works, but because every function must begin with a unique call to the initialization program, it is awkward to code. Moreover, to be completely effective, the local declarations must include character variables at each end of the program.

Because pointers always reference only one byte of a multibyte variable, a noncharacter variable's address may not be the last address in the block of locals.

Figure 7.5 shows the stack for a case where the first variable is a 32-bit long integer. Note that &ch is ØxEEEC but that the last byte is ØxEEEF.

It would be far more convenient if every call to the initialization function were exactly alike. A simple filter that recognizes opening function braces and variable declarations could be used to insert initialization calls into existing code. This filter would guarantee that the calls were made at every function entry and would relieve some typing overhead. The filter presented in Appendix D performs a similar task and could be the base for such a utility.

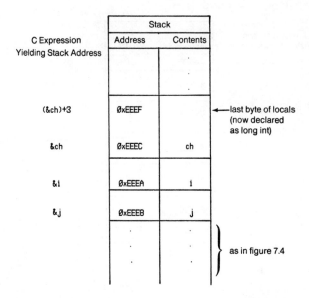

	Stack	
C Expression Yielding Stack Address	Address	Contents
		.
		.
		.
(&ch)+3	ØxEEEF	
&ch	ØxEEEC	ch
&i	ØxEEEA	i
&j	ØxEEE8	j
	.	.
	.	.
	.	.

←—last byte of locals (now declared as long int)

} as in figure 7.4

Fig. 7.5. Stack detail: multibyte local variable complicates computation of local variable address space.

One way to control the calls to initloc() is to eliminate the parameters. A careful examination of how the stack is used will show that initloc() doesn't need parameters; it can gather what it needs directly from information already in the stack.

The following section explains why this is so. Although the discussion, illustrations, and code fragments presented assume an MS-DOS environment, the techniques illustrated are applicable to any environment.

Whenever one function calls another, several communication and information structures must be constructed. The calling function must evaluate actual parameters (the values in the calling argument list) and arrange to communicate these values to the subordinate function. The calling function must store the address of the instruction to be resumed after the subordinate function has completed.

The stack address of the calling function's local variables must be saved so that the calling function can still reference its variables after the subordinate function has finished. Typically, the calling function places its "return address" and the actual parameter values on the stack. Then the subordinate function saves a pointer to the calling function's locals (a frame pointer) and allocates stack space for its own locals.

Figure 7.6 illustrates the stack structure in the case when foo() calls bar() with

bar(6+17,'c',"tx");

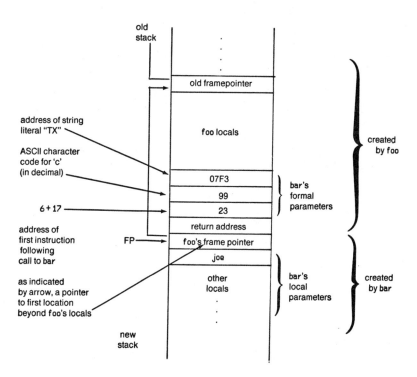

Fig. 7.6. Stack detail: creation of new stack frame as function foo *calls function* bar.

The labels FP and SP, which are mnemonics for *frame pointer and stack pointer*, indicate where internal machine registers (typically the *BP* and *SP* on an 8086) point while bar is executing.

Note that instead of pointing at local variables each frame pointer points at the next older frame pointer (as indicated by the arrow along the stack's left edge). This arrangement creates a chain of pointers that, working backward through each stack frame in the stack, allows the creation of "walk-back" functions like the one developed in Chapter 8.

Although the frame pointer doesn't point to the locals, it always points to the pair of bytes adjacent to the locals. If the programmer knows the frame pointer's value, computing the top end of a block of locals is a trivial matter.

Assuming that the highest placed local variable in bar is named *joe* and is character type, the programmer can compute a pointer to the highest byte of foo's locals with this expression:

```
toploc = *(&joe + 1) -1;
```

Computing the address of the other end of the locals, however, relies on knowing exactly how many actual parameters were set up by foo. It isn't as great a limitation as it may seem.

If the subordinate function is the initialization function, it will always be called with zero actual parameters and result in the stack structure illustrated in figure 7.7. In this special case, a pointer to the bottom of foo's locals can be computed with

endloc = &joe + 5;

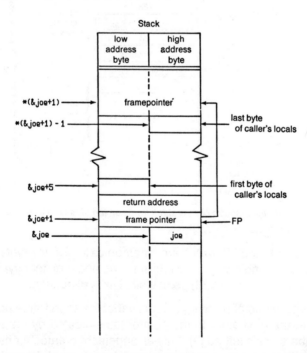

Fig. 7.7. Stack structure created by calling a function with no parameters and a single char type local variable (joe). Column at left shows how each important address can be calculated with pointer arithmetic.

Under MS-DOS, the following version of initloc(), which works without knowing anything about the order or type of the calling function's local variables, will initialize all local variables of the calling function

```
void initloc()

{
    char joe;    /* necessary only to get an address into the stack */
    char *endloc, *toploc;

    toploc = *(&joe + 1) -1;
    endloc = &joe + 5;
    while (toploc >= endloc) *toploc-- = 0;
}
```

This function should be called at the beginning of every function, just after all variable declarations but before any other statements. An enhanced version of the utility in Appendix D could effect the code changes conveniently.

RETURN

Bugs caused by uninitialized pointers are easier to recognize and to localize if the faulty pointer is always forced to assume a disastrous value.

Forcing the initialization of all pointers requires bulk initialization of unallocated memory and local variables. Each process presents special challenges.

If programmers practice a disciplined approach to the invocation sequence during testing, the necessary initialization routines can be made relatively convenient to use. However, these initialization routines are extremely machine- and compiler-dependent. Under the circumstances, it is not unusual for users to create unique versions for each environment in which they work.

In operating system environments (not MS-DOS) that zero all memory each time a program is loaded, there is no need to worry about initializing unallocated memory.

A final thought for this chapter: a good lint will locate most uninitialized variables. The consistent and frequent use of lint during the debugging process will limit the need for initializing techniques.

8

Special Trace Techniques

Errant pointers defy conventional trace techniques by corrupting the virtual machine. Programs executed on the impaired machine cease to exhibit the high-level locality properties essential to conventional trace-based debugging because of damage to the stack, to the variables, or to the code space.

This chapter presents two families of debugging techniques that are effective, even when the virtual machine has been destroyed. One family of techniques monitors directly the condition of the virtual machine. These techniques rely on a temporal proximity between a faulty pointer reference and damage to the virtual machine.

The second family of techniques abandons high-level tracing for tracing at the machine-level, where low-level versions of the proximity properties are always inviolable.

Monitoring the Virtual Machine

The code block, because it is the most static portion of the virtual machine is conceptually the easiest portion to monitor. (The execution overhead, however, can be high.) The stack, although highly dynamic, preserves certain patterns that can be exploited to test its integrity.

Globals, the least predictable resource of the virtual machine, don't require special monitoring because their condition is easily and reliably monitored by traditional snapshots.

The following sections will explain three methods of monitoring the state of the virtual machine.

Checksums on Code Space

Checksums are a powerful technique for detecting errant pointers that write on code. Checksumming is borrowed from communications applications in which changes in a body of code, such as the differences between what is sent and what is received, must also be detected.

Checksums are generated by summing each byte in a block of code as though each byte represented a small integer. The total is known as a checksum.

In the communications environment, a checksum generated by the transmitter before data is transmitted is compared to a checksum generated at the receiver after that data has been received. If the two checksum's match, the data is assumed to be correct.

Figure 8.1, which shows a tiny 7-byte block, illustrates how the checksum technique works for both an error-free transmission and for a noise-corrupted transmission.

Because checksums detect changes that have occurred in the code body between one computation of a checksum and another, adapting the method to the debugging environment is a trivial matter.

The user simply recomputes the checksum at regular intervals during the program's execution. If the checksum at one computation differs from the checksum at the previous computation, an intervening pointer reference must have modified the code.

The debugging system presented in Appendix B will compute an error detection function known as a cyclic redundancy check (CRC) rather than a checksum. Although CRCs are more time-consuming to compute, they offer greater security. Simple checksums are more likely to be "fooled" by offsetting changes in a code block than are CRCs.

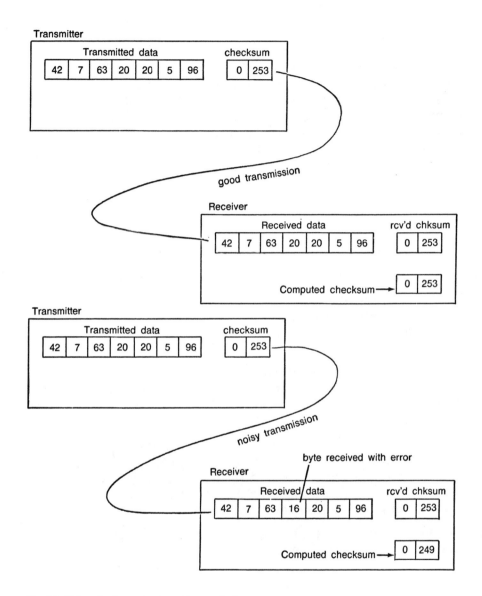

Fig. 8.1. Using checksums to detect tramsmission errors.

Checksums under CP/M

Checksums are particularly easy to generate in the uniform address space of a CP/M environment. In that environment, the code always begins at 100H and normally ends immediately before the global area. Dereferencing the first declared global variable will provide the first address following the code body. Assuming that startinit is a char and the first declared global, a function to checksum the code will look like this:

```
long sumcode()

{
    long sum;
    char *pnt;

    sum = 0;
    pnt = (char *) 0x100;
    while (pnt < &startinit) sum += *pnt++;
    return sum;
}
```

To use this function, the programmer must first call it from several spots in the program. Each calling location represents a mile post. He or she then compares the result of each checksum computation with the result of the prior computation.

If this process uncovers a discrepancy, the code has changed and a warning must be printed. Otherwise, it is appropriate to proceed quietly to the next section of code. To simplify the coding of this set of operations, the checksum function should actually perform the comparison as well as other operations.

The following skeletal listing presents a more complete function and illustrates checksum's use:

```
      char startinit;
      long lasttot;

main()
{
      lasttot = checkcode("first ck",0L);

        .  /* some application code */
        .

      lasttot = checkcode("second ck", lasttot);

        .  /* some more application code */
        .

      lasttot = checkcode("last ck",  lasttot);
}

long checkcode(msg, lastck)
char *msg;
long lastck;
{
      long sum;
      char *pnt;

      sum = 0;
      pnt = (char *) 100H;
      while (pnt < startinit) sum += *pnt++;
      if ((lastck != sum) && (lastck != 0L))
      printf("\nWARNING: code change detected at %s",msg);
      return sum;
}
```

In the first call to checkcode, zero is passed instead of lasttot. Because this is the first call to checkcode, lasttot does not yet have a value. The zero serves as a flag, warning checkcode that the purpose of the call is only to get an initial value. Zero is a safe value for this call because the sum over a "meaningful" body of code will never be zero.

The global lasttot is declared long so that it will be large enough to preserve all the bits in the total. On a CP/M machine, the maximum code space is 64K bytes (each of which corresponds to an integer value of 255 or less). Thus, the maximum total (255 * 64K, or 24 bits) will fit in a long.

Problems with CP/M Checksums

Compilers for CP/M machines sometimes are forced to use self-modifying code to implement specific functions. For example, if the compiler outputs 8080 assembly language as opposed to Z80 assembly language, the only means of implementing dynamically addressed port operations is to modify selected code sections as the program runs.

Moreover, the compiler run-time package will set up internal workspaces within the run-time package (to expedite retrieval of function arguments or to facilitate extended precision arithmetic, for example). It may also simulate static variables by allocating storage in the parent function's code block. Thus, certain spots in the compiler's run-time package (and in certain library functions) are supposed to change.

These intended changes, which look like pointer errors to the `checksum` routine, will generate misleading error messages. The only practical way to handle the problem is to adapt the `checksum` program to "skip over" the dynamic portions of the code.

Unfortunately, compiler vendors don't always identify these locations in the documentation. If information that would allow the programmer to be more selective isn't available, an alternative is to skip the entire run-time package. Most of the dynamic code can be avoided. The disadvantage to this approach lies in not catching pointers that write on the run-time package.

Checksums under MS-DOS

The discussion of code checksumming becomes complicated when it includes 8086 processors. The processor employs a segmented memory space and in some cases distinguishes between code and data space. In practice, however, these features may eliminate the need for checksumming. Any of the several placement policies may govern the positioning of code and data within the 8086's segmented memory. For debugging purposes, all of the policies fit into one of two classes:

- code and data space overlaid
- code and data space separate

If the code and data segments have the same base (occupy the same memory), checksumming under MS-DOS is identical to checksumming under CP/M. This unusual arrangement for MS-DOS C compilers is referred to as a *64K model.*

More often, code and data occupy distinct memory. The most common implementation is the *128K model,* in which code occupies one 64K segment and data occupies a different 64K segment. Less common are *large model* implementations, in which data may reside in more than one 64K segment. If data and code are in distinct segments of memory, checksumming is unnecessary (and unproductive) because data pointers aren't able to "reach" the code to write on it.

For similar reasons, checksumming isn't necessary or useful on large multiuser machines. These mainframe systems always have some form of hardware memory-protect mechanism that immediately traps any attempt to write on code or to write outside the active user's data area.

Managing Checksums

Using a checksumming function is similar to using a snapshot function. Embedding a checksum in a snapshot function is convenient. (Such a modification is suggested in the comments accompanying Appendix B.) With the checksum function buried in the snapshot function, a single granularity control will govern the behavior of both.

Granularity controls coupled with start and stop limits are the best option for controlling checksum execution overhead (a greater problem than output volume). By coupling these two controls, the programmer can perform a low-detail run that involves only five or ten checksum computations.

Then, knowing which large segment of the program is suspect, a run can be executed that more frequently checksums only the suspect portion. If instead the programmer tried to perform detailed checksumming throughout the entire program, he or she might never reach the suspect part. (Summing all of memory takes time.)

Stack Walk-Back

Chapter 7 presented the idea that the frame pointers for all active functions form a chain, each frame pointer pointing to the frame pointer of its invoking function.

The chain can be exploited by periodically following it back to the deepest part of the stack, dumping the most critical parts of each stack frame along the way. If any but the most recent stack entries change from one stack trace to the next, the programmer can be reasonably sure that a faulty pointer has been referenced between the two dumps.

As explained in Chapter 7, the stack saves four kinds of information: parameters, local variables, return addresses, and frame pointers. Of these, return addresses and frame pointers are the most critical to the virtual machine and the least visible to conventional trace techniques.

The routines presented in this chapter will process only return addresses and frame pointers. Expanding the routines to dump parameter lists and local variables should be a relatively straightforward procedure. Listing 8.1 illustrates a stack-trace function for Eco-C88 for MS-DOS.

```
void dumpstk(id)
char *id;


{
     char *mark;
     unsigned char *framepointer;
     extern char *stacktop;

     printf("\n%s\n", id);
     framepointer = &mark + 1;
          /*now step over dumpstk's frame since it's unimportant*/
     framepointer = *((unsigned char **) framepointer);
     while (framepointer < stacktop){
          printf("%04.4x-%02.2x %02.2x   %02.2x %02.2x\n",
                    framepointer, *framepointer,
                    *(framepointer + 1), *(framepointer + 2),
                    *(framepointer + 3));
          framepointer = *((unsigned char **) framepointer);
          }
}
```

Listing 8.1.

This code and the local initialization routine from Chapter 7 rely on the same trick: manipulating the address of a local variable to produce the address of the newest frame pointer. Because each frame pointer is stored immediately beneath a return address, the `while` loop can print both the frame pointer and the return address by indexing off the address of the framepointer.

To avoid printing the stack frame that belongs to the debug routine, `framepointer` is advanced beyond that stack frame before the loop is entered. Each call to `printf` then prints a stack address and the value of the return address and frame pointer stored at that stack address.

There are compilers that will insist that `printf` sign-extend the byte values referenced in the `printf`. Four-character values are generated for the high-memory references if the programmer doesn't insist that the pointer reference an `unsigned char`.

The ugly type coercion in the last statement forces `framepointer` to be loaded with a 16-bit value. (WARNING: this code assumes 16-bit pointers. To work in environments with different sized pointers, the code would require serious modification.)

`stacktop` is a global variable that holds the address of the oldest stack entry. Some compilers initialize such a variable for the programmer. If the compiler doesn't, `stacktop` can be initialized in `main` by assigning it the address of `main`'s first declared local variable. This code fragment illustrates the trick:

```
char *stacktop;

main()
{
  char ch;
  int i;
      .
      .    /* other declarations */
      .
  stacktop = &ch;
      .
      .    /* balance of code */
```

A Sample Walk-Back

At best, the trace generated by a stack walk-back function is arcane. To use `dumpstk()` effectively, it isn't necessary to understand every line of the trace. The programmer needs only to adhere to the straightforward rules governing usage and to learn to recognize the pattern generated by a correct running program.

This do-nothing program (see listing 8.2) illustrates the appropriate technique for calling dumpstk() and the stack trace generated by a correct program.

Step 1: Calling dumpstk():

```
#include <stdio.h>

char *stacktop;

main()
{
    char mark;

    stacktop = &mark;

    printf("\napproaching first call\n");
    level1(1);
    printf("\napproaching second call\n");
    level1(6);
    printf("\napproaching third call\n");
    level1(2);
}

void level1(depth)
int depth;
{
    dumpstk("at level1 entry");
    if (depth > 1) level2( depth - 1);
    dumpstk("at level1 exit");
}

void level2(depth)
int depth;
{
    dumpstk("at level2 entry");
    if (depth > 1) level3( depth - 1);
    dumpstk("at level2 exit");
}
```

```
void level3(depth)
int depth;
{
    dumpstk("at level3 entry");
    if (depth > 1) level3( depth - 1);
    dumpstk("at level3 exit");
}
```

Listing 8.2.

The main function in this program makes three separate calls to a lower-level function (level1), which in turn calls other lower-level functions.

The lowest-level function, level3(), is recursive—in other words, under certain conditions it calls itself. The parameter to level1() specifies how deep the calls are to nest.

With a parameter of one, only level1() is called. With a parameter of six, however, level1() calls level2(), which calls level3(), which calls itself enough times to exhaust the depth argument. Between all top-level calls to level1(), printf is called to print a marker message.

Using the trick discussed in the preceding section, main initializes stacktop. Each function calls dumpstk immediately upon entry, passing an identifying string as the only parameter and immediately before exit again passing an identifying string.

When run on a "PC clone," the program generated this output:

Step 2: The Stack Trace.

```
approaching first call

at level1 entry
fff4-fc ff  1e 00

at level1 exit
fff4-fc ff  1e 00
```

```
approaching second call

at level1 entry
fff4-fc ff  32 00

at level2 entry
ffee-f4 ff  6d 00
fff4-fc ff  32 00

at level3 entry
ffe8-ee ff  99 00
ffee-f4 ff  6d 00
fff4-fc ff  32 00

at level3 entry
ffe2-e8 ff  c5 00
ffe8-ee ff  99 00
ffee-f4 ff  6d 00
fff4-fc ff  32 00

at level3 entry
ffdc-e2 ff  c5 00
ffe2-e8 ff  c5 00
ffe8-ee ff  99 00
ffee-f4 ff  6d 00
fff4-fc ff  32 00


at level3 exit
ffdc-e2 ff  c5 00
ffe2-e8 ff  c5 00
ffe8-ee ff  99 00
ffee-f4 ff  6d 00
fff4-fc ff  32 00

at level3 exit
ffe2-e8 ff  c5 00
ffe8-ee ff  99 00
ffee-f4 ff  6d 00
fff4-fc ff  32 00

at level3 exit
ffe8-ee ff  99 00
ffee-f4 ff  6d 00
fff4-fc ff  32 00

at level2 exit
ffee-f4 ff  6d 00
fff4-fc ff  32 00

at level1 exit
fff4-fc ff  32 00
```

```
approaching third call

at level1 entry
fff4-fc ff  46 00

at level2 entry
ffee-f4 ff  6d 00
fff4-fc ff  46 00

at level2 exit
ffee-f4 ff  6d 00
fff4-fc ff  46 00

at level1 exit
fff4-fc ff  46 00
```

To interpret this output, the programmer first correlates its structure to that of the main program. Notice that between the opening approaching marker and the second approaching marker, there is one block of entry and a matching block of exit stack trace.

The second and third approaching markers bracket six entry/exit pairs of stack-tracing blocks. The third marker precedes two entry/exit pairs of stack trace.

In each case, the number of entry/exit pairs correlates perfectly with the depth parameter passed in each of main()'s calls to level1(). Each entry block of stack trace corresponds to the stack history at the entry to one level in the calling hierarchy.

In a correct function, each entry block should match exactly each exit block because the stack (calling) history doesn't change between the beginning and end of a function. The output from the sample listing exhibits this correct behavior.

The stack trace can be used effectively with no deeper understanding than this. The user simply must be consistent about calling dumpstk() at the beginning and end of each function, and then compare sequential entry trace blocks and corresponding entry and exit trace blocks. Any discrepancy between these blocks signals a pointer error in the intervening code.

A Pointer Bug that Writes on the Stack

In listing 8.3, level1() and level2() functions from the preceding program have been modified to introduce a pointer bug that writes on the stack.

```
#include <stdio.h>

char *stacktop;

main()
{
char mark;

stacktop = &mark;

    printf("\napproaching first call\n");
    level1(1);
    printf("\napproaching second call\n");
    level1(6);
    printf("\napproaching third call\n");
    level1(2);
}

void level1(depth)
int depth;
{
     char buffer[15];
     dumpstk("at level1 entry");
     if (depth > 1) level2( depth - 1, &buffer);
     dumpstk("at level1 exit");
}

void level2(depth, pntr)
int depth;
char *pntr;
{
     int i;

     dumpstk("at level2 entry");
     if (depth > 1) {
         for (i = 0; i < 23; i++){
             *pntr++ = '\0';
             }
         level3( depth - 1);
         }
     dumpstk("at level2 exit");
}
```

```
void level3(depth)
int depth;
{
    dumpstk("at level3 entry");
    if (depth > 1) level3( depth - 1);
    dumpstk("at level3 exit");
}


void dumpstk(id)
char *id;

{
char *mark;
    unsigned char *framepointer;
    extern char *stacktop;

    printf("\n%s\n", id);
    framepointer = &mark + 1;
        /*now step over dumpstk's frame since it's unimportant*/
    framepointer = *((unsigned char **) framepointer);
    while (framepointer < stacktop){
    printf("%04.4x-%02.2x %02.2x  %02.2x %02.2x\n",
            framepointer, *framepointer,
            *(framepointer + 1), *(framepointer + 2),
            *(framepointer + 3));
    if (framepointer == (unsigned char *) NULL) return;
    framepointer = *((unsigned char **) framepointer);
    }
}
```

Listing 8.3.

In this version of the program, level1() allocates a 15-position string and passes a pointer to level2().

Level2() then initializes this string whenever it is called with a depth parameter greater than one. Unfortunately, level2() is overly aggressive, initializing far more than 15-character elements.

This program, if run without the stack trace, produces the following (seemingly impossible) output:

```
approaching first call

approaching second call

approaching first call

approaching second call

approaching first call
        .
        .
        .
```

The output is a typical example of the kinds of impossible behavior generated by writing on the stack. Conventional trace mechanisms will indicate only that at some point level2() completed normally but passed execution to main, rather than back to its caller.

The stack trace, on the other hand, generates some useful clues about what is happening.

```
approaching first call

at level1 entry
fff4-fc ff  1e 00

at level1 exit
fff4-fc ff  1e 00

approaching second call

at level1 entry
fff4-fc ff  32 00

at level2 entry
ffdc-f4 ff  74 00
fff4-fc ff  32 00

at level3 entry
ffd4-dc ff  be 00
ffdc-f4 ff  74 00
fff4-00 00  00 00          /* notice change from preceding block*/
0000-00 00  00 00
```

```
at level3 entry
ffce-d4 ff   ec 00
ffd4-dc ff   be 00
ffdc-f4 ff   74 00
fff4-00 00   00 00
0000-00 00   00 00

at level3 entry
ffc8-ce ff   ec 00
ffce-d4 ff   ec 00
ffd4-dc ff   be 00
ffdc-f4 ff   74 00
fff4-00 00   00 00
0000-00 00   00 00

at level3 entry
ffc2-c8 ff   ec 00
ffc8-ce ff   ec 00
ffce-d4 ff   ec 00
ffd4-dc ff   be 00
ffdc-f4 ff   74 00
fff4-00 00   00 00
0000-00 00   00 00

at level3 exit
ffc2-c8 ff   ec 00
ffc8-ce ff   ec 00
ffce-d4 ff   ec 00
ffd4-dc ff   be 00
ffdc-f4 ff   74 00
fff4-00 00   00 00
0000-00 00   00 00

at level3 exit
ffc8-ce ff   ec 00
ffce-d4 ff   ec 00
ffd4-dc ff   be 00
ffdc-f4 ff   74 00
fff4-00 00   00 00
0000-00 00   00 00

at level3 exit
ffce-d4 ff   ec 00
ffd4-dc ff   be 00
ffdc-f4 ff   74 00
fff4-00 00   00 00
0000-00 00   00 00
```

```
at level3 exit
ffd4-dc ff  be 00
ffdc-f4 ff  74 00
fff4-00 00  00 00
0000-00 00  00 00

at level2 exit
ffdc-f4 ff  74 00
fff4-00 00  00 00
0000-00 00  00 00

at level1 exit
fff4-00 00  00 00          /* return address is zero! */
0000-00 00  00 00

approaching first call

at level1 entry
ffee-f6 ff  1e 00

at level1 exit
ffee-f6 ff  1e 00

approaching second call

at level1 entry
ffee-f6 ff  32 00

at level2 entry
ffd6-ee ff  74 00
ffee-f6 ff  32 00

at level3 entry
ffce-d6 ff  be 00
ffd6-ee ff  74 00
ffee-00 00  00 00
0000-00 00  00 00
        .
        .
        .
```

To get this stack trace, dumpstk(); has been slightly enhanced; an alternate exit from the trace loop has been added. The exit is taken whenever the framepointer contains zero, a value that always indicates either a pointer bug or stack overflow.

Using a return in this location if (framepointer == 0); dumpstk(); allows the program to run until it (the program) attempts to use the faulty portion of the stack.

Although the return is instructive in this example, it's a nuisance in real life because it allows the program to enter an infinite loop. A practical version of dumpstk() would include the test for zero (or, perhaps, for any small number) but would exit instead of returning.

Notice that the contents of stack location fff4 changed sometime after level2() was entered but before level3() was entered. (That line and a later one have been marked to make them easy to spot.) This kind of discrepancy signals a bug. If level2() were a large function, the problem could be localized further by including additional calls to dumpstk() within level2().

This example clearly illustrates also how bugs that write on the stack destroy temporal proximity. The error, which occurs before the first comment, manifests no behavioral symptoms until after the second comment, when the program attempts to return to location zero, which happens to be the beginning of main(). Had the string been initialized with something other than zeros (blanks, perhaps), the return would have been to some other impossible location.

Interpreting the Stack-Trace Detail

Programmers better understand the context in which their program executes if they have a general understanding of a stack trace. A solid understanding of the execution context is helpful, particularly when debugging C.

Each block of the stack trace lists selected values from the then current stack. Each line of the block represents information that relates to a single, as yet incomplete, function call.

The block's upper lines are the newest information (the most recent function calls); its lower lines are the oldest information.

In a correct program, changes occur only as a new function is called or an old one completed, adding or deleting a line, respectively, at the top of the block. Thus, when level2() calls level3(), the block grows by one line, a line representing the reactivation information for the partially complete level2().

As functions call functions (winding deeper into the program's hierarchy), the blocks will grow in size, reflecting the growing list of partially complete functions. As functions complete and return to their caller, the blocks will shrink.

Each line in the stack trace consists of three entries:

- a stack address
- a frame pointer at that address
- the return address

Each of these entries is a 16-bit address (four hexadecimal digits). The stack address, which is printed with the most significant byte first, looks like a reasonable address.

The frame pointer and return address, however, are printed with the most significant byte last, reflecting the natural byte order on an 8086. Therefore, the first dump from the preceding test output

```
at level1 entry
fff4-fc ff  1e 00
```

reports three addresses:

```
stack address ....... fff4
frame pointer........ fffc
return address....... 001e
```

The address 0xfff4 is high in the current data segment (0xffff is the absolute top of that segment), reflecting the stack's position in high memory. In contrast, the return address is low in the code segment, reflecting the MS-DOS practice of loading code into the lowest available address. Remember that the code and data segments reside, at least conceptually, in disjointed parts of physical memory.

Return Addresses

To invoke a function, the compiler generates an assembly language call. The return address is the address (in the code segment) of the first instruction following such a call.

To examine the code and verify this relationship, the programmer can load the executable program under DEBUG and then, using the Unassemble command, disassemble the code. To find the appropriate beginning address for the Unassemble command, a load map is needed. The pertinent entries from the load map for the correct program of listing 8.2 are:

```
0000:00D4          _dumpstk
0000:0050          _level1
0000:007C          _level2
0000:00A8          _level3
0000:0000          _main
0000:019C          _printf
01F8:0346          _stacktop
```

Because level1() is first called from main(), the return address in the first block should be the address on an instruction in the code representing main(). Specifically, the return address should be the address of the first instruction following a call to 0x0050—the address of level1().

This listing records a session with DEBUG in which the code for main() was disassembled to verify the relationship.

```
A>DEBUG NEST.EXE
-U
0BF6:0000  55        PUSH   BP
0BF6:0001  8BEC      MOV    BP, SP
0BF6:0003  83C4FE    ADD    SP, -02
0BF6:0006  8D5EFF    LEA    BX, [BP-01]
0BF6:0009  891E4603  MOV    [0346], BX
0BF6:000D  BB1000    MOV    BX, 0010
0BF6:0010  53        PUSH   BX
0BF6:0011  E88801    CALL   019C
0BF6:0014  83C402    ADD    SP, +02
0BF6:0017  BA0100    MOV    DX, 0001
0BF6:001A  52        PUSH   DX
0BF6:001B  E83200    CALL   0050
0BF6:001E  83C402    ADD    SP, +02
-U
0BF6:0021  BB2900    MOV    BX, 0029
0BF6:0024  53        PUSH   BX
0BF6:0025  E87401    CALL   019C
0BF6:0028  83C402    ADD    SP, +02
0BF6:002B  BA0600    MOV    DX, 0006
0BF6:002E  52        PUSH   DX
0BF6:002F  E81E00    CALL   0050
0BF6:0032  83C402    ADD    SP, +02
0BF6:0035  BB4300    MOV    BX, 0043
0BF6:0038  53        PUSH   BX
```

```
0BF6:0039  E86001       CALL    019C
0BF6:003C  83C402       ADD     SP, +02
0BF6:003F  BA0200       MOV     DX, 0002
-U
0BF6:0042  52           PUSH    DX
0BF6:0043  E80A00       CALL    0050
0BF6:0046  83C402       ADD     SP, +02
0BF6:0049  B80000       MOV     AX, 0000
0BF6:004C  8BE5         MOV     SP, BP
0BF6:004E  5D           POP     BP
0BF6:004F  C3           RET
                .
                .
                .
```

In this listing, the first column is a physical memory location in
segment:offset format. The second column is the machine-
code instruction which debug found at that address. The third and
fourth columns are the assembly language representation of that
machine-code instruction.

Each of the three calls to 0x0050 corresponds to one call to
level1() in main(). The first call appears at location 0x001B and the
following instruction starts at location 0x001E—exactly what
dumpstk() reported for a return address for that first call.

The later calls to level1() generate these stack traces (excerpts
from Step Two: The Stack Trace):

```
approaching second call

at level1 entry
fff4-fc ff  32 00


        .
        .
        .

approaching third call

at level1 entry
fff4-fc ff  46 00
```

Similarly, these return addresses (0x0032 and 0x0046) are the starting addresses for the first instructions following the call instruction at addresses 0x002F and 0x0043.

The Stack Address and the Frame Pointer

In this program, the stack address is the location within the data segment at which the frame pointer (the address of the preceding frame pointer) is stored.

In other words, each frame pointer is the stack address for a previous frame pointer. The chain-like relationship is reflected in each stack trace block; each stack address appears (in byte-inverted form) as a frame pointer in the line above. In the block

```
at level2 entry
ffd6-ee ff  74 00
ffee-f6 ff  32 00
```

Oxffee is a stack address when it appears in the third line and a frame pointer when it appears (inverted, as ee ff) in the second line.

Machine-Level Tracing

So far, this chapter has focused on monitoring virtual machine resources with high-level (C language) structures. These high-level facilities, used in conjunction with the initialization techniques discussed in Chapter 7, usually are adequate for localizing a pointer bug. However, there are times when trace code can't be inserted without destabilizing and "losing track" of a bug.

For example, an uninitialized pointer could pick up "stable" garbage that remains on the stack. In such a case, the pointer might point consistently at a local variable on the stack, generating an easily reproducible and detectable symptom—until trace statements are added to the code.

Because they also use the stack, the trace statements can change that remaining garbage. The value loaded into the uninitialized pointer may change also, and the bug's symptom may become "invisible" or at least much more difficult to detect.

Should this happen, the programmer needs to be able to trace the program's execution. He or she needs to monitor also those local variables related to the symptom, without changing the code or run-time environment. (At least, the changes should be as subtle as is practical.) A breakpoint machine-level debugger (and, to a lesser extent, a source-level breakpoint debugger like the one discussed in Chapter 9) enables the programmer to do this.

Nevertheless, a machine-level debugger should be treated as a tool of last resort, used only after all other avenues prove fruitless. Working at such a microscopic level is a tedious, time-consuming approach that is prone to errors.

Specifically, the programmer should try to checksum code (in environments other than MS-DOS), to initialize memory (if the compiler doesn't), to initialize local variables, and to use stack traces.

If by installing the high-level trace techniques the bug's symptoms vanish instead of reappearing in a different form, the programmer should experiment with changes that modify the program's utilization of memory.

Almost any change to the program's structure, to the program's variables, or to the sequence in which the program is assembled will shift the position of code and variables. Alterations impact significantly not only the load map but also the behavior of certain bugs. After each of these changes the programmer should try to make the symptom reappear with the debugging aids in place.

Experimenting with these tricks may be a valuable exercise:

- by declaring extra unused globals at the beginning of your global section, change the position of all other globals

- by declaring extra unused locals at the beginning of main(), change the position of almost everything in the stack

- by relinking modules in a different order or adding some do-nothing print statements early in main(), change the placement of code

Trace Preparation

To be successful in battle, warriors must be prepared. Not only do they need appropriate weapons and supplies (including a compass and a map), but they also must know certain commands.

Learning the command set for most debugging programs isn't particularly challenging. Usually, these programs have only a handful of commands, all of which are abbreviated to a terse one-letter mnemonic. (The details of the commands can be learned from the user's manual.) Simply knowing the commands won't be of much use. To use the commands effectively, the programmer must know how to find his or her way around the machine environment.

Instead of focusing on the commands, this section explains how, by using commands combined with information that's available through the debugger, to achieve specific debugging tasks. The three primary tasks are:

- displaying and tracing specific code
- finding and displaying global variables
- finding and displaying local variables

Chapter 7 explained how to go about finding and displaying global variables. Because the program's execution must first be traced to find the program's local variables, this chapter discusses that first task (tracing and displaying code) before it discusses the second task (finding and displaying local variables). The process, although presented here in MS-DOS's DEBUG environment, is similar in other environments.

As a warrior against bugs in C, the programmer also must be prepared for battle. Before attempting to use a debugger to trace code, you need:

- a printed copy of the load map
- a printed listing of the source code
- lots of additional paper for the printer and an extra-large cup of patience—whatever brand is preferred.

This is not the time to be parsimonious with the paper. Not when attempting this kind of debugging! To keep from getting lost—record every step taken.

The only way to capture that record is to echo the entire debug session to the printer. The easiest way to do this on CP/M and MS-DOS is with a control-P. On UNIX systems, using "tee" or attaching a printer directly to the terminal may work. Whatever it takes, do it—it'll save days of agony.

Displaying the Code for a Specific Function

As pointed out in the preceding sections on stack traces, the code for a specific function can be displayed in assembly language form.

Doing so requires that the programmer "Unassemble" the function's address, as it is listed in the load map. The default mode for Unassemble is to list 13 instructions, beginning at the requested address. The starting address for subsequent Unassemble requests will default to the next following address. Thus, to list 26 instructions beginning at address Øx37, the programmer enters:

```
-U37
   .
   .        /* 13 instructions listed */
   .

-U
   .
   .        /* next 13 instructions listed */
   .
```

Listing the code for the function is easy. Correlating that code to the source code it represents is more difficult. But there are certain easy-to-spot features that can be used as reference points:

- function calls: always a `call` to the address of the called function

- function returns: always a `ret`

- references to simple global variables: the variable's address appears in one of the operand columns.

With few exceptions, well-designed C source code makes such frequent use of function calls that function calls alone should provide ample reference points for code tracing.

To see how users can relate the assembly features to the source code, compare the following annotated DEBUG listing (listing 8.4) with its source code (listings 8.1 and 8.2).

Pertinent entries from load map

```
0000:00D4        _dumpstk
0000:0050        _level1
0000:007C        _level2
0000:00A8        _level3
0000:0000        _main
0000:019C        _printf
01F8:0346        _stacktop
```

The disassembly listing

```
-u0
0CBB:0000 55          PUSH     BP             start of main
0CBB:0001 8BEC        MOV      BP,SP
0CBB:0003 83C4FE      ADD      SP, -02
0CBB:0006 8D5EFF      LEA      BX,[BP-01]
0CBB:0009 891E4603    MOV      [0346],BX      reference of stacktop
0CBB:000D BB1000      MOV      BX,0010
0CBB:0010 53          PUSH     BX
0CBB:0011 E88801      CALL     019C           first call to printf
0CBB:0014 83C402      ADD      SP,+02
0CBB:0017 BA0100      MOV      DX,0001
0CBB:001A 52          PUSH     DX
0CBB:001B E83200      CALL     0050           first call to level1
0CBB:001E 83C402      ADD      SP,+02
-u
0CBB:0021 BB2900      MOV      BX,0029
0CBB:0024 53          PUSH     BX
0CBB:0025 E87401      CALL     019C           second call to printf
0CBB:0028 83C402      ADD      SP,+02
0CBB:002B BA0600      MOV      DX,0006
0CBB:002E 52          PUSH     DX
0CBB:002F E81E00      CALL     0050           second call to level1
0CBB:0032 83C402      ADD      SP,+02
0CBB:0035 BB4300      MOV      BX,0043
0CBB:0038 53          PUSH     BX
0CBB:0039 E86001      CALL     019C           third call to printf
0CBB:003C 83C402      ADD      SP,+02
0CBB:003F BA0200      MOV      DX,0002
-u
0CBB:0042 52          PUSH     DX
0CBB:0043 E80A00      CALL     0050           third call to level1
```

```
ØCBB:ØØ46 83C4Ø2      ADD      SP,+Ø2
ØCBB:ØØ49 B8ØØØØ      MOV      AX,ØØØØ
ØCBB:ØØ4C 8BE5        MOV      SP,BP
ØCBB:ØØ4E 5D          POP      BP
ØCBB:ØØ4F C3          RET                     end of main
ØCBB:ØØ5Ø 55          PUSH     BP             beginning of level1
ØCBB:ØØ51 8BEC        MOV      BP,SP
ØCBB:ØØ53 BB5CØØ      MOV      BX,ØØ5C
ØCBB:ØØ56 53          PUSH     BX
ØCBB:ØØ57 E87AØØ      CALL     ØØD4           entry call to dumpstk
ØCBB:ØØ5A 83C4Ø2      ADD      SP,+Ø2
ØCBB:ØØ5D 837EØ4Ø1    CMP      WORD PTR [BP+Ø4],+Ø1
ØCBB:ØØ61 7EØD        JLE      ØØ7Ø
-u
ØCBB:ØØ63 8B46Ø4      MOV      AX,[BP+Ø4]
ØCBB:ØØ66 2DØ1ØØ      SUB      AX,ØØØ1
ØCBB:ØØ69 5Ø          PUSH     AX
ØCBB:ØØ6A E8ØFØØ      CALL     ØØ7C           call to level2
ØCBB:ØØ6D 83C4Ø2      ADD      SP,+Ø2
ØCBB:ØØ7Ø BB6CØØ      MOV      BX,ØØ6C
ØCBB:ØØ73 53          PUSH     BX
ØCBB:ØØ74 E85DØØ      CALL     ØØD4           exit call to dumpstk
ØCBB:ØØ77 83C4Ø2      ADD      SP,+Ø2
ØCBB:ØØ7A 5D          POP      BP
ØCBB:ØØ7B C3          RET                     end of level1
ØCBB:ØØ7C 55          PUSH     BP             beginning of level2
ØCBB:ØØ7D 8BEC        MOV      BP,SP
ØCBB:ØØ7F BB7BØØ      MOV      BX,ØØ7B
ØCBB:ØØ82 53          PUSH     BX
-u
ØCBB:ØØ83 E84EØØ      CALL     ØØD4           entry call to dumpstk
ØCBB:ØØ86 83C4Ø2      ADD      SP,+Ø2
ØCBB:ØØ89 837EØ4Ø1    CMP      WORD PTR [BP+Ø4],+Ø1
ØCBB:ØØ8D 7EØD        JLE      ØØ9C
ØCBB:ØØ8F 8B46Ø4      MOV      AX,[BP+Ø4]
ØCBB:ØØ92 2DØ1ØØ      SUB      AX,ØØØ1
ØCBB:ØØ95 5Ø          PUSH     AX
ØCBB:ØØ96 E8ØFØØ      CALL     ØØA8           call to level3
ØCBB:ØØ99 83C4Ø2      ADD      SP,+Ø2
ØCBB:ØØ9C BB8BØØ      MOV      BX,ØØ8B
ØCBB:ØØ9F 53          PUSH     BX
ØCBB:ØØAØ E831ØØ      CALL     ØØD4           exit call to dumpstk
```

```
-u
0CBB:00A3 83C402         ADD      SP, +02
0CBB:00A6 5D             POP      BP
0CBB:00A7 C3             RET                    end of level2
0CBB:00A8 55             PUSH     BP            beginning of level3
0CBB:00A9 8BEC           MOV      BP, SP
0CBB:00AB BB9A00         MOV      BX, 009A
0CBB:00AE 53             PUSH     BX
0CBB:00AF E82200         CALL     00D4          entry call to dumpstk
0CBB:00B2 83C402         ADD      SP, +02
0CBB:00B5 837E0401       CMP      WORD PTR [BP+04], +01
0CBB:00B9 7E0D           JLE      00C8
0CBB:00BB 8B4604         MOV      AX, [BP+04]
0CBB:00BE 2D0100         SUB      AX, 0001
0CBB:00C1 50             PUSH     AX
0CBB:00C2 E8E3FF         CALL     00A8          recursive call to level3
-u
0CBB:00C5 83C402         ADD      SP, +02
0CBB:00C8 BBAA00         MOV      BX, 00AA
0CBB:00CB 53             PUSH     BX
0CBB:00CC E80500         CALL     00D4          exit call to dumpstk
0CBB:00CF 83C402         ADD      SP, +02
0CBB:00D2 5D             POP      BP
0CBB:00D3 C3             RET                    end of level3
0CBB:00D4 55             PUSH     BP            beginning of dumpstk
0CBB:00D5 8BEC           MOV      BP, SP
0CBB:00D7 83C4FC         ADD      SP, -04
0CBB:00DA FF7604         PUSH     [BP+04]
0CBB:00DD BBB900         MOV      BX, 00B9
0CBB:00E0 53             PUSH     BX
0CBB:00E1 E8B800         CALL     019C          call to printf
0CBB:00E4 83C404         ADD      SP, +04
-u
0CBB:00E7 8D5EFE         LEA      BX, [BP-02]
0CBB:00EA 83C302         ADD      BX, +02
0CBB:00ED 895EFC         MOV      [BP-04], BX
0CBB:00F0 8B5EFC         MOV      BX, [BP-04]
0CBB:00F3 8B1F           MOV      BX, [BX]
0CBB:00F5 895EFC         MOV      [BP-04], BX
0CBB:00F8 8B5EFC         MOV      BX, [BP-04]
0CBB:00FB 3B1E4603       CMP      BX, [0346]    reference to stacktop
0CBB:00FF 7340           JNB      0141
0CBB:0101 8B5EFC         MOV      BX, [BP-04]
0CBB:0104 83C303         ADD      BX, +03
```

```
-u
ØCBB:0107 8A07          MOV     AL, [BX]
ØCBB:0109 32E4          XOR     AH, AH
ØCBB:010B 50            PUSH    AX
ØCBB:010C 8B5EFC        MOV     BX, [BP-04]
ØCBB:010F 83C302        ADD     BX, +02
ØCBB:0112 8A07          MOV     AL, [BX]
ØCBB:0114 32E4          XOR     AH, AH
ØCBB:0116 50            PUSH    AX
ØCBB:0117 8B5EFC        MOV     BX, [BP-04]
ØCBB:011A 83C301        ADD     BX, +01
ØCBB:011D 8A07          MOV     AL, [BX]
ØCBB:011F 32E4          XOR     AH, AH
ØCBB:0121 50            PUSH    AX
ØCBB:0122 8B5EFC        MOV     BX, [BP-04]
ØCBB:0125 8A07          MOV     AL, [BX]
-u
ØCBB:0127 32E4          XOR     AH, AH
ØCBB:0129 50            PUSH    AX
ØCBB:012A FF76FC        PUSH    [BP-04]
ØCBB:012D BBBE00        MOV     BX, 00BE
ØCBB:0130 53            PUSH    BX
ØCBB:0131 E86800        CALL    019C         call to printf
ØCBB:0134 83C40C        ADD     SP, +0C
ØCBB:0137 8B5EFC        MOV     BX, [BP-04]
ØCBB:013A 8B1F          MOV     BX, [BX]
ØCBB:013C 895EFC        MOV     [BP-04], BX
ØCBB:013F EBB7          JMP     00F8
ØCBB:0141 8BE5          MOV     SP, BP
ØCBB:0143 5D            POP     BP
ØCBB:0144 C3            RET                  end of dumpstk
ØCBB:0145 00B8B30E      ADD     [BX+SI+0EB3], BH
```

Listing 8.4.

Study the annotated lines and observe that machine-code versions of each function are loaded in the same order in which the functions appear in the source.

Compilers usually load modules in this order. With Eco-C, main is a true function with an entry and exit structure identical to those of other functions. With other compilers, this may not be true; main may exit directly to the system or by jumping to a predefined exit function.

Each function begins with a PUSH BP instruction that saves the parent function's frame pointer (which ordinarily is kept in BP) on the stack. Each function's second, third, and fourth instructions calculate the function's own frame pointer, and allocate necessary local-variable space on the stack. Function parameters are placed on the stack by the PUSH instructions that precede a CALL.

Be forewarned: code created by individual users may not exhibit such a clear-cut correlation between CALLs and function invocations, or between RETs and function ends.

Many more complicated operations (floating-point math, for example) will be performed by means of a call to a "run-time function," which will generate additional CALLs in the code. If a function with more than one exit is written, the compiler may or may not generate multiple RETs (the alternate exits may generate jumps to a common return).

Tracing Execution

A machine-level debugging program allows the programmer to interrupt the execution of the program with a facility known as a *breakpoint*. Execution will stop when the program reaches an instruction associated with a preset breakpoint, and the debugger will resume control.

A breakpoint suspends program execution, rather than aborting it. This break gives the programmer the opportunity to examine variables and the stack, and to move the breakpoint. Execution of the program can always be resumed from the last encountered breakpoint.

The debugging program allows a breakpoint to be placed anywhere in machine code. Practically speaking, however, if the programmer chooses a point that doesn't correlate clearly to a high-level action, he or she won't know what high-level tasks should have been completed at that point. Breakpoints clearly marking the beginning or end of such high-level tasks as a function call or return should be chosen.

For example, in main() from listing 8.2, each call to level1 and to printf constitutes a reasonable breakpoint. If the programmer stops only at these breakpoints, he or she can inspect memory (stacktop, for instance) for appropriate values and be certain that the actions should have been completed. Stopping at other points in the listing will offer no such clear assurance.

In the following sample debug session (see listing 8.5), a breakpoint is set at each printf() and level(1) call to illustrate how, when using the "Go" command, the programmer would walk through such a sequence of function calls. At each breakpoint, the contents of global variable stacktop are dumped, illustrating how (within a debugger) the equivalent of a "snapshot" is achieved.

The listing is annotated with comments in C-style delimiters so that it can be followed easily. This annotation will mean more if each breakpoint is matched with the associated entries in listing 8.4, as well as with corresponding statements in the original source code (listings 8.1 and 8.2).

```
     C>debug next.exe        /* invoke debugger on program
"nest.exe" */
     -G,0                     /* set break point at zero, begin execution */

     AX=0000  BX=0001  CX=0000  DX=80D3  SP=FFFE  BP=0000  SI=0000  DI=0366
     DS=0DEE  ES=0DEE  SS=0DEE  CS=0BF6  IP=0000    NV UP DI PL ZR NA PE NC
     0BF6:0000 55          PUSH   BP
     -D346,347               /* check on stacktop */
     0DEE:0346  00 00        /* right now it's zero...main hasn't started */
     -G,19C                  /* resume execution, new breakpoint at 19C */
                             /* 19C is beginning of printf() */
     AX=0000  BX=0010  CX=0000  DX=80D3  SP=FFF6  BP=FFFC  SI=0000  DI=0366
     DS=0DEE  ES=0DEE  SS=0DEE  CS=0BF6  IP=019C    NV UP DI NG NZ AC PE CY
     0BF6:019C 55          PUSH   BP
     -D346 L 2               /* display stacktop */
     0DEE:0346  FB FF        /* now it has a value...assignment worked */
     -G,50                   /* resume execution, new breakpoint at 50 */
                             /* 50 is beginning of level1() */
approaching first call /* note this line is output from program */
                             /* not from debugger */
     AX=0018  BX=0028  CX=0000  DX=0001  SP=FFF6  BP=FFFC  SI=0124  DI=0366
     DS=0DEE  ES=0DEE  SS=0DEE  CS=0BF6  IP=0050    NV UP DI NG NZ NA PE NC
     0BF6:0050 55          PUSH   BP
     -D346 L 2               /* display stacktop */
     0DEE:0346  FB FF        /* it should never change again ! */
     -G,19C                  /* resume execution, break at second printf() */
```

```
AX=0018  BX=00B9  CX=0000  DX=0001  SP=FFE4  BP=FFEE  SI=0124  DI=0366
DS=0DEE  ES=0DEE  SS=0DEE  CS=0BF6  IP=019C    NV UP DI NG NZ AC PO CY
0BF6:019C 55            PUSH    BP
-D346 L 2                       /* display stacktop */
0DEE:0346 FB FF
-G,50                           /* resume, stopping at second call to level1() */

at level1 entry
fff4-fc ff  1e 00               /* output generated by program */

at level1 exit
fff4-fc ff  1e 00

approaching second call

AX=0019  BX=0042  CX=0000  DX=0006  SP=FFF6  BP=FFFC  SI=0124  DI=0002
DS=0DEE  ES=0DEE  SS=0DEE  CS=0BF6  IP=0050    NV UP DI NG NZ NA PE NC
0BF6:0050 55            PUSH    BP
-D346 L 2                       /* display stacktop */
0DEE:0346  FB FF
-G,19C                          /* resume, stopping at third printf() */

AX=0019  BX=00B9  CX=0000  DX=0006  SP=FFE4  BP=FFEE  SI=0124  DI=0002
DS=0DEE  ES=0DEE  SS=0DEE  CS=0BF6  IP=019C    NV UP DI NG NZ AC PO CY
0BF6:019C 55            PUSH    BP
-D346 L 2                       /* display stacktop */
0DEE:0346  FB FF
-G,50                           /* resume, stopping at third level1() */

at level1 entry
fff4-fc ff  32 00

at level2 entry
ffee-f4 ff  6d 00
fff4-fc ff  32 00

at level3 entry                 /* lots of normal program output */
ffe8-ee ff  99 00
ffee-f4 ff  6d 00
fff4-fc ff  32 00

at level3 entry
ffe2-e8 ff  c5 00
ffe8-ee ff  99 00
ffee-f4 ff  6d 00
fff4-fc ff  32 00
```

```
at level3 entry
ffdc-e2 ff  c5 00
ffe2-e8 ff  c5 00
ffe8-ee ff  99 00
ffee-f4 ff  6d 00
fff4-fc ff  32 00

at level3 entry
ffd6endc ff  c5 00
ffdc-e2 ff  c5 00
ffe2-e8 ff  c5 00
ffe8-ee ff  99 00
ffee-f4 ff  6d 00
fff4-fc ff  32 00

at level3 exit
ffd6-dc ff  c5 00
ffdc-e2 ff  c5 00
ffe2-e8 ff  c5 00
ffe8-ee ff  99 00
ffee-f4 ff  6d 00
fff4-fc ff  32 00

at level3 exit
ffdc-e2 ff  c5 00
ffe2-e8 ff  c5 00
ffe8-ee ff  99 00
ffee-f4 ff  6d 00
fff4-fc ff  32 00

at level3 exit
ffe2-e8 ff  c5 00
ffe8-ee ff  99 00
ffee-f4 ff  6d 00
fff4-fc ff  32 00

at level3 exit
ffe8-ee ff  99 00
ffee-f4 ff  6d 00
fff4-fc ff  32 00

at level2 exit
ffee-f4 ff  6d 00
fff4-fc ff  32 00

at level1 exit
fff4-fc ff  32 0x0
```

```
approaching third call

AX=018  BX=005B  CX=0000  DX=0002  SP=FFF6  BP=FFFC  SI=0124  DI=0002
DS=0DEE  ES=0DEE  SS=0DEE  CS=0BF6  IP=0050    NV UP DI NG NZ NA PE NC
0BF6:0050 55             PUSH    BP
-D346 L 2                /* display stacktop */
0DEE:0346  FB FF
-G,4F                    /* resume, stopping just before main exits */

at level1 entry
fff4-fc ff  46 00

at level2 entry
ffee-f4 ff  6d 00        /* normal program output */
fff4-fc ff  46 00

at level2 exit
ffee-f4 ff  6d 00
fff4-fc ff  46 00

at level1 exit
fff4-fc ff  46 00

AX=0000  BX=FFFC  CX=0000  DX=030A  SP=FFFE  BP=0000  SI=0124  DI=0002
DS=0DEE  ES=0DEE  SS=0DEE  CS=0BF6  IP=004F    NV UP DI PL ZR NA PE NC
0BF6:004F C3             RET
-D346 L 2                /* one last time...display stacktop */
0DEE:0346  FB FF
-Q                       /* return to operating system */
```

Listing 8.5.

Monitoring Local Variables with DEBUG

Because stack space is allocated dynamically (as the program executes) to local variables, the load map can't be used to locate local variables.

Instead, the program must be executed with a breakpoint, at the beginning of the function that declares the target local variables. When this breakpoint is encountered, the machine registers are examined to find the current frame pointer. To find the addresses of the current local variables, the appropriate offsets are added to the current frame pointer.

A DEBUG session, used with a short program that generates boxes of varying sizes, illustrates the process. In this session, to more accurately reflect the way DEBUG is typically used, only parts of the program are unassembled. Ordinarily, instead of unassembling the entire program before a session, the user will select pertinent sections, unassembling them as the session progresses.

Your understanding of the relationship between source code and DEBUG listings can be expanded by correlating carefully each small segment of unassembled code in listing 8.6 with the source in the session of listing 8.7.

```c
#include <stdio.h>

#define START  3
#define STOP   7
#define CHANGE 1
#define ROWS   2
#define COLS   8

main()

{
    printf( "\n" );
    varycols(START, STOP, CHANGE, ROWS);
    varyrows(START, STOP);
}

void varycols(start, stop, change, rows)
int start, stop, change, rows;

{
    int i;

    for ( i = start; i <= stop; i += change) box( i, rows);
}
```

```
void varyrows( start, stop)
int start, stop;

{
    int i;
    for (i = start; i <= stop; i += 1) box (COLS, i);
}

void box( col, row)
int col, row;

{
    int c, r;

    for ( r = 1; r <= row; r++){
        if ((r == 1) || (r == row)) {
            for ( c = 1; c <= col; c++) {
                printf( "*" );
                }
            printf("\n");
            }
        else {
            printf( "*" );
            for ( c = 2; c < col; c++ ) {
                printf( " " );
                }
            printf( "*\n" );
            }
        }
    printf("\n\n");
}
```

Listing 8.6.

Listing 8.7 represents a DEBUG session captured on the printer. In this session, breakpoints are set at the beginning of each function (at addresses found in the load map) so that the function's code may be unassembled.

```
-g, 0                                      /*Begin Execution, breaking */
                                           /*  when main is reached     */
AX=0000  BX=0001  CX=0000  DX=80D3  SP=FFFE  BP=0000 SI=0000  DI=02A0
DS=0EB0  ES=0EB0  SS=0EB0  CS=0CBB  IP=0000   NV UP DI PL ZR NA PE NC
0CBB:0000 BB10000        MOV      BX, 0010
-u
0CBB:0000 BB1000         MOV      BX, 0010 /* Unassemble main() */
0CBB:0003 53             PUSH     BX
0CBB:0004 E86501         CALL     016C
0CBB:0007 83C402         ADD      SP, +02
0CBB:000A BA0200         MOV      DX, 0002
0CBB:000D 52             PUSH     DX
0CBB:000E BA0100         MOV      DX, 0001
0CBB:0011 52             PUSH     DX
0CBB:0012 BA0700         MOV      DX, 0007
0CBB:0015 52             PUSH     DX
0CBB:0016 BA0300         MOV      DX, 0003
0CBB:0019 52             PUSH     DX
0CBB:001A E81500         CALL     0032
0CBB:001D 83C408         ADD      SP, +08
-u
0CBB:0020 BA0700         MOV      DX, 0007
0CBB:0023 52             PUSH     DX
0CBB:0024 BA0300         MOV      DX, 0003
0CBB:0027 52             PUSH     DX
0CBB:0028 E83300         CALL     005E
0CBB:002B 83C404         ADD      SP, +04
0CBB:002E B80000         MOV      AX, 0000
0CBB:0031 C3             RET
0CBB:0032 55             PUSH     BP
0CBB:0033 8BEC           MOV      BP, SP
0CBB:0035 83C4FE         ADD      SP, -02
0CBB:0038 8B4604         MOV      AX, [BP+04]
0CBB:003B 8946FE         MOV      [BP-02], AX
0CBB:003E 8B46FE         MOV      AX, [BP-02]
-g, 32                            /* resume, set breakpoint */
                                  /* at varycols() entry */

AX=0001  BX=0011  CX=0000  DX=0003  SP=FFF4  BP=0000 SI=0060  DI=02A0
DS=0EB0  ES=0EB0  SS=0EB0  CS=0CBB  IP=0032   NV UP DI NG NZ NA PO NC
0CBB:0032 55             PUSH     BP
-u
0CBB:0032 55             PUSH     BP         /* list varycols() code */
0CBB:0033 8BEC           MOV      BP, SP
0CBB:0035 83C4FE         ADD      SP, -02
0CBB:0038 8B4604         MOV      AX, [BP+04]
```

```
0CBB:003B 8946FE       MOV     [BP-02],AX
0CBB:003E 8B46FE       MOV     AX,[BP-02]
0CBB:0041 3B4606       CMP     AX,[BP+06]
0CBB:0044 7F14         JG      005A
0CBB:0046 FF760A       PUSH    [BP+0A]
0CBB:0049 FF76FE       PUSH    [BP-02]
0CBB:004C E83A00       CALL    0089
0CBB:004F 83C404       ADD     SP,+04
-g,38                                   /* resume, stopping once */
                                        /* new frame pointer ready*/
AX=0001  BX=0011  CX=0000  DX=0003  SP=FFF0  BP=FFF2  SI=0060  DI=02A0
DS=0EB0  ES=0EB0  SS=0EB0  CS=0CBB  IP=0038  NV UP DI NG NZ AC PE CY
0CBB:0038 8B4604       MOV     AX,[BP+04]                        SS:FFF6=0003
-dfff0 1 2                             /* list contents of varycols() local i */
                                       /* at function start, it's garbage */
                                       /* see figure 8.2 */
0EB0:FFF0  BB 0C                                                 ;
-g,4c                                  /* resume, stop at call to box() */


AX=0003  BX=0011  CX=0000  DX=0003  SP=FFEC  BP=FFF2  SI=0060  DI=02A0
DS=0EB0  ES=0EB0  SS=0EB0  CS=0CBB  IP=004C  NV UP DI NG NZ AC PE CY
0CBB:004C E83A00          CALL    0089
-dffec 1 4                             /* show parameters to box and ... */
0EB0:FFEC  03 00 02 00                                           ...
-dfff0 1 2                             /* show varycol local variables */
                                       /* see figure 8.3 */
0EB0:FFF0  03 00                                                 ..
-g,89                                  /* resume, stop at box() entry */


AX=0003  BX=0011  CX=0000  DX=0003  SP=FFEA  BP=FFF2  SI=0060  DI=02A0
DS=0EB0  ES=0EB0  SS=0EB0  CS=0CBB  IP=0089   NV UP DI NG NZ AC PE CY
0CBB:0089 55           PUSH    BP
-u
0CBB:0089 55           PUSH    BP      /* list box function */
0CBB:008A 8BEC         MOV     BP,SP
0CBB:008C 83C4FC       ADD     SP,-04
0CBB:008F C746FC0100   MOV     WORD PTR [BP-04],0001
0CBB:0094 8B46FC       MOV     AX,[BP-04]
0CBB:0097 3B4606       CMP     AX,[BP+06]
0CBB:009A 7F6B         JG      0107
0CBB:009C 837EFC01     CMP     WORD PTR [BP-04],+01
0CBB:00A0 7408         JZ      00AA
0CBB:00A2 8B46FC       MOV     AX,[BP-04]
0CBB:00A5 3B4606       CMP     AX,[BP+06]
0CBB:00A8 7528         JNZ     00D2
```

```
-u
0CBB:00AA C746FE0100    MOV    WORD PTR [BP-02],0001
0CBB:00AF 8B46FE        MOV    AX,[BP-02]
0CBB:00B2 3B4604        CMP    AX,[BP+04]
0CBB:00B5 7F0F          JG     00C6
0CBB:00B7 BB1200        MOV    BX,0012
0CBB:00BA 53            PUSH   BX
0CBB:00BB E8AE00        CALL   016C
0CBB:00BE 83C402        ADD    SP,+02
0CBB:00C1 FF46FE        INC    WORD PTR [BP-02]
0CBB:00C4 EBE9          JMP    00AF
0CBB:00C6 BB1400        MOV    BX,0014
0CBB:00C9 53            PUSH   BX
-g,8f                           /* resume, stop after locals */
                                /* allocated */
AX=0003 BX=0011 CX=0000 DX=0003 SP=FFE4 BP=FFE8 SI=0060 DI=02A0
DS=0EB0 ES=0EB0 SS=0EB0 CS=0CBB IP=008F NV UP DI NG NZ AC PE CY
0CBB:008F C746FC0100    MOV    WORD PTR [BP-04],0001        SS:FFE4=0089
-dffe4 1 4                      /* dump uninitialized box() locals */
                                /* see figure 8.4 */
0EB0:FFE4  89 00 BB 0C                                  ..;.
-g,bb                           /* resume, stop at printf() call */

AX=0001 BX=0012 CX=0000 DX=0003 SP=FFE2 BP=FFE8 SI=0060 DI=02A0
DS=0EB0 ES=0EB0 SS=0EB0 CS=0CBB IP=00BB NV UP DI NG NZ AC PO CY
0CBB:00BB E8AE00        CALL   016C
-dffe2 1 2                      /* dump printf() pointer parameter */
0EB0:FFE2  12 00                                        ..
-d12 1 2                        /* dump string at pointer */
0EB0:0012  2A 00                                        *.
-dffe4 1 4                      /* dump box() locals */
0EB0:FFE4  01 00 01 00                                  ....
-dfff0 1 2                      /* dump varycol's local i */
0EB0:FFF0  03 00                                        ..
-d ffec 1 4                     /* dump parameters to box() */
                                /* see figure 8.5 */
0EB0:FFEC  03 00 02 00                                  ....
-g,5e                           /* resume, stop at varyrows() */
***
***                             /* boxes drawn by varycols() */
```

```
****
****

*****
*****

******
******

*******
*******
```

```
AX=0008  BX=001F  CX=0000  DX=0003  SP=FFF8  BP=0000  SI=0060  DI=02A0
DS=0EB0  ES=0EB0  SS=0EB0  CS=0CBB  IP=005E    NV UP DI NG NZ PO NC
0CBB:005E 55          PUSH    BP
-u                                  /* list varyrows function */
0CBB:005E 55          PUSH    BP
0CBB:005F 8BEC        MOV     BP,SP
0CBB:0061 83C4FE      ADD     SP,-02
0CBB:0064 8B4604      MOV     AX,[BP+04]
0CBB:0067 8946FE      MOV     [BP-02],AX
0CBB:006A 8B46FE      MOV     AX,[BP-02]
0CBB:006D 3B4606      CMP     AX,[BP+06]
0CBB:0070 7F13        JG      0085
0CBB:0072 FF76FE      PUSH    [BP-02]
0CBB:0075 BA0800      MOV     DX,0008
0CBB:0078 52          PUSH    DX
0CBB:0079 E80D00      CALL    0089          /* call to box() */
0CBB:007C 83C404      ADD     SP,+04
-g,64                               /* resume, stop after locals */
                                    /* allocated */
AX=0008  BX=001F  CX=0000  DX=0003  SP=FFF4  BP=FFF6  SI=0060  DI=02A0
DS=0EB0  ES=0EB0  SS=0EB0  CS=0CBB  IP=0064  NV UP DI NG NZ AC PO CY
0CBB:0064 8B4604      MOV     AX,[BP+04]                   SS:FFFA=0003
-dfff4 1 2                          /* dump varyrows local i (garbage) */
                                    /* see figure 8.6 */
0EB0:FFF4  BB 0C                                           ; .
-g,79                               /* resume, stop at call to box */

AX=0003  BX=001F  CX=0000  DX=0008  SP=FFF0  BP=FFF6  SI=0060  DI=02A0
DS=0EB0  ES=0EB0  SS=0EB0  CS=0CBB  IP=0079  NV UP DI NG NZ AC PE CY
0CBB:0079 E80D00      CALL    0089
-dfff0 1 4                          /* dump box parms */
0EB0:FFF0   08 00 03 00                                    ....
-dfff4 1 2                          /* dump varyrows local i */
                                    /* see figure 8.7 */
```

```
ØEBØ:FFF4    Ø3 ØØ                                         ..
-g,8f                            /* resume, stop after box() */
                                 /* locals allocated */


AX=ØØØ3  BX=ØØ1F  CX=ØØØØ  DX=ØØØ8  SP=FFE8  BP=FFEC  SI=ØØ6Ø  DI=Ø2AØ
DS=ØEBØ  ES=ØEBØ  SS=ØEBØ  CS=ØCBB  IP=ØØ8F    NV UP DI NG NZ AC PE CY
ØCBB:ØØ8F C746FCØ1ØØ    MOV    WORD PTR [BP-Ø4],ØØØ1              SS:FFE8=FFF2
-dffe8 1 4                       /* dump box locals (garbage) */
                                 /* see figure 8.8 */
ØEBØ:FFE8    F2 FF 79 ØØ                                   r.y.
-g,16c                           /* resume, stop at printf() entry */


AX=ØØØ1  BX=ØØ12  CX=ØØØØ  DX=ØØØ8  SP=FFE4  BP=FFEC  SI=ØØ6Ø  DI=Ø2AØ
DS=ØEBØ  ES=ØEBØ  SS=ØEBØ  CS=ØCBB  IP=Ø16C    NV UP DI NG NZ AC PE CY
ØCBB:Ø16C 55          PUSH   BP
-dffe8 1 4                       /* dump box locals r and c */
ØEBØ:FFE8    Ø1 ØØ Ø1 ØØ                                   ....
-dfff4 1 2                       /* dump varyrows local i */
ØEBØ:FFF4    Ø3 ØØ                                         ..
-dfffØ 1 4                       /* dump box parameters */
                                 /* see figure 8.9 */
ØEBØ:FFFØ    Ø8 ØØ Ø3 ØØ                                   ....
-g                               /* resume, run to termination */
********                         /* output from varyrows */
*      *
********

********
*      *
*      *
********

********
*      *
*      *
*      *
********
```

```
********
*      *
*      *
*      *
*      *
********

********
*      *
*      *
*      *
*      *
*      *
********
```

```
Program terminated normally
-q
```

Listing 8.7.

A breakpoint is then set at a point a few instructions into the function. At this point, the stack pointer contains the frame pointer. The selected point, which represents the earliest instruction within the function where the frame pointer is known, is identified by an addition operation on the stack pointer.

The following annotated fragment explains a typical function "preamble"—the first few instructions of every function that contains a local variable.

PUSH	BP	Save caller's frame pointer
MOV	BP, SP	Capture pointer to input parameters
ADD	SP, -02	Allocate local variable space (2 bytes), SP becomes local frame pointer.
MOV	AX, [BP+04]	First nonpreamble instruction. This particular instruction fetches a parameter out of the stack.

In this example, a breakpoint at the last MOV instruction would stop the program after the new frame pointer had been placed in SP.

The programmer can look for one of two landmarks if he or she has trouble identifying this point in the compiler's output:

- the first parameter pushed as the current function prepares to call a subordinate

- the first function call (at this point, the SP will not hold the frame pointer but will hold a value that the programmer can adjust to get the frame pointer)

The first parameter push can be located by counting pushes backward from the call to the subordinate function. If the subordinate function is called with three parameters, the third push preceding the call is the spot for the breakpoint. This method of identifying an adequate breakpoint is most dependable if there are no computations on the parameters in the call.

Subordinate Call	Reliability
foo(a, b)	counting pushes works fine
foo(a+b, c)	counting pushes may not work because the compiler may insert extra calls to compute a + b.

The local frame address can be computed directly from the stack pointer value if a breakpoint is set at the first call to a subordinate routine. When this breakpoint is reached, the stack pointer can be adjusted "backward" to yield the frame pointer. The necessary computations for this procedure are

```
      current stack pointer
  +   (size of) actual parameters
      _____

      frame pointer
```

The register dumps that accompany the g, 38 and g, 4c instructions in listing 8.7 reflect this relationship.

In the dump immediately following g, 38, the stack pointer contains the true frame pointer (Øxfffø), because Øx38 is the first instruction following the allocation of local-variable stack space.

The frame pointer can be computed from the stack pointer value at the next breakpoint (Øx4c, the call to box()), by adding the size of box()'s parameters to the stack pointer contents. Because box's parameter list consists of two 16-bit integers (four bytes), the computation looks like this:

0xffec	stack pointer contents at 0x4c breakpoint
+ 4	bytes in parameter list

0xfff0	true frame pointer

Annotations in listing 8.7 explain the purpose of each debug command and will help you to identify key landmarks. Refer also to the following list of entry points for all functions:

0000:0089	_box
0000:0000	_main
0000:016C	_printf
0000:0032	_varycols
0000:005E	_varyrows

Additionally, figures 8.2 through 8.9 show the contents of the stack at critical breakpoints during the session.

Created by	Object	Address	Value	
main				
	parameters	FFF6		
	return	FFF4	1D 00	
	frame pointer	FFF2	? ?	
varycols	local i	FFF0	BB 0C	←SP

Fig. 8.2. Stack detail from sample debugging session (refer to listing 8.7).

Created by	Object	Address	Value	
main	parameters	FFF6		
	return	FFF4	1D 00	
	frame pointer	FFF2	? ?	
varycols	local i	FFF0	03 00	
	parameter 1	FFEE	02 00	
	parameter 2	FFEC	03 00	←SP

Fig. 8.3. Stack detail from sample debugging session (refer to listing 8.7).

Created by	Object	Address	Value
main	parameters	FFF6	
	return	FFF4	1D 00
	frame pointer	FFF2	? ?
	local i	FFF0	03 00
varycols	parameter 1	FFEE	02 00
	parameter 2	FFEC	03 00
	return	FFEA	4F 00
	frame pointer	FFE8	F2 FF
box	local c	FFE6	BB 0C
	local r	FFE4	89 00 ←—SP

Fig. 8.4. Stack detail from sample debugging session (refer to listing 8.7).

Created by	Object	Address	Value
main	parameters	FFF6	
	return	FFF4	1D 00
	frame pointer	FFF2	? ?
	local i	FFF0	03 00
varycols	parameter 1	FFEE	02 00
	parameter 2	FFEC	03 00
	return	FFEA	4F 00
	frame pointer	FFE8	F2 FF
	local c	FFE6	01 00
box	local r	FFE4	01 00
	parameter	FFE2	12 00 ←—SP

Fig. 8.5. Stack detail from sample debugging session (refer to listing 8.7).

Notice that, beginning with figure 8.6, the high-address portion of the stack "moves up" four bytes. That is, the return to main() is at 0xfff4 prior to figure 8.6 and at 0xfff8 through the rest of the example.

This reflects the fact that varyrows() is called with fewer parameters than varycols(). The parameter space allocated by main for these functions is in an (unshown) higher-address portion of the stack. Because the four parameters of varycols() require four bytes more than do the two parameters of varyrows(), the space used by varyrows() begins "higher" in memory.

Figures 8.5 and 8.8 clearly reflect how local variables "move" from one location to another during program execution. In figure 8.5, box()'s locals (r and c) reside at 0xffe4–0xffe7. In figure 8.8 (where box is called from varyrows(), rather than from varycols()), box()'s locals are at 0xffe8–0xffeb.

Created by	Object	Address	Value	
main	return	FFF8	2B 00	
	frame pointer	FFF6	? ?	
varyrows	local i	FFF4	BB 0C	←SP

Fig. 8.6. Stack detail from sample debugging session (refer to listing 8.7).

Created by	Object	Address	Value	
main	return	FFF8	2B 00	
	frame pointer	FFF6	? ?	
varyrows	local i	FFF4	03 00	
	parameter 1	FFF2	03 00	
	parameter 2	FFF0	08 00	←SP

Fig. 8.7. Stack detail from sample debugging session (refer to listing 8.7).

Created by	Object	Address	Value	
main	return	FFF8	2B 00	
	frame pointer	FFF6	? ?	
	local i	FFF4	03 00	
varyrows	parameter 1	FFF2	03 00	
	parameter 2	FFF0	08 00	
	return	FFEE	7C 00	
	frame pointer	FFEC	F6 FF	
box	local c	FFEA	79 00	
	local r	FFE8	F2 FF	←SP

Fig. 8.8. Stack detail from sample debugging session (refer to listing 8.7).

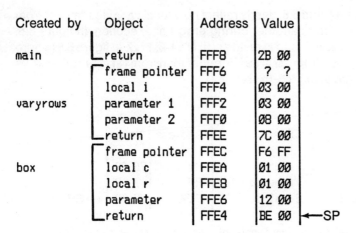

Created by	Object	Address	Value
main	└return	FFF8	2B 00
	┌frame pointer	FFF6	? ?
	local i	FFF4	03 00
varyrows	parameter 1	FFF2	03 00
	parameter 2	FFF0	08 00
	└return	FFEE	7C 00
	┌frame pointer	FFEC	F6 FF
box	local c	FFEA	01 00
	local r	FFE8	01 00
	parameter	FFE6	12 00
	└return	FFE4	BE 00 |←—SP

Fig. 8.9. Stack detail from sample debugging session (refer to listing 8.7).

This example is simplified by the uniform use of integer variables only. The bookkeeping is simplified because integers, frame pointers, and return addresses are all 16-bit values and all stack addresses, therefore, are even. Using local variables that aren't 16-bit values will result in less tidy stack addresses.

RETURN

Chapter 7 focuses on stabilizing bugs with general-purpose variable-initializing tools. This chapter presents techniques for localizing an error after it has been stabilized.

Both chapters examine techniques for attacking pointer bugs. Each of the techniques presented is designed to counter a specific kind of bug.

As programmers gain experience, they learn to select their debugging techniques based on the differences in visible bug symptoms. The following can be used as a guide for selecting efficient and effective debugging techniques.

Behavior	Probable Cause	Best Technique
Program "gets lost" between lines	Pointer writing on return linkage in stack	Periodic call to stack dump function
Bug changes when debug code is added	Pointer writing on code, or uninitialized pointer among local variables	Periodic checksum of code areas, and initialize all locals at start of each function
Local variable changes value without being referenced	Pointer writing on local-variable area of stack frame	Initialize all variables. Include suspect variable in snapshot (via pointer stored in a global). Experiment with changes that change the load map. As a last resort, trace with breakpoint debugger.

In this chapter, and in the preceding chapters, I have discussed only "homemade" debugging tools. That is, I've looked at techniques that rely only on access to a compiler and to the low-level debugging program that normally is supplied with the operating system.

These tools wield enough power to find any normal bug. But using these tools isn't always efficient or convenient. Many of the techniques presume extensive low-level knowledge of the machine, the compiler, and the run-time environment.

Chapters 9 and 10 examine several commercial products that offer significant improvements in both efficiency and convenience.

9
Source-Level Debuggers

Using a breakpoint debugging program very nearly becomes a requirement as you track certain particularly troublesome C bugs. Assembly-oriented debuggers, such as DEBUG and DDT, are hardly convenient.

In fact, for the systems programmer who takes up C to avoid assembly language, being coerced into debugging "high-level" code at the assembly level seems the ultimate humiliation.

Using DEBUG or DDT forces the high-level programmer to:

- translate symbolic names into physical memory addresses

- correlate compiler-generated assembly language with the source code

- manually translate familiar high-level numeric values and operations into machine-oriented representations

- be constantly aware of such implementation issues as where certain globals are placed, how the stack is used, and how parameters are passed to functions

Humans aren't oriented naturally to these tasks. Compilers were developed primarily to relieve us of such tedious bookkeeping activities. By grafting the compiler's "bookkeeping capabilities" onto a basic breakpoint debugger, source-level debugging programs extend the basic machine-level capability to debugging programs such as DEBUG and DDT.

Source-level debugging programs permit variables to be referenced by their symbolic name and code to be referenced by its position within the original source (either by line numbers or labels, such as function names).

Language-specific source-level debugging programs (designed to be used with code generated by a single programming language) implement a substantial subset of the language's operators. These programs format dumps and other output in forms appropriate to the language's high-level view of the machine.

This chapter explores the capabilities of two representative source-level debugging programs: *sdb*, the source-level debugging program available on UNIX systems, and *CodeView*™, the source-level debugging program included with the Microsoft C Compiler (beginning with version 4.0).

sdb: UNIX's Symbolic Debugging Program

Under UNIX, *sdb* plays two roles:

- it aids in postmortem analysis of *core dumps* (files containing a literal copy of the contents of memory space at the time that the operating system aborts a program)

- it supports interactive execution and debugging of C, assembly language, and (to a lesser extent) of other high-level languages such as Fortran 77

Because *sdb* is an assembly language breakpoint debugger, it can be used with any executable file. However, its full range of symbolic capabilities is available only when *sdb* is used to manipulate an executable image compiled from a C program using the special compiler option *-g*.

This option causes the compiler and linker to save special tables of information about the program, and to attach them to the load module. From these tables, *sdb* gets information about variable names, function names, and line numbers. The option also automatically links several debugging functions from a special library.

The UNIX documentation for *sdb* (a scant 16 pages in the *3B/2 Programming Guide*) outlines most of the commands, but doesn't help the programmer understand how to apply the package's capabilities to specific problems. Several important commands and options (command *m* and option *w*, for example) are mentioned only in the *sdb* manual page. The description of individual commands is not organized (in either document) for quick reference.

Furthermore, *sdb*'s case-sensitive interpreter is not particularly helpful to newcomers. *sdb* is not easily accessible to the user who is trying to learn independently. A more usable command summary appears in Appendix E, and although the summary is sketchy, it is a convenient learning resource and reference.

The "real" *sdb*, available only on "real" UNIX systems, has strongly influenced the design of debugging programs in many other systems. Even if you don't expect to work on a "real" UNIX system, being familiar with *sdb*'s capabilities is useful. (All of the examples in this chapter were run on an AT&T 3B/2-300 running UNIX System V, Release 2. The *sdb* described is Issue 3.)

Using sdb

sdb allows the user to interactively examine and change variable contents, control execution, and examine code. These operations are all accomplished by single-letter mnemonic commands, much as they are with DEBUG and DDT. Rather than requiring physical addresses, however, *sdb* commands accept, as their arguments, symbolic variable names and program line numbers.

In fact, the programmer who is comfortable using either DEBUG or DDT, will quickly adapt to the more pleasant and powerful *sdb* environment. The next three sections explain how commands are formed. Later sections describe how the commands are applied to specific problems.

Command Format

Commands in *sdb* have three parts:

- a locator
- the command (often a single letter)
- an optional list of arguments

Unfortunately, because some of the most frequently used commands are punctuation marks, the boundaries between command parts are sometimes obscured. (Humans tend to view punctuation

as the terminal member of a string, rather than as a separate entity.)
The rest of the commands are fairly mnemonic. In many cases, the
command letters were chosen to parallel commands with similar
functions in the UNIX line editor *ex*.

Here are some examples of commands:

locator	command	args	as typed
foo:i	/	l c	foo:i/lc
15	b	i/	15b i/
default	z	none	z
none	r	<infile >outfile	r <infile >outfile
buffer	$m	3	buffer$m 3
/ch == 'a'/	none	none	/ch == 'a'/
1402	!	7	1402!7
foo:g->nextin	/	none	foo:g->nextin/

The *locator* names the object that the command will manipulate.

There are four classes of object in *sdb*'s world.

- variables
- files
- lines (of source code)
- functions

To keep track of the most recently referenced object in each of
these classes, *sdb* maintains internal currency pointers. The behavior of many commands is influenced by *sdb*'s notion of current
line, variable, function, and file.

Function and Variable Locators

To distinguish, and in some cases to separate them from variable
names, function names that appear in the locator field must end
with a colon.

foo: refers to function named foo

foo   refers to a variable named foo

Functions may be identified by name or by the physical address
of their code body.

Variables may be located by name, with a C expression (consisting
of operators, not functions), or by physical address. Several unique

variables frequently have the same name (the counter *i*, for example, in several functions). Such a variable name may be made more precise by prepending the name of the function (terminated by a colon) in which that variable is declared.

With certain commands, the wildcards * and *?* are permitted in function and variable names, allowing a single locator field to name more than one variable. The *asterisk* matches any number of characters, whereas the *?* matches one character. The *period* always references the last-named variable.

A variable name carrying a null function name prefix is identified as a global. Whenever there is no colon in the locator field, the reference is presumed to be a variable in the current function.

All of the following locate variables:

i	the variable i in the current function
foo:i	the variable i in function foo
*:i	all variables i in any currently active scope
foo?:*	all local variables in functions with four-letter names that begin with foo (foo1, foo2, foo3, fooa, fooy ...)
:joe	the global variable joe
.	all local variables
:*	all global variables
arry[*]	all elements of arry (works only if size of arry is known in current scope)
arry[3; 6]	elements 3 through 6 of arry

As is hinted in the last example of the preceding table, *sdb* is knowledgeable even about structures and about pointers to structures.

To distinguish between instances of the same variable in different activations of a recursive function, an activation index is appended to the locator.

foo:joe, 2	the local variable joe in the second oldest activation of foo

Other Locators

Programs number from the beginning of the file. Certain lines are located by their line number, and specified in absolute or relative form. Relative forms are offsets from the current line or from a function or file name.

15	sets current line to 15, an absolute reference
+15	the current line plus 15, a relative reference
foo:15	line 15, must appear in function foo
foo:+15	15th line after the beginning of function foo
test:15	line 15 in file test

Notice, in the last two examples, that file names are used as though they were function names. File names are used infrequently, usually as arguments of the e command rather than as modifiers of a line number.

Alternatively, a search pattern can be used as a locator (full regular expressions are supported, as in the UNIX line editor ex). For example, /regular expression/ searches forward from the current line in the current file, whereas ?regular expression? searches backward. Both update the current line.

Commands that Display Code

Three commands, named after similar ex functions, facilitate the display of source text. The programmer can print (*p*) the current line, display a window (*w*) of text centered on a certain line, or scroll (*z* or *Control-D*) through the next window of text.

control-D scrolls much like *z* but produces a cleaner display. Although only the *scroll* command updates the current line, a line locator can be used with one of these commands to update the current line. As illustrated in the session captured in listing 9.1, the three display commands are used most often with the e command.

Although the programmer can't edit source while in *sdb*, he or she can think of *e* (which names the block of code to be investigated next), as starting a tiny "read-only" edit session.

The e command requires either a function or file name as an argument. Typically, *e* is used to select a function. Then *w* or *z* is used to list the first few lines of that function. This combination of commands creates a convenient, name-oriented mechanism for browsing through the code. The uppercase *Q* will generate a list of available procedures and files.

```
No core image
*!cat <list1a.c                    /*escape to operating system to */
                                   /*show the program being examined */
                                   /*It's the stack exercising */
                                   /*from Chapter 8 with some added */
                                   /*(nonfunctioning) data structures */
#include "stdio.h"

int index_g;
int oned_g[4] = {
2, 3, 4, 5};

int table_g[3][4] = {
    {2,  3,  4,  5},
    {4,  3,  2,  1},
    {15, 7,  6,  5}
    };

struct block {
    int bag;
    int ave;
    int street;
    char *name;
    } lone_g = { 0, 0, 0, "oops"};

struct block city_g[] = {
    {0,0,0, "origin"},
    {0,1,2, "east"},
    {1,0,1, "west"},
    {1,1,0, "diagonal"}
    };

struct block *ptr_g;
```

```
main()
{
ptr_g = &city_g[2];
printf("\ncalling level 1");
level1(1);
printf("\ncalling second time");
level1(6);
printf("\ncalling third time");
level1(2);
}

level1(depth)
int depth;
{
char *lbl_l1 = "first subordinate";

level2(depth -1,  lbl_l1);
}

level2(depth, pnt)
int depth;
char *pnt;
{
int count_l2;

count_l2 = city_g[0, 0]. bag++;

printf("\nentering level2");
if (depth > 0) level2(depth-1, pnt);
}                                       /*end of program source */

*/level1/                               /*search for a string *,

33: level1(1);

*w                                      /*print a window around line 33 */
```

```
28:
29: main()
30: {
31: ptr_g = &city_g[2];
32: printf("\ncalling level 1");
33: level1(1);
34: printf("\ncalling second time");
35: level1(6);
36: printf("\ncalling third time");
37: level1(2);
```

*/level1(depth)/   /*search again with more info*/

```
40: level1(depth)
```

*w   /*and window */

```
35: level1(6);
36: printf("\ncalling third time");
37: level1(2);
38: }
39:
40: level1(depth)
41: int depth;
42: {
43: char *lbl_l1 = "first subordinate";
44:
```

*1z   ~~~/*scroll through window beginning*/

```
1: #include "stdio.h"                   /*with line one */
2:
3: int index_g;
4: int oned_g[4] = {
5:    2,3,4,5};
6:
7: int table_g[3][4] = {
8:    {2, 3, 4, 5},
9:    {4, 3, 2, 1},
10:   {15, 7, 6, 5}
```

```
*z                                      /*scroll through next window */

10:    {15, 7, 6, 5}                    /*notice line 10 is repeated */
11:    };
12:
13: struct block {
14:    int bag;
15:    int ave;
16:    int street;
17:    char *name;
18:    } lone_g = { 0, 0, 0, "oops"};
19:
20: struct block city_g[] = {            /*clean scroll produced by */
21:    {0,0,0,"origin"},                 /*invisible Control-d */
22:    {0,1,2,"east"},
23:    {1,0,1,"west"},
24:    {1,1,0,"diagonal"}
25:    };
26:
27: struct block *ptr_g;
28:
29: main()                               /*another Control-d was typed*/
30: {
31: ptr_g = &city_g[2];
32: printf("\ncalling level 1");
33: level1(1);
34: printf("\ncalling second time");
35: level1(6);
36: printf("\ncalling third time");
37: level1(2);

*e level2                               /*work with ("edit") level2 */

level2() in "list1a.c"                  /*wherever it is */
```

```
*w                                    /*Window on new current line */

46: }
47:
48: level2(depth, pnt)
49: int depth;
50: char *pnt;
51: {
52: int count_12;
53:
54: count_12 = city_g[0, 0]. bag++;
55:

*e main                               /*work with ("edit") main */

main() in "list1a. c"

*z                                    /*notice scroll doesn't print */

30: {                                 /*main() definition line */
31: ptr_g = &city_g[2];
32: printf("\ncalling level 1");
33: level1(1);
34: printf("\ncalling second time");
35: level1(6);
36: printf("\ncalling third time");
37: level1(2);
38: }
39:
```

```
*/level1/                           /*search again */

33: level1(1);

*p                                  /*print current line */

33: level1(1);

*/level1/                           /*search again */

35: level1(6);

*+5p                                /*print relative offset */

40: level1(depth)

*q
```

Listing 9.1. Commands that display source code.

Commands that Display Variables

A variable locator followed by a slash (/) displays the named variable or variables. The slash is the *display* or *dump* command (not all the commands are mnemonic).

The slash has four governing parameters:

- the variable locator
- the size of the variable
- the representation to be used
- the number of such objects to be displayed

Simple dumps need name only the variable locator; the format and length will be inferred from the variable's declared type or from the format used in the most recent display command. The number of objects will default to *1*. Alternative representations and lengths can be named explicitly with characters like those used in printf.

Several variations and the display they generate are shown in the session captured in listing 9.2. This session (and that shown in listing 9.1) manipulate the same program.

```
No core image
**_g/                                  /*just to illustrate what happens*/
index_g/ No process and/or no file     /*if you try to view variables*/
                                       /*before starting a test run */


*32b                                   /*set a breakpoint and start */
main:32 b                              /*the process    */


*R

Breakpoint at
main:32: printf("\ncalling level 1");

**_g/                                  /*now look at tagged globals */

index_g/ 0
oned_g[0]/ 2
table_g[0][0]/ 2
lone_g.bag/ 0
lone_g.ave/ 0
lone_g.street/ 0
lone_g.name/ oops
ptr_g/ 0x8088009c

*city_g. */                            /*a bug in release 2 kept this */

city_g.bag/ 0                          /*one from printing */
city_g.ave/ 0                          /*when array elements aren't */
city_g.street/ 0                       /*subscripted, element 0 is used */
city_g.name/ origin

*city_g[1;2]. */                       /*look at other elements */

city_g[1].bag/ 0
city_g[1].ave/ 1
city_g[1].street/ 2
city_g[1].name/ east
city_g[2].bag/ 1
city_g[2].ave/ 0
city_g[2].street/ 1
city_g[2].name/ west
```

```
*index_g.*/                        /*if you imply a structure (.) */

index_g.bag/ 0                     /*but don't specify the elements,  */
index_g.ave/ -2138570596           /*the last-used type is assumed, even */
index_g.street/ 0                  /*if it makes no sense...index is int! */
index_g.name/ ^?^?^?^?^?^?^?^?^?^?^?^?^?^?^?
^?^?^?^?^?^?^?^?^?^?^?^?^?^?^?^?^?^?^?^?^?^?^?^?^?^?^?^?^?^?^?^?^?^?^?^?^?^?
^?^?^?^?^?^?^?^?^?^?^?^?^?^?^?^?^?^?^?^?^?^?^?^?^?^?^?^?^?^?^?^?^?^?^?^?^?^?
^?^?^?^?^?^?^?^?^?^?^?^?^?^?^?^?^?^?^?^?^?^?^?^?^?^?^?^?^?^?^?^?^?^?^?^?^?^?
                                   /*The ^?^?... is the result of trying */
                                   /*to print an uninitialized string */


*ptr_g->bag/                       /*sdb understands pointers to structures */

1

*ptr_g->*/                         /* asterisk still gets all fields */

ptr_g->bag/ 1
ptr_g->ave/ 0
ptr_g->street/ 1
ptr_g->name/ west

*ptr_g->name/x                     /* gets the address of name in hex */

0x808800cd

*0x808800cd/1c                     /* notice how the format descriptors */

w e s t                            /* affect the display */

*0x808800cd/4bx

0x77    0x65    0x73    0x74

*0x808800cd/4bc

w       e       s       t

*0x808800ce/3bx
```

```
0x65     0x73     0x74

*0x808800ce/1bx

0x65
                              /* now the program is executed to a */
                              /* much later breakpoint so that */
                              /* there will be local variables on */
                              /* the stack. */
*56b

level2:56 b

*c 6

Breakpoint at
level2:56: printf("\nentering level2");
                              /*the traceback shows that there are */
                              /*five calls to level2 pending, note */
                              /*the parameters for each */

*t

level2(depth=1,pnt=first subordinate)    [list1a.c:56]
level2(depth=2,pnt=first subordinate)    [list1a.c:57]
level2(depth=3,pnt=first subordinate)    [list1a.c:57]
level2(depth=4,pnt=first subordinate)    [list1a.c:57]
level2(depth=5,pnt=first subordinate)    [list1a.c:57]
level1(depth=6)   [list1a.c:45]
main(1,-1073610644,-1073610636)    [list1a.c:35]

**:*/                         /* list all variables...note that */
                              /* calling parameters are included */

level2:count_12/ 5            /* newest invocation */
level2:pnt/ first subordinate
level2:depth/ 1
level2:count_12/ 4            /* second newest */
level2:pnt/ first subordinate
level2:depth/ 2
level2:count_12/ 3            /* third newest */
level2:pnt/ first subordinate
level2:depth/ 3
```

```
level2:count_12/ 2
level2:pnt/ first subordinate
level2:depth/ 4
level2:count_12/ 1
level2:pnt/ first subordinate
level2:depth/ 5
level1:lbl_l1/ first subordinate
level1:depth/ 6
Assuming .data is int.                /*these are globals...note how */
 data/ 2                              /*many system variables appear */
Assuming environ is int.
environ/ -1073610636
index_g/ 0
oned_g[0]/ 2
table_g[0][0]/ 2
lone_g.bag/ 0
lone_g.ave/ 0
lone_g.street/ 0
lone_g.name/ oops
ptr_g/ 0x8088009c
Assuming _iob is int.
_iob/ 0
Assuming _bufendtab is int.
_bufendtab/ 0
Assuming _ctype is int.
_ctype/ 2105376
Assuming _bigpow is int.
_bigpow/ 1086457317
Assuming _litpow is int.
_litpow/ 1192048951
Assuming _lastbuf is int.
_lastbuf/ -2138568308
Assuming errno is int.
errno/ 25
Assuming _stdbuf is int.
_stdbuf/ -2138567500
Assuming _smbuf is int.
_smbuf/ 0
Assuming _sibuf is int.
_sibuf/ 0
Assuming _sobuf is int.
_sobuf/ 174285164
```

```
Assuming _fp_hw is int.
_fp_hw/ 0
Assuming _asr is int.
_asr/ 0
Assuming _fpftype is int.
_fpftype/ 0
Assuming _fpfault is int.
_fpfault/ 0
Assuming __dbargs is int.
__dbargs/ 0
```

```
*l*:*/                              /*exploit naming convention to get */

level2:count_l2/ 5                  /*just our local variables */
level2:pnt/ first subordinate
level2:depth/ 1
level2:count_l2/ 4
level2:pnt/ first subordinate
level2:depth/ 2
level2:count_l2/ 3
level2:pnt/ first subordinate
level2:depth/ 3
level2:count_l2/ 2
level2:pnt/ first subordinate
level2:depth/ 4
level2:count_l2/ 1
level2:pnt/ first subordinate
level2:depth/ 5
level1:lbl_l1/ first subordinate
level1:depth/ 6


*l*:*_l*/                           /*refine pattern to exclude parameters */
```

```
level2:count_12/ 5
level2:count_12/ 4
level2:count_12/ 3
level2:count_12/ 2
level2:count_12/ 1
level1:lbl_l1/ first subordinate

*level2:count_12, 2/          /* list count from just the second */

4                            /* newest invocation */

*q
```

Listing 9.2. Dumping the contents of variables.

The session in listing 9.2 begins with several commands that will be discussed later as "Commands that Control Execution." These commands set a breakpoint and then initiate execution. Variable values cannot be displayed successfully unless a run has been started or a core file (the result of an aborted program) has been loaded. If variables aren't available *sdb* reminds the user (as shown in the first three lines of listing 9.2) that no program is running.

If a uniform naming convention for variables is used when drafting code, a simple wildcard pattern can be used to produce selective snapshots. For example, if the programmer consistently ends local variables with _l and global variables with _g, he or she can get a dump of all local variables with

   :*_g

This may seem redundant—after all, :*/ also prints all global variables. The difference is that :*_g prints only globals that have been declared explicitly.

The more general :*/ prints all global variables, including those declared in the headers for the various libraries that the program references. The system-declared globals probably will eclipse the user's, particularly if *curses* (a terminal-independent screen handler) or some other large function library has been used.

More elaborate tags can be used to classify globals according to use, and to classify functions according to purpose. All globals associated with a central data structure (a circular queue and its head and tail pointers, for example) should have the same identifying tag, perhaps _gq. All functions that manipulate this queue could be similarly tagged. Several operations near the end of listing 9.2 exploit naming conventions.

Commands that Manipulate Breakpoints

The *b* command sets breakpoints at a line specified by a line locator. Breakpoints may have an argument that specifies an attached action. This attached action is a list of *sdb* commands that are executed automatically whenever the associated breakpoint is encountered. When the line locator is just a function name, the breakpoint is placed at the first line of that function.

Here are some examples of breakpoint commands:

23b	Place a simple breakpoint at line 23, which must be a line in the current function.
foo:23b	Set a simple breakpoint at line 23, which must be in function foo. Changes the current function.
*foo:b :*_gq/*	Set a breakpoint at the first line of function foo. Whenever this breakpoint is encountered, dump all globals with names that end in _gq.

The attached action (as illustrated by the preceding example) is one of *sdb*'s most general and powerful features. An attached action may be more than one command. Multiple commands are separated by semicolons and, although not quite a macro facility, are almost as powerful as a macro facility. (The attached command is used in the session of listing 9.7.)

Listing 9.3 (among others) includes several examples of breakpoint manipulation.

```
No core image

*main:b                           /*set a breakpoint at beginning of main*/

0x80800116 (main:30+2) b

*R                                /*begin execution                    */

Breakpoint at
0x80800116 in main:30: {

*z                                /*it's easier to keep your bearings */

30: {                             /*with the code handy               */
31: ptr_g = &city_g[2];
32: printf("\ncalling level 1");
33: level1(1);
34: printf("\ncalling second time");
35: level1(6);
36: printf("\ncalling third time");
37: level1(2);
38: }
39:

*s                                /* take a step */

main:31: ptr_g = &city_g[2];

*s                                /* and another */

main:32: printf("\ncalling level 1");

*S                                /* but avoid going inside printf */

main:33: level1(1);

*s                                /* now step into level1 */

level1:43: char *lbl_l1 = "first subordinate";
```

```
*z                                /* and get a new listing of the code */

43: char *lbl_l1 = "first subordinate";
44:
45: level2(depth -1,   lbl_l1);
46: }
47:
48: level2(depth, pnt)
49: int depth;
50: char *pnt;
51: {
52: int count_l2;

*52c                              /* resume, stopping at line 52 */

Breakpoint at                     /* sdb stops at line 54 instead */
                                  /* (it's the first executable line) */
level2:54: count_l2 = city_g[0,0].bag++;

*z                                /* again get one's bearings */

54: count_l2 = city_g[0,0].bag++;
55:
56: printf("\nentering level2");
57: if (depth > 0) level2(depth - 1, pnt);
58: }

*57b                              /* set a breakpoint at end of level2 */

level2:57 b

*c                                /* resume, no limit */

Breakpoint at
level2:57: if (depth > 0) level2(depth - 1, pnt);

*t                                /*find out how we got here */

level2(depth=0, pnt=first subordinate)   [list1a.c:57]
level1(depth=1)   [list1a.c:45]
main(1, -1073610644, -1073610636)   [list1a.c:33]
```

```
*c                              /*run deeper */

Breakpoint at
level2:57: if (depth > 0) level2(depth - 1, pnt);

*c                              /*and deeper */

Breakpoint at
level2:57: if (depth > 0) level2(depth - 1, pnt);

*c                              /*and deeper, using same breakpoint */

Breakpoint at                   /*to maintain control          */
level2:57: if (depth > 0) level2(depth - 1, pnt);

*t                              /*a check shows only three level2()s */
                                /*are active */

level2(depth=3, pnt=first subordinate)   [list1a. c:57]
level2(depth=4, pnt=first subordinate)   [list1a. c:57]
level2(depth=5, pnt=first subordinate)   [list1a. c:57]
level1(depth=6)   [list1a. c:45]
main(1, -1073610644, -1073610636)   [list1a. c:35]

*c 3                            /*resume, stopping on 3nd breakpoint */

Breakpoint at
level2:57: if (depth > 0) level2(depth - 1, pnt);
                                /*deepest point reached. */

*t

level2(depth=0, pnt=first subordinate)   [list1a. c:57]
level2(depth=1, pnt=first subordinate)   [list1a. c:57]
level2(depth=2, pnt=first subordinate)   [list1a. c:57]
level2(depth=3, pnt=first subordinate)   [list1a. c:57]
level2(depth=4, pnt=first subordinate)   [list1a. c:57]
level2(depth=5, pnt=first subordinate)   [list1a. c:57]
level1(depth=6)   [list1a. c:45]
main(1, -1073610644, -1073610636)   [list1a. c:35]
```

```
*s                              /*step through if...it finally fails */

level2:58: }

*s                              /*stepping out of level2 unwinds all */

level1:46: }                    /*pending level2 calls              */

*s                              /*stepping out of level1 reaches main*/

main:36: printf("\ncalling third time");

*s

main:37: level1(2);

*s

level1:43: char *lbl_l1 = "first subordinate";

*s

level1:45: level2(depth - 1, lbl_l1);

*z

45: level2(depth - 1, lbl_l1);
46: }
47:
48: level2(depth, pnt)
49: int depth;
50: char *pnt;
51: {
52: int count_l2;
53:
54: count_l2 = city_g[0,0].bag++;

*S

Breakpoint at
level2:57: if (depth > 0) level2(depth - 1, pnt);
```

```
*c

Breakpoint at
level2:57: if (depth > 0) level2(depth - 1, pnt);

*c
```

```
calling level 1                    /* program output */
entering level2                    /* it's collected here as a */
calling second time                /* side-effect of mechanism used */
entering level2                    /* to log the session...normally */
entering level2                    /* appears at appropriate points */
entering level2                    /* within the session. */
entering level2
entering level2
entering level2
calling third time
entering level2
entering level2Process terminated
```

```
*q
```

Listing 9.3.

Ordinarily, attached commands do not return control to *sdb*. Instead, breakpoints with attached commands automatically resume execution of the program as soon as the commands have been performed. However, if *k* is included in the string of attached commands, the program will be halted and control passed to the *sdb* command interface. Note that:

- breakpoints can be generated using *b*

- currently active breakpoints can be listed using *B*

- lowercase *d* removes breakpoints one at a time (a line number must be specified or a prompt responded to for each active breakpoint)

- uppercase *D* removes all breakpoints

Commands that Control Execution

To control the execution of a program, four lowercase commands and three uppercase variants are used:

- command *r*, or *R*, to run a program
- command *s*, or *S*, to single step
- command *c*, or *C*, to continue to a temporary breakpoint
- command *g*, to resume at a line other than the current line

A new run is started with *r* or *R*. The uppercase variant starts the program with no arguments. The lowercase version always supplies command-line arguments to the program before executing it.

If arguments are supplied with the *r* command, they are used as the program's command-line arguments. If no arguments are supplied, the last supplied arguments are reused.

The locator field of a *run* command can be used to suppress a specified number of breakpoints, a useful feature if the programmer believes that the early parts of a program have been debugged but he or she doesn't feel ready to remove the breakpoints.

Lowercase *s* steps through the program by source lines. Frequently, the uppercase version of this command is more useful than the lowercase version. *S* "steps over" function calls. That is, *S* treats a function call and all the code it invokes as a single line. The *step* commands accept an optional single-integer argument that specifies how many steps are to be performed before control is returned to the *sdb* command interpreter.

The *continue* command (*c*, or *C*) resumes execution following a breakpoint. When accompanied by a line locator, *continue* places a temporary breakpoint at the named line before continuing. Unlike breakpoints set with the *b* command, temporary breakpoints cause a halt only when they are first reached. *Continue* is useful for stepping through code in large blocks or for stepping over loops. *Continue* may be followed by an integer argument count, in which case count-1 breakpoints will be ignored.

In addition to stopping for breakpoints, *sdb* catches and stops to report all signals encountered by the program under test. (A signal is an interrupt that is either hardware- or software-generated. A signal handler is a user-coded interrupt service routine.)

The *continue* command also resumes execution after these signal-generated breakpoints. Command *C* forwards the signal to the program so that it can be handled in a normal fashion, whereas command *c* consumes the signal so that the program under test never sees it.

A related but undocumented command, *control-C,* facilitates the debugging of user-written signal handlers. The programmer probably doesn't need to worry about signals and signal handlers unless he or she is working on real-time or multiple-process applications.

Under certain circumstances, however, system code (such as the start-up code preceding `main()`) can process signals. If an unexpected signal is encountered, normal debugging can be resumed using the *C* command to continue.

Every interactive debugging session should start by setting at least one breakpoint, followed by the *run* command. To ensure that *sdb* regains control sometime before the program terminates, at least one *breakpoint* command must be set before beginning the run. After receiving control at this breakpoint, *step* and *continue* commands can be used to walk through the rest of the program.

Direct Function Evaluation

Execution can be initiated not only by using the *run, step,* and *continue* commands but also by invoking a function directly from *sdb*'s command level. This feature can be used to test individual functions, or (when stopped at a breakpoint) to dump selected variables with a custom snapshot.

When the user debugs programs processed by *ctrace,* (see the later section on other UNIX debugging aids), the functions *ctron* and *ctroff* can be invoked directly to adjust dynamically the level of trace detail.

WARNING: You can't substitute reliably the direct evaluation of `main()` for the *run* command. Although `main()` is the logical beginning of a program, it isn't the beginning of the code generated by the compiler.

Code to perform certain system-dependent housekeeping functions (like opening standard input and standard output) always precedes the code for main. If main is invoked directly, this start-up code is skipped. The results aren't predictable. Generally, functions shouldn't be evaluated directly unless a program is halted at a breakpoint. Otherwise, files and explicitly set variable values may disappear "mysteriously."

The Monitor Command

The two-letter *monitor* command (*$m*) specifies that a variable is to be monitored. When the monitored variable is referenced, the program will return control to *sdb*.

The command is preceded by a variable locator and may be followed by a count argument. If the count is supplied, *sdb* will not receive control until count references have been detected. (The later sections on pointer debugging demonstrate the use of the *$m* command.)

The Stack Traceback Command

The *traceback* command (*t*) extracts the currently active calling hierarchy from the stack. The command is similar to the stack trace function described in Chapter 8. However, the *traceback* command, which "knows" the names of functions, not only reports function linkages but also dumps parameters. This command takes no arguments and requires no locator.

Later sections explore pointer debugging and include illustrations of the command. (Refer to listing 9.3 for sample *traceback* reports.)

sdb *Application: Postmortem*

When a program aborts under UNIX, a literal image of the program's memory space is captured to the *core* file in the default directory.

When *sdb* is invoked, it tries (unless an option to tell it otherwise is used) to load this file and the object file that is specified on the command line.

By default, the linker output or object file is in a. out during normal program development and *sdb* knows it. To invoke *sdb* on the most recently produced object file and core dump, invoke *sdb* with no arguments. The debugging program will then load *a.out* and *core* by default.

As the programmer examines this frozen image of the "dead" program, he or she is, in effect, performing a postmortem. The range of tests or examinations that can be performed is not wide. Nevertheless, important information can be gathered from the core dump.

The most important step in a postmortem is: performing a trace back, a step that identifies what the program was doing when it died. Next, the programmer dumps all local variables and global variables to search for unreasonable values. There's really not much else that can be done. Listing 9.4 captures a postmortem session with a program aborted by a floating-point exception.

Usually, core dumps are triggered by such hardware-detectable program errors as "divide by zero" or a reference to nonexistent memory. With an abort() call, the programmer deliberately triggers core dumps.

It's good practice to use abort() for error exits (instead of exit()) whenever a program detects an internal error (an error that should never occur). For example, if the control variable in a switch statement should assume only the values *'R'*, *'L'*, or *'z'*, the default clause (which, if all is correct, will never execute) should perform an abort (after any user files have been saved). The abort will capture the program status that led to the unexpected condition.

```
0x808001bf in level2:55: printf("the magic number is %d", count_12/depth);

*w                            /*sdb says problem was line 55...get */

50: char *pnt;               /*the code in that area */
51: {
52: int count_12;
53:
54: count_12 = city_g[0, 0]. bag++;
55: printf("the magic number is %d", count_12/depth);
56: printf("\nentering level2");
57: if (depth > 0) level2(depth-1, pnt);
58: }
```

```
*t                              /*how was this spot reached ? */

level2(depth=0, pnt=first subordinate)    [list4.c:55]
level1(depth=1)    [list4.c:45]
main(1, -1073610644, -1073610636)    [list4.c:33]

*depth/                         /*what values did variables in divide */

0                               /*have at abort ? */

*count_12/

0

*q                              /*that's enough */
```

Listing 9.4. A postmortem session.

sdb *Application: Locating Pointer Bugs that Write on Globals*

The *monitor* command is perfect for locating pointer bugs that target globals. For example, if the user knows that global bufndx is being damaged by a pointer, but is uncertain which pointer is responsible,

```
:bufndx$m
```

can be used to initiate monitoring. Then, when the program is executed, each time bufndx is modified, *sdb* will reclaim control. At each such interruption, the programmer should perform a trace back and examine the source line responsible for the modification. Monitoring should be resumed if the breakpoint line is supposed to perform the modification. It's usually obvious if a line should not be modifying the monitored variable. Unfortunately, *sdb* doesn't offer a tidy command for repeating this operation. The entire *monitor* command must be retyped.

Clearly, this can be a time-consuming process if thousands of correct references precede the faulty one. In this situation, the portion of the program that needs monitoring can be narrowed by check-ing the validity of the monitored variable at several widely spaced breakpoints (the first stage of the technique suggested in Chapter 8). After identifying the the bug's locale, *monitor* can be used to zero in on it quickly.

sdb *Application: Locating Pointer Bugs that Write on Locals*

Because the *monitor* command accesses directly only variables known within the current scope, the command doesn't work as cleanly with local variables as it does with globals.

Pointers that damage locals within the current scope are relatively easy to identify; on the other hand, pointers that damage a local somewhere deep in the stack (in an enclosing scope) are ex-tremely perplexing. Although the *monitor* command won't accept symbolic names for variables outside the current scope, the com-mand always recognizes physical addresses. The session cap-tured in listing 9.5 shows how to obtain the physical address of a local variable, and demonstrates the *monitor* command's special form (*:m*), which is used with physical addresses.

```
No core image

*e level2                        /*work in level2 */

level2() in "list1a. c"

*z                               /*a listing to find the line number */

51: {
52: int count_12;
53:
54: count_12 = city_g[0, 0]. bag++;
55:
56: printf("\nentering level2");
57: if (depth > 0) level2(depth-1, pnt);
58: }
```

```
*56 b                           /*set a breakpoint so that count_l2 */

level2:56 b                     /*is active when reached */

*R                              /*and run */

Breakpoint at
level2:56: printf("\nentering level2");

*count_l2=x                     /*get the address of count_l2 in hex */

0xc0020118

*0xc0020118:m                   /*monitor it */

Prev stmt changed loc 0xc0020118  from 0(0) to 1(0x1).
level2:56: printf("\nentering level2");

*0xc0020118:m                   /*again */

Prev stmt changed loc 0xc0020118  from 1(0x1) to 7(0x7).
level2:56: printf("\nentering level2");

*q
```

Listing 9.5. Monitoring a local variable.

sdb *Application: Locating Pointer Bugs that Destroy Return Addresses*

Because *sdb*'s *traceback* function depends on information that has been left in the stack, postmortems aren't always useful. For example, when the demonstration program from Chapter 8 (overwriting the stack with zeros) runs, the postmortem yields listing 9.6.

No useful return addresses are left for *traceback* to follow, because the stack was destroyed before *core* was dumped. Because the bug in this example also writes on local variables, some of its effects can be viewed during the postmortem. This bug attacks return addresses and locals. The *monitor* command (as described earlier) can be used to watch for the effect on locals.

```
: address Ø

*1z                                 /*The offending program */

1: char buffer[25];
2: main()
3: {
4: printf("\ncalling level 1");
5: level1(1);
6: printf("\ncalling second time");
7: level1(6);
8: printf("\ncalling third time");
9: level1(2);
10: }                              /*listed with Control-Ds */
11:
12: level1(depth)
13: int depth;
14: {
15: char local[15];
16: level2(depth -1, local);
17: }
18:
19: level2(depth, pnt)
20: int depth;
21: char *pnt;
22: {
23: int i;
24:
25: if (depth > 1) level2(depth-1, pnt);
26: if (depth == 4) {
27:    for (i=0; i<35; i++) *pnt++ = 0;
28:    }
29: }

*t                                  /*WOW!...traceback yields nothing */

**:*/                               /*only findable variables are */
```

```
Assuming .data is int.          /*system-declared */
.data/ 174285164
Assuming environ is int.
environ/ -1073610636
buffer/
Assuming _iob is int.
_iob/ 0
Assuming _bufendtab is int.
_bufendtab/ 0
Assuming _ctype is int.
_ctype/ 2105376
Assuming _bigpow is int.
_bigpow/ 1086457317
Assuming _litpow is int.
_litpow/ 1192048951
Assuming _lastbuf is int.
_lastbuf/ -2138568544
Assuming errno is int.
errno/ 0
Assuming _stdbuf is int.
_stdbuf/ -2138567716
Assuming _smbuf is int.
_smbuf/ 0
Assuming _sibuf is int.
_sibuf/ 0
Assuming _sobuf is int.
_sobuf/ 174285164
Assuming _fp_hw is int.
_fp_hw/ 0
Assuming _asr is int.
_asr/ 0
Assuming _fpftype is int.
_fpftype/ 0
Assuming _fpfault is int.
_fpfault/ 0
Assuming __dbargs is int.
__dbargs/ 0

*:i*/

i* not found

*q
```

Listing 9.6. Postmortem, with damaged stack.

If, however, the bug attacks only a return address, the stack trace will still be rendered uninformative and there will be no sign of the damage. The *monitor* command isn't particularly useful in such cases, because there is no clear indication of the address under attack.

To assault this bug, the programmer should set *sdb* breakpoints with attached commands that effectively dump the stack using a traceback and a local variables dump. On large programs, it is necessary to make several passes through the program. Each of these passes tests a smaller area with more frequently placed breakpoints. Listing 9.7 captures a session localizing such a stack error.

```
: address Ø

*1z                                  /*getting oriented */

1: char buffer[25];
2: main()
3: {
4: printf("\ncalling level 1");
5: level1(1);
6: printf("\ncalling second time");
7: level1(6);
8: printf("\ncalling third time");
9: level1(2);
1Ø: }

*6b t                        /* set some breakpoints to act */

main:6 b                     /* as mile posts for first (course) */

*8b t                        /* test run */

main:8 b

*1Øb t

main:1Ø b
```

```
*R                            /* Begin execution */

main(1, -1073610644, -1073610636)   [demo2.c:6]
Illegal Instruction (4) (sig 4)
 at                           /* abort was after line 6, before */
: address 0                   /* line 8...must be in level1() */


*

*D                            /* delete all to prepare more detailed */

All breakpoints deleted       /* test run */

*7b                           /* to gain control before level1 executed */

main:7 b

*R                            /* Begin second test */

Breakpoint at
main:7: level1(6);            /* Level1 is very trivial... */
                              /* we'll look for problem in level2 */

*e level2

level2() in "demo2.c"

*z

22: {
23: int i;
24:
25: if (depth > 1) level2(depth-1, pnt);
26: if (depth == 4) {
27:    for (i=0; i<35; i++) *pnt++ = 0;
28:    }
29: }

*25b t; 1*:*/                 /* set breakpoints at entry and exit */

level2:25 b                   /* use trace and local variable dump */
```

```
*29b t;1*:*/                        /* to report entire stack contents. */

level2:29 b

*c                                  /* resume */

level2(depth=5, pnt=@)   [demo2.c:25]
level1(depth=6)   [demo2.c:16]
main(1, -1073610644, -1073610636)   [demo2.c:7]  /* report at entry */
level2:i/ 5
level2:pnt/ @
level2:depth/ 5
level1:local/ @
level1:depth/ 6


level2(depth=4, pnt=@)   [demo2.c:25]
level2(depth=5, pnt=@)   [demo2.c:25]
level1(depth=6)   [demo2.c:16]
main(1, -1073610644, -1073610636)   [demo2.c:7]   /* second report at entry */
level2:i/ -1073610460
level2:pnt/ @
level2:depth/ 4
level2:i/ 5
level2:pnt/ @
level2:depth/ 5
level1:local/ @
level1:depth/ 6


level2(depth=3, pnt=@)   [demo2.c:25]
level2(depth=4, pnt=@)   [demo2.c:25]
level2(depth=5, pnt=@)   [demo2.c:25]
level1(depth=6)   [demo2.c:16]                    /*third report at entry */
main(1, -1073610644, -1073610636)   [demo2.c:7]
level2:i/ -1073610412
level2:pnt/ @
level2:depth/ 3
level2:i/ -1073610460
level2:pnt/ @
level2:depth/ 4
level2:i/ 5
```

```
level2:pnt/ @
level2:depth/ 5
level1:local/ @
level1:depth/ 6

level2(depth=2, pnt=@)    [demo2.c:25]
level2(depth=3, pnt=@)    [demo2.c:25]
level2(depth=4, pnt=@)    [demo2.c:25]
level2(depth=5, pnt=@)    [demo2.c:25]
level1(depth=6)    [demo2.c:16]
main(1, -1073610644, -1073610636)    [demo2.c:7] /* 4th report at entry */
level2:i/ -1073610364
level2:pnt/ @
level2:depth/ 2
level2:i/ -1073610412
level2:pnt/ @
level2:depth/ 3
level2:i/ -1073610460
level2:pnt/ @
level2:depth/ 4
level2:i/ 5
level2:pnt/ @
level2:depth/ 5
level1:local/ @
level1:depth/ 6

level2(depth=1, pnt=@)    [demo2.c:25]
level2(depth=2, pnt=@)    [demo2.c:25]
level2(depth=3, pnt=@)    [demo2.c:25]
level2(depth=4, pnt=@)    [demo2.c:25]
level2(depth=5, pnt=@)    [demo2.c:25]
level1(depth=6)    [demo2.c:16]
main(1, -1073610644, -1073610636)    [demo2.c:7] /*5th report at entry */
level2:i/ -1073610316
level2:pnt/ @
level2:depth/ 1
level2:i/ -1073610364
level2:pnt/ @
level2:depth/ 2
level2:i/ -1073610412
level2:pnt/ @
```

```
level2:depth/ 3
level2:i/ -1073610460
level2:pnt/ @
level2:depth/ 4
level2:i/ 5
level2:pnt/ @
level2:depth/ 5
level1:local/ @
level1:depth/ 6

level2(depth=1,pnt=@)    [demo2.c:29]
level2(depth=2,pnt=@)    [demo2.c:25]
level2(depth=3,pnt=@)    [demo2.c:25]
level2(depth=4,pnt=@)    [demo2.c:25]
level2(depth=5,pnt=@)    [demo2.c:25]
level1(depth=6)    [demo2.c:16]
main(1,-1073610644,-1073610636)   [demo2.c:7] /* 6th report at entry */
level2:i/ -1073610316
level2:pnt/ @
level2:depth/ 1
level2:i/ -1073610364
level2:pnt/ @
level2:depth/ 2
level2:i/ -1073610412
level2:pnt/ @
level2:depth/ 3
level2:i/ -1073610460
level2:pnt/ @
level2:depth/ 4
level2:i/ 5
level2:pnt/ @
level2:depth/ 5
level1:local/ @
level1:depth/ 6

level2(depth=2,pnt=@)    [demo2.c:29]
level2(depth=3,pnt=@)    [demo2.c:25]
level2(depth=4,pnt=@)    [demo2.c:25]
level2(depth=5,pnt=@)    [demo2.c:25]
level1(depth=6)    [demo2.c:16]
main(1,-1073610644,-1073610636)   [demo2.c:7]   /*exit from 6th level */
level2:i/ -1073610364
```

```
level2:pnt/ @
level2:depth/ 2
level2:i/ -1073610412
level2:pnt/ @
level2:depth/ 3
level2:i/ -1073610460
level2:pnt/ @
level2:depth/ 4
level2:i/ 5
level2:pnt/ @
level2:depth/ 5
level1:local/ @
level1:depth/ 6

level2(depth=3, pnt=@)   [demo2.c:29]
level2(depth=4, pnt=@)   [demo2.c:25]
level2(depth=5, pnt=@)   [demo2.c:25]
level1(depth=6)   [demo2.c:16]
main(1, -1073610644, -1073610636)   [demo2.c:7]  /*exit from 5th level */
level2:i/ -1073610412
level2:pnt/ @
level2:depth/ 3
level2:i/ -1073610460
level2:pnt/ @
level2:depth/ 4
level2:i/ 5
level2:pnt/ @
level2:depth/ 5
level1:local/ @
level1:depth/ 6

level2(depth=4, pnt=h)   [demo2.c:29]
level2(depth=0, pnt=^?^?^?^?^?^?^?^?^?^?^?^?^?^?
^?^?^?^?^?^?^?^?^?^?^?^?^?^?^?^?^?^?^?^?^?^?^?^?^?^?^?^?^?^?^?^?^?^?^?^?^?^?^?
^?^?^?^?^?^?^?^?^?^?^?^?^?^?^?^?^?^?^?^?^?^?^?^?^?^?^?^?^?^?^?^?^?^?^?^?^?^?^?^?
)   [demo2.c:25]               /*Attempted report at exit from 4th level */
level2:i/ 35                  /*Notice garbage and sudden change in */
level2:pnt/ h                 /*trace back...Problem is between return from*/
level2:depth/ 4               /*5th level and exit from 4th level !*/
level2:i/ 5                   /*That leaves only the for statement.*/
level2:pnt/ ^?^?^?^?^?^?^?^?^?^?^?^?^?^?
^?^?^?^?^?^?^?^?^?^?^?^?^?^?^?^?^?^?^?^?^?^?^?^?^?^?^?^?^?^?^?^?^?^?^?^?^?^?^?
^?^?^?^?^?^?^?^?^?^?^?^?^?^?^?^?^?^?^?^?^?^?^?^?^?^?^?^?^?^?^?^?^?^?^?^?^?^?^?^?
```

```
level2:depth/ Ø
level2(depth=Ø, pnt=^?^?^?^?^?^?^?^?^?^?^?^?^?^?
^?^?^?^?^?^?^?^?^?^?^?^?^?^?^?^?^?^?^?^?^?^?^?^?^?^?^?^?^?^?^?^?^?^?^?^?^?^?^?
^?^?^?^?^?^?^?^?^?^?^?^?^?^?^?^?^?^?^?^?^?^?^?^?^?^?^?^?^?^?^?^?^?^?^?^?^?^?^?
)    [demo2. c:29]
level2:i/ 5
level2:pnt/ ^?^?^?^?^?^?^?^?^?^?^?^?^?^?
^?^?^?^?^?^?^?^?^?^?^?^?^?^?^?^?^?^?^?^?^?^?^?^?^?^?^?^?^?^?^?^?^?^?^?^?^?^?^?
^?^?^?^?^?^?^?^?^?^?^?^?^?^?^?^?^?^?^?^?^?^?^?^?^?^?^?^?^?^?^?^?^?^?^?^?^?^?^?
level2:depth/ Ø
Illegal Instruction (4) (sig 4)
 at
: address Ø

*g
```

Listing 9.7. Localizing a stack error.

Testing Modules

The most convenient way to test low-level modules is to evaluate them directly. Functions that don't reference nonlocal data are easily tested in this way. The programmer begins by including a do-nothing main in the file with the function to be tested. A breakpoint is set at the first line of main, and the run is started.

Once the breakpoint has been reached, the function is invoked with appropriate test arguments. If the function references nonlocal variables, declarations for the variables should be included in the otherwise empty main. The *!* command can be used to assign variables reasonable values after the breakpoint has been reached. If the function under test changes these variables, the programmer may need to reset the variables whenever the test function is evaluated.

If the function manipulates a large, complex data structure, the testing can be accelerated by coding a support function (setup, for instance) that only initializes the data structure. Then, whenever the data structure needs rebuilding, the programmer can invoke *setup* directly. This can be an effective way to test a suite of functions (functions to add, to delete, and to copy nodes in a large tree, for example) that all manipulate the same data structure.

Caution

3B/2 users may be surprised by what appears to be a failure of *sdb* when it is invoked on programs that use floating-point arithmetic. When a *run* command is issued, *sdb* will catch a signal(12) instead of reaching the first breakpoint. This signal is generated by the operating system's response to a query from the start-up code about the presence of floating-point hardware. The programmer can recover from this interrupt by issuing a *continue* command.

sdb *Weaknesses*

The method used in listing 9.7 is surprisingly similar to the code-based techniques discussed in Chapter 8. The major difference between these methods is that, with *sdb*, code isn't modified. Granted—keeping the code static is important in certain instances. However, expecting "sophisticated" debugging tools to automate some of the more mundane debugging tasks seems reasonable.

Using *sdb* would be more convenient if the programmer could:

- use a single command to set a breakpoint at the beginning of every function (using *: b* doesn't work)
- reexecute the previous command (especially a *monitor* command) without retyping it
- attach commands to monitor command interrupts

The cost of implementing these extensions would be minimal. A macro facility would be a great improvement.

Other UNIX Debugging Aids

In all fairness, *sdb* is not used in a vacuum. Some of its deficiencies are addressed by other UNIX tools and facilities. A preprocessor named *ctrace* inserts trace calls throughout a body of C source code, allowing function-by-function (and even statement-by-statement) traces to be generated quickly and painlessly. The utility in this book's Appendix D is a "poor man's" *ctrace*.

By combining *ctrace* with *sdb*, detailed traces of a specific section of code can be produced quickly—without extensive, time-consuming single-stepping.

If *ctrace* is directed to insert trace calls but to suppress the output, and if the resulting program is run under *sdb*, execution can be halted (with a breakpoint) in the area of interest and detailed tracing can be started (with direct evaluation of *ctron*). If the trace indicates that the error is elsewhere, trace detail can be turned off (with direct evaluation of *ctroff*). Then, without the overhead of recompilation, execution can be restarted and trace detail can be enabled in a different part of the program. Thus, the combination of *ctrace* and *sdb* significantly mitigates the damage caused by the lack of a "set breakpoint at every function" ability.

The lack of macro capability can be offset by redirecting command input. *sdb* allows commands to be input from a file instead of from the keyboard. The form of the request is:

<filename

After the command file has been exhausted, control returns to standard input. Retyping a complex sequence of commands can be avoided by simply placing the commands in a file (a short name, preferably) and, whenever commands are needed, requesting input from that file. Several files can be used in a single session, but redirection commands are not allowed within a file.

I/O redirection at the operating system level can be used to capture a complete record of a debugging session. (That's how the listings used throughout this chapter were created.) Because *sdb* makes disciplined use of standard input and standard output, a copy of *sdb*'s dialog can be diverted by fitting it between a pair of tees:

tee –a sdbdialog | sdb | tee –a sdbdialog

The *–a* option directs *tee* to append all output to the file *sdbdialog*. Another file name can be used, of course, in place of *sdbdialog*. (For information about UNIX I/O redirection, tee, and pipes, see any of the UNIX references of Appendix A.)

CodeView: Microsoft's Source-Level Debugger

CodeView, an MS-DOS debugging program, is a descendant of SYMDEB. (SYMDEB is Microsoft's symbolic version of DEBUG, the standard MS-DOS breakpoint debugger.) CodeView's lineage parallels that of *sdb*, which was developed in the mid-70s from a pure assembly level debugging program known as *adb*.

When *adb* was rewritten to become *sdb*, the traditional teletype-oriented interface was retained. This conservative user interface was appropriate for the diverse range of hardware supported by a portable, multiuser operating system like UNIX.

CodeView, on the other hand, was developed ten years later to be used on PC clones. CodeView's designers were able to fully exploit a uniform hardware base to support a sophisticated window-oriented user interface.

CodeView is remarkably convenient to use. Its most striking feature is its user interface. But, except for this user interface and a newfound understanding of C expressions, CodeView is little changed from its predecessor, SYMDEB. The basic execution controls and memory-examination commands are virtually unchanged in syntax or capability. Moreover, most of CodeView's commands have a direct parallel in *sdb*. This section, then, will focus on CodeView's user interface and on some of its unique capabilities.

CodeView is not only more pleasant to use than *sdb* but also much more accessible to the independent learner. Microsoft's 250-page manual is a thorough and well-organized learning tool and reference resource.

User Interface

CodeView presents two command interfaces: one employs modern single-stroke menu techniques (or, alternatively, a mouse); the other produces a conventional teletype-style dialog. Displays for both command interfaces and a window of code are continuously present on the screen. Figure 9.1 shows a screen with the `evaluate` function selected and a temporary dialog box open.

This operation can be performed also in conventional teletype-style from the continuously open dialog screen on the lower half of the screen. Generally, the "dialog" versions of each command (as Microsoft refers to them) are more flexible than the menu version. Figure 9.2 shows the expression of figure 9.1 being evaluated in dialog mode.

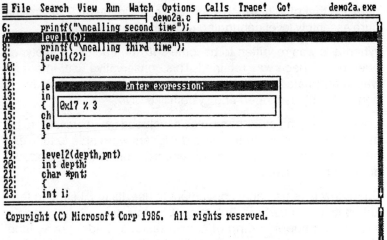

```
 File  Search  View  Run  Watch  Options  Calls  Trace!  Go!      demo2a.exe
                           demo2a.c
6:       printf("\ncalling second time");
7:       level1(6);
8:       printf("\ncalling third time");
9:       level1(2);
10:      }
11:
12:      le          Enter expression:
13:      in
14:      {   0x17 % 3
15:      ch
16:      le
17:      }
18:
19:      level2(depth,pnt)
20:      int depth;
21:      char *pnt;
22:      {
23:      int i;
```

Copyright (C) Microsoft Corp 1986. All rights reserved.

Figure 9.1. Codeview screen with an open dialog box.

```
 File  Search  View  Run  Watch  Options  Calls  Trace!  Go!      demo2a.exe
                           demo2a.c
6:       printf("\ncalling second time");
7:       level1(6);
8:       printf("\ncalling third time");
9:       level1(2);
10:      }
11:
12:      level1(depth)
13:      int depth;
14:      {
15:      char local[15];
16:      level2(depth -1,local);
17:      }
18:
19:      level2(depth,pnt)
20:      int depth;
21:      char *pnt;
22:      {
23:      int i;
2
>? 0x17 % 3
2
>
```

Figure 9.2. Figure 9.1 operation performed in the continuously open dialog window at the bottom of the screen.

A comprehensive on-line help facility augments the compact main screen with several pages of well-organized command and mode summaries. Figures 9.3, 9.4, and 9.5 show the sequence of help screens that the user moves through to find an explanation of display-formatting options.

PGDN=Next PGUP=Previous HOME=Top END=Exit

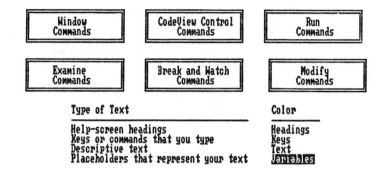

Figure 9.3. Top level help menu.

PGDN=Next PGUP=Previous HOME=Top END=Exit

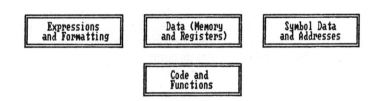

Figure 9.4. Expressions submenu.

```
PGDN=Next  PGUP=Previous  HOME=Top  END=Exit
Display Expression
```

? expression[,format]   Evaluates expression and displays the value. If
                         format is given, the value is displayed in the
                         corresponding printf format, as shown below:

Specifier	Input Type	Output Format
d or i	Integer	Signed decimal integer
u	Integer	Unsigned decimal integer
o	Integer	Unsigned octal integer
x or X	Integer	Hexadecimal integer
f	Real	Floating point
e or E	Real	Scientific notation
g or G	Real	More compact of f or e/E
c	Character	Single character
s	String	Null-terminated string

Types d, u, i, o, x, and X can have one
of the following prefixes:

    l for long integer
    s for short integer

Figure 9.5. Expressions help page.

Output from the application program is always directed to the output screen. A single function key is used to move between the normal debugger screen and the output screen.

Expression Evaluation

CodeView's command interpreter understands C expressions and evaluates them directly. Although the interpreter can evaluate invocations of user-written functions, it cannot evaluate printf and other library functions, presumably because these functions weren't compiled with the special debugging option. As with *sdb*, this capability facilitates not only the interactive evaluation of program expressions but also the forcing of variables, the interactive testing of low-level modules, and the use of custom snapshot routines.

Watch Windows

CodeView's *watch* commands (including *watch*, *watchpoint*, and *tracepoint*) are related to *sdb*'s *monitor* command. Not only are CodeView's commands more powerful and convenient to use than the *sdb* command, but they are also more permanent. (Because a *watch* remains in effect until canceled, there is no need to type and retype the same command to *watch* throughout a body of text.)

Each CodeView *watch* opens a new line in the watch window at the top of the screen. The value of the watched expression or variable is displayed continuously in this window. This is a convenient mechanism for locating pointers that write on data or for tracing the effects of obscure code.

Figures 9.6, 9.7, and 9.8 illustrate how watch windows and *trace* commands (single step) are used to explore the behavior of a *crc* generator. A cyclic redundancy check, *crc* is a sophisticated version of a checksum.

In CodeView, a simple *watch* command causes the named expression's value to be updated in the watch window whenever execution is interrupted. In *sdb* terms, a *watch* command attaches a *dump* command to every breakpoint and interrupt. The simple *watch* command is a convenient means of keeping important variables available at every breakpoint.

Although the simple *watch* command has no effect until an independent mechanism causes a break, the *watchpoint* and *tracepoint* forms of the command cause breaks.

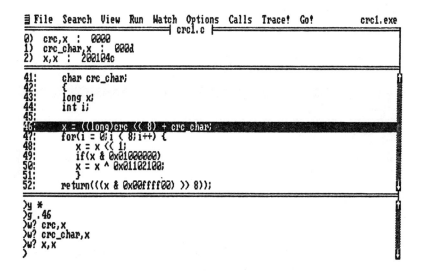

Figure 9.6. Using Code View to trace a section of code. Notice the watch window at the top of the display. Variable x contains garbage. The highlighted line is the line which will execute next.

```
≣ File  Search  View  Run  Watch  Options  Calls  Trace!  Go!        crc1.exe
╠══════════════════════════╡ crc1.c ╞══════════════════════════════════
0)   crc,x  :  0000
1)   crc_char,x  :   000d
2)   x,x  :  000d
╠══════════════════════════════════════════════════════════════════════
41:      char crc_char;                                                  ↑
42:      {
43:      long x;
44:      int i;
45:
46:      x = ((long)crc << 8) + crc_char;
47:      for(i = 0; i < 8; i++) {
48:          x = x << 1;
49:          if(x & 0x01000000)
50:          x = x ^ 0x01102100;
51:          }
52:      return(((x & 0x00ffff00) >> 8));                                 ↓
╠══════════════════════════════════════════════════════════════════════
)g .46                                                                    ↑
)w? crc,x
)w? crc_char,x
)w? x,x
)t; t
)                                                                         ↓
```

Figure 9.7. Variable x has been assigned a value.

```
≣ File  Search  View  Run  Watch  Options  Calls  Trace!  Go!        crc1.exe
╠══════════════════════════╡ crc1.c ╞══════════════════════════════════
0)   crc,x  :  0000
1)   crc_char,x  :   000d
2)   x,x  :  001a
╠══════════════════════════════════════════════════════════════════════
40:      int crc;                                                        ↑
41:      char crc_char;
42:      {
43:      long x;
44:      int i;
45:
46:      x = ((long)crc << 8) + crc_char;
47:      for(i = 0; i < 8; i++) {
48:          x = x << 1;
49:          if(x & 0x01000000)
50:          x = x ^ 0x01102100;
51:          }                                                            ↓
╠══════════════════════════════════════════════════════════════════════
)w? crc,x                                                                 ↑
)w? crc_char,x
)w? x,x
)t; t
)t
)                                                                         ↓
```

Figure 9.8. The value in x has been shifted left one place.

The *watchpoint* command, which will break whenever the named
expression is true, is an excellent tool for localizing pointers that
write on data. For example, suppose that a variable count in function foo should take on only positive values but that, for some rea-

son, the variable count mysteriously has become negative during one portion of the program. The programmer can identify the statement responsible for the negative assignment by using the following *watchpoint* command:

WP? foo.count < 0

If this *watchpoint* is set, execution will halt immediately following the statement that sets count negative.

Tracepoints also cause breaks but, in this case, the break is triggered by any change in the named variable or expression. Like *watchpoints*, *tracepoints* are effective against pointers that write on data, but *tracepoints* are less selective than *watchpoints*.

With a *tracepoint*, for instance, the programmer doesn't need to know which value is being assigned incorrectly. The *tracepoint* will generate a breakpoint at every assignment to the named variable. This lack of selectivity can be a real handicap if the variable is heavily used by all parts of the program.

With a heavily used variable, the problem can be localized more rapidly by using a simple *watch* and explicitly set breakpoints. The programmer should make several passes through the program, refining the granularity of the breakpoints and monitoring the variable's value in the watch window with each pass.

Because they require that memory be tested following every statement, *watchpoints* and *tracepoints* slow program execution significantly. With most large programs, explicit breakpoints and a simple *watch* should be used to narrow the range of the search before a *watchpoint* or *tracepoint* is used.

CodeView Weaknesses

CodeView is a strong product that is much easier to learn and use than the traditional breakpoint debugger. CodeView's features are particularly well-suited for bug hunting. The program is also far more useful for program verification than were its predecessors. However, CodeView's usefulness as a program verification tool would be enhanced if these capabilities were added:

- a means of breaking automatically at the beginning and end of every function. A preprocessor derived from that in Appendix D could overcome this weakness by modifying the source to include calls to an empty debug function at the beginning and end of each function. Then, placing a single breakpoint in this empty debug function when CodeView is used would cause execution to halt at each function exit and entrance.

- an option (like that in *sdb*) to pass a certain number of breakpoints. CodeView does allow a breakpoint to have a *passcount*. These passcounts, however, are associated with a specific breakpoint (in other words, if breakpoint 3's passcount is 7, breakpoint 3 must be passed seven times).

- a command (again, as in *sdb*) to restart a program with new arguments. Being forced to exit and reload CodeView, simply to change the application program's command-line arguments, is inconvenient and time-consuming.

- a special logical channel that would direct output from the application program to the debug screen. Currently, snapshot output goes to the program's output screen. It would be nice if only this output could be directed to the debug screen, where it could be captured as part of the session record.

RETURN

CodeView, *sdb*, and similar source-level debugging programs are directly descended from machine-oriented breakpoint debuggers. DEBUG, SYMBUG, DDT, ZSID, and *adb* were developed as tools for the assembly language programmer. Generally, these parent tools were primitive and awkward-to-use weapons of last resort. The high-level programmer turned to them only when he or she had no other choice. Thus, these assembly level debugging programs usually were used in bug-hunting mode to find a specific, particularly nasty bug that had evaded conventional code-based testing.

This heritage, clearly evident in the command set of both modern descendants, exerts strong influence on the use of *sdb*. According to David Raanan of AT&T Information Systems, *sdb* is used primarily to "poke around" and see what happens to "one or two variables."

CodeView may be convenient and powerful enough to transcend its heritage. Although automatic function-by-function breakpoints aren't provided, the user interface makes manually setting and moving breakpoints easy. CodeView's ease of use and watch windows create an effective environment for both program verification and bug hunting.

Although it is an excellent product, CodeView may be one example of a mature technology reaching its prime as it is displaced by an immature but more effective technology. Integrated development environments (discussed in Chapter 10) offer CodeView's debugging and verification support and modern user interface in a fast, interactive code-development environment.

10
Interpreters and Integrated Environments

Although the source-level debuggers discussed in Chapter 9 better preserve the programmer's high-level view than do machine-level debuggers, there are certain productivity issues that source-level debuggers don't address. For example, a simple code change (such as adding a simple trace statement) can be a lengthy process. Pointer problems can violate the virtual machine and in doing so, require special, time-consuming debugging.

Interpreters not only provide the symbolic and breakpoint capabilities of source-level debuggers but also address productivity issues by integrating the development environment and enforcing the integrity of the virtual machine.

Edit-Compile-Link Costs

The edit-compile-link cycle wastes programmer time directly and indirectly. The cycle wastes time directly by forcing the programmer to wait while a series of comparatively slow disk operations process information.

The time-consuming edit-compile-link cycle often includes a great deal of redundant processing because the information being processed remains substantially unchanged between cycles. Changing even a single semicolon, requires that the editor load and save the source file; and that the source file be loaded again, this time by the compiler.

Each compiler pass creates an intermediate file that will be loaded by its successor. Whenever the cycle is repeated, a compiler, a linker, and a loader (unchanged since the earlier cycle) are loaded to process source and intermediate files almost identical to the files processed in the earlier cycle.

Redundant disk activity is an obvious and direct waste of programmer time. However, it may not be as costly as the indirect impact of edit-compile-link delays.

Because the delay for modifying the code (or, more precisely, for modifying the testing structure built into the code) is significant, the programmer may avoid adding tests, arguing that he or she "knows what would probably happen anyway." In an attempt to save time, the programmer will use sketchy or obsolete results to "figure it out." Often, compilations are used to test "corrections" rather than to support information-collecting runs that are less obviously productive.

The edit-compile-link delay encourages programmers to adopt techniques that can be counterproductive. The delay distorts efficiency measures by hiding the real cost of working with inadequate or obsolete test results.

Integrated development environments address these problems by combining the editor, the compiler, and the linker into a single memory-resident load module. Because the editor, the compiler, and the linker are always resident in memory, the programmer doesn't have to wait for them to be loaded from the disk.

Similarly, the programmer's application program is always resident in memory, probably stored in tokenized form (each keyword replaced with a small numeric code) rather than as a simple text file. Integrated systems frequently eliminate disk activity completely. They are far more memory-intensive than traditional compiler environments. (The system discussed in this chapter is not a practical tool unless the programmer has 300K to 600K of memory available.)

Integrated environments try to avoid redundant compilation of unchanged modules by implementing some form of incremental translation.

The incremental technique can range from true interpretation, in which each statement is analyzed and translated (at least into actions) whenever it is executed, to incremental compilation, in which modules are recompiled only if they have been changed after the last compilation.

True interpretation protects the virtual machine, but incremental compilation improves run-time speed. High-performance commercial products tend to use incremental compilation techniques to identify syntax errors and tokenize the code. These products use also some form of interpretation to execute the tokens.

In an effective design, integrating the development tools into an incremental translation system shortens the modify-test cycle to 10 to 30 seconds (even when the program is several hundred lines long). By contrast, the typical edit-compile-link cycle consumes several minutes. The contrast is particularly dramatic on floppy-based personal computers.

Interpretation versus Compilation

Integrated development environments are almost always built around an interpreter or an interpreter-like execution vehicle. Interpreters better fit the dynamic nature of the integrated environment; and especially in C, interpreters better accommodate measures that protect the virtual machine.

The advantages, however, are not without cost. Interpreted code executes 15 to 100 times slower than compiled code. The various interpreter-like schemes are attempts to strike a balance between the security and interactiveness of interpreted code, and the speed of compiled code.

Controlling Debugging Facilities

One issue that interpreter designers face is where to house the control for debugging facilities. Breakpoints, execution, data, and stack traces can be enabled and disabled either from the interpreter's command interface or from within the user's program. Each alternative has advantages and disadvantages.

Because control functions that are embedded in the program as function calls won't exist in the compiled environment, some provision must be made for removing them from the production code. Preprocessor directives seem the best alternative, although manual insertion and deletion are appropriate for specific special-purpose testing. Alternatively, the interpreter can provide special editing capabilities to remove such function references.

On the other hand, embedding control in the command interface restricts the flexibility and generality of the debugging capabilities, and can significantly complicate the user interface.

The balance of this chapter is devoted to a design that places much of the debugging control in special functions.

Readers who are interested in a command-based design might investigate Interactive-C™, from IMPACC Associates, Inc., P.O. Box 93, Gwynedd Valley, PA 19437–0093. Interactive-C controls all of its debugging aids directly from the user interface. All operations are conducted directly from a single multiwindow screen.

Interactive-C emphasizes its dynamic but sometimes risky nature by allowing the programmer to "patch" code and data values, and to continue execution following any type of interruption. Ironically, immediate-mode execution (one of the most powerful dynamic features of an interpreter) is severely limited in Interactive-C. Only externally compiled functions can be executed in immediate mode.

C-terp™ (Gimpel Software, 3207 Hogarth Lane, Collegeville, PA 19426) is a powerful, nicely balanced, integrated-development environment with only a few debugging features built into the command interface. C-terp extends its dynamic control with several trace functions that can be invoked either from within the code or as immediate-mode commands.

The result is surprisingly dynamic and interactive without being a radical departure from conventional trace mechanisms. All major subsystems (the editor, compiler, interpreter, and operating-system interface) are accessed from a main menu. All interactive debugging, however, is controlled from an interactive two-window screen. C-terp observes the conservative rule that an interrupted execution may not be continued following a code change or a run-time error.

An Overview of C-terp

In C-terp, few debugging features are controlled from the command interface. Instead, fairly powerful and general trace and breakpoint facilities are controlled by means of special library functions. Only step modes are selected through the command interface, and then only after debug mode has been reached. Debug mode may be entered only when a program has encountered an error or a breakpoint. C-terp supports unrestricted immediate-mode execution only while the program is halted in debug mode.

Employing a technique that the designers call "semicompilation," C-terp requires "recompilation" whenever any portion of code is modified. With each change in the code, the main menu must be accessed and a new test run begun. Nevertheless, "semicompilation," which requires only a few seconds for a file of 500–600 lines, is much faster than conventional compilation.

Like most interpreters, C-terp will not allow execution to continue after an error has been executed; the code must be modified, recompiled, and the test rerun from the beginning.

C-terp Debugging Functions

The C-terp standard library includes four functions specifically designed to support debugging:

- Trace(), which turns on various execution traces, most of which echo important data values and report on the flow of control
- Dumpv(), which dumps (in appropriate formats) the value of various variables
- Check(), which turns on pointer checking
- Breakpt(), which suspends execution and puts the interpreter into debug mode

Although these functions may be called from the code, with the exception of Breakpt() they are really designed to be used as extensions of the command interface. By invoking the functions in immediate mode, the programmer uses them to control trace output dynamically during a test run.

The trace() Function

The function trace() enables and disables several levels of built-in execution trace. The trace output, ordinarily directed to the screen, can be redirected (with an option from the main menu) to a file. The integer argument to trace is bit-mapped, with each bit selecting a different type of trace detail. The options (which can be combined) are

- *Statement Tracing*, which prints the line number and code for every statement executed

- *Function Tracing*, which prints the name of the function and the value of all arguments at each call, and the name and return value at each return

- *Assignment Tracing*, which prints the name of the variable on the left (provided it's a simple type) and the value it received

- *Clause Tracing*, which prints the value of the conditional expression in for, if, and while clauses

Calls to trace may be interspersed throughout the code or executed in immediate mode to enable and disable various kinds of trace. If the programmer is having trouble understanding what is happening in a complex loop, he or she can turn on clause and assignment tracing (and, perhaps, function and statement tracing) just before the loop is entered and then turn them off immediately after exiting the loop.

Listing 10.1 includes a small test program and the trace output it generates.

```
/*This program plays the game "Tower of Hanoi" */
#include "stdio.h"

main()

{
int n, count;

count = 0;
printf("\nEnter number of disks in the game...\n");
trace(002);
scanf("%d", &n);
trace(033);
tower(n,'A','B', 'C',&count);
trace(000);
printf("\n%d disk problem solved in %d steps\n", n, count);
}
```

```
void tower(n, from, to, aux, count)
int n,  *count;
char from, to, aux;

{

*count += 1;  /*increment counter each time function is called */
if (n == 1)  /*the terminal case */
    printf("\nMove disk 1 from peg %c to peg %c", from, to);
else {
    tower(n-1, from, aux, to, count);
    printf("\nMove disk %d from peg %c to peg %c", n, from, to);
    tower(n-1, aux, to, from, count);
    }
}
```

Program output:

```
Move disk 1 from peg A to peg B
Move disk 2 from peg A to peg C
Move disk 1 from peg B to peg C
Move disk 3 from peg A to peg B
Move disk 1 from peg C to peg A
Move disk 2 from peg C to peg B
Move disk 1 from peg A to peg B
3 disk problem solved in 7 steps
```

Trace output:

```
| Returned 0
| scanf(3e3d:39 "%d", 4adf:20)
| Returned 1
| trace(27)
| Returned 2
| 14:          tower(n,'A','B', 'C',&count);
| tower(3, 65, 66, 67, 4adf:22)
| | 25:    *count += 1; /*increment counter each time function is called */
| | 4adf:22 = 1
| | 26:  if (n == 1)  /*the terminal case */
| | Conditional: 0
| | 28:  else {
| | 29:      tower(n-1, from, aux, to, count);
| | tower(2, 65, 67, 66, 4adf:22)
```

```
| | | 25:                    *count += 1; /*increment counter each time function is calle
| | | 4adf:22 = 2
| | | 26:   if (n == 1)  /*the terminal case */
| | | Conditional: 0
| | | 28:    else {
| | | 29:     tower(n-1, from, aux, to, count);
| | | tower(1, 65, 66, 67, 4adf:22)
| | | | 25:      *count += 1; /*increment counter each time function is called */
| | | | 4adf:22 = 3
| | | | xe26:    if (n == 1)  /*the terminal case */
| | | | Conditional: 1
| | | | 27:         printf("\nMove disk 1 from peg %c to peg %c",from,to);
| | | | printf(3e3d:61 "
Move disk 1 from peg %c to peg %c", 65, 66)
| | | | Returned 32
| | | Returned 0
| | | 30:    printf("\nMove disk %d from peg %c to peg %c",n,from,to);
| | | printf(3e3d:84 "
Move disk %d from peg %c to peg %c", 2, 65, 67)
| | | Returned 32
| | | 31:    tower(n-1,aux,to,from,count);
| | | tower(1, 66, 67, 65, 4adf:22)
| | | | 25:      *count += 1; /*increment counter each time function is called */
| | | | 4adf:22 = 4
| | | | 26:      if (n == 1)  /*the terminal case */
| | | | Conditional: 1
| | | | 27:          printf("\nMove disk 1 from peg %c to peg %c",from,to);
| | | | printf(3e3d:61 "
Move disk 1 from peg %c to peg %c", 66, 67)
| | | | Returned 32
| | | Returned 0
| | Returned 0
| | 30:          printf("\nMove disk %d from peg %c to peg %c",n,from,to);
| | printf(3e3d:84 "
Move disk %d from peg %c to peg %c", 3, 65, 66)
| | Returned 32
| | 31:          tower(n-1,aux,to,from,count);
| | tower(2, 67, 66, 65, 4adf:22)
| | | 25: *count += 1; /*increment counter each time function is called */
| | | 4adf:22 = 5
| | | 26: if (n == 1)  /*the terminal case */
| | | Conditional: 0
| | | 28: else {
```

```
I I I 29:    tower(n-1, from, aux, to, count);
I I I tower(1, 67, 65, 66, 4adf:22)
I I I I 25:     *count += 1; /*increment counter each time function is called */
I I I I 4adf:22 = 6
I I I I 26:     if (n == 1)  /*the terminal case */
I I I I Conditional: 1
I I I I 27:        printf("\nMove disk 1 from peg %c to peg %c", from, to);
I I I I printf(3e3d:61 "
Move disk 1 from peg %c to peg %c", 67, 65)
I I I I Returned 32
I I I Returned 0
I I I 30:    printf("\nMove disk %d from peg %c to peg %c", n, from, to);
I I I printf(3e3d:84 "
Move disk %d from peg %c to peg %c", 2, 67, 66)
I I I Returned 32
I I I 31:    tower(n-1, aux, to, from, count);
I I I tower(1, 65, 66, 67, 4adf:22)
I I I I 25:     *count += 1; /*increment counter each time function is called */
I I I I 4adf:22 = 7
I I I I 26:     if (n == 1)  /*the terminal case */
I I I I Conditional: 1
I I I I 27:        printf("\nMove disk 1 from peg %c to peg %c", from, to);
I I I I printf(3e3d:61 "
Move disk 1 from peg %c to peg %c", 65, 66)
I I I I Returned 32
I I I Returned 0
I I Returned 0
I Returned 0
I 15: trace(000);
I trace(0)
```

Listing 10.1.

Function trace() is a powerful, general-purpose tool that probably makes conventional control-flow tracing unnecessary in all cases except those involving complex structures and pointers to pointers.

The dumpv() Function

What trace() does for control-flow monitoring, dumpv() does for data monitoring. dumpv() exploits the information available in the interpreter's symbol table to generate reasonably formatted dumps of local or global variables. dumpv()'s integer parameter is bit-mapped, and permits the various dumps to be selected individually or in combination.

In programs with few global variables and in functions with few local variables, dumpv() is an effective and convenient snapshot function. In more complex environments, a conventional snapshot function can be written. Because immediate-mode execution in C-terp is unrestricted, custom snapshot functions may be invoked "on the fly" in debug mode.

In figure 10.1, dumpv() has been called from the command window in immediate mode to generate a listing of all local variables.

```
25    int i;
26
27    printf("\nlevel2 called with %d",depth);
28    if (depth > 1) {
29       for (i=0; i<23; i++){
30          *pntr++ = '\0';
31       }
32       level3(depth - 1);
33       }
34    }
35
36    void level3(depth)
37    int depth;
                                        Insert    nest2.c
(D/d)isplay Trcbk Flip Continue (N/n)ext-step (S/s)ide-step Edit Restore Window
     expression: dumpv(1);;
pntr: 5dc5:2c "!▄"
depth: 5
i: 15

| | | level2 called from
| | level1 called from
| main
```

Fig. 10.1.

The check() Function

C-terp's default thoroughly tests pointer references. Normally, every pointer reference is tested to verify that it targets an area set aside as user variable space.

Calls to check() can reduce checking to either of two less stringent modes. The least restrictive test identifies pointers with "integer" values—in other words, pointers that have never been initialized or that have values produced by "promoting" an integer.

The other mode essentially checks to be certain that the pointer isn't trying to write on code or on the operating system. Writing on code is a real possibility with C-terp because C-terp uses the 8086 large-memory model, in which a pointer may reach any part of physical memory.

C-terp's default pointer-checking effectively locates pointers that would otherwise write on return addresses in the stack.

Figure 10.2 shows the debug screen that results from running a slightly modified version of listing 8.3. Note that the interpreter has reported the stack error. When debug mode is entered, the cursor will be on the assignment statement responsible for the violation.

```
approaching first call
level1 called with 1
approaching second call
level1 called with 6
level2 called with 5Error 107,  Out of bounds assignment

Type any key to enter debug
```

Fig. 10.2.

This is an excellent example of how an interpreter can protect the virtual machine and simplify the debugging task. The checking, however, won't spot pointers that write on data areas.

If level1() is modified, as it is in the following fragment, level2() will write on the extra local string (buff2) rather than on a return address.

```
void level1(depth)
int depth;
{
    char buff2[15];      /*add this string */
    char buffer[15];

        .
        .
        .
```

The error is not, and should not be, detected by C-terp's pointer checking. Such errors can never be detected by the interpreter because the programmer must be free to use a pointer to point at any variable of the appropriate type.

The breakpt() Function

When a running program encounters a breakpt() call or an execution error, the program is halted and the interpreter enters debug mode.

Debug Mode

Debug mode is easily identified by the screen configuration shown in figure 10.1.

The edit window at the top of the screen displays the suspended program. The command window in the lower part of the screen displays responses to debug-mode commands.

Using the commands named in the one-line menu at the top of this command window, the user can examine the run-time environment or exit debug mode. Program output does not appear on the debug screen. Instead, all program output is routed to a separate hidden screen. The program-output screen is displayed automatically whenever the program executes, or when the program screen is selected from the debug menu.

(D/d)isplay

This case-sensitive option is used to display the value of any C expression entered from the keyboard. This is true immediate-mode execution. Expressions with side-effects (assignment or increment, for example) change the current value of referenced program variables.

Functions (including dumpv or the programmer's snapshot function) can be invoked directly. If the programmer chooses lowercase d, output generated by the expression is displayed in the command window. Uppercase D temporarily directs output to the program-output screen. The debug menu's F option (Flip) is selected to view the program-output screen.

display is the most important feature of debug mode. To fully exploit C-terp's power, the programmer should use display as a platform on which to build his or her own extensions to the command interface. C-terp's dynamic resources can be customized by building debugging functions (such as snapshots, breakpoint control, and watch mechanisms) and invoking them with display.

Traceback

The *traceback* option (trcbk) triggers a display (in the command menu) of the calling sequence executed by the program to reach the suspension point.

The command window shown in figure 10.1 includes a traceback.

(N/n)ext-Step

The (N/n)ext-step option single-steps the interpreter through the next program statement, reentering debug mode after the statement has been completed.

Uppercase *N* causes display of the program-output screen during the step. Lowercase *n* permits the debug screen to remain displayed. If the next statement is a function call, *next-step* will descend into the called function and halt there. If accompanied by a numeric argument n, *next-step* will execute n lines before stopping.

(S/s)ide-step

The (S/s)ide-step option single-steps through lines in the current function, executing at full speed the code in subordinate functions.

This command returns to the debug screen after the statement and its subordinate functions have been completed. In most test applications, this is the more useful of the step commands.

With *side-step*, a ten-line function is completed with ten step commands (assuming that there are no loops or branches), even if all ten lines are calls to complex functions. *side-step* also accepts a numeric argument requesting that a specific number of side-steps be executed before halting.

Continue

The continue option is similar to DEBUG's *go* command. Supplied alone, it resumes execution of the program, returning to debug mode only if an error or explicit breakpoint is encountered. Supplied with a numeric argument that represents a line number, it continues until the named line is reached.

Because line numbers always are displayed in the code window, the *continue* option is a convenient facility for stepping over short loops. The programmer simply picks a visible line number after the loop and *continue*s to it. Using the *continue* option with a line number, the programmer can walk through the code, function by function.

However, if the target function doesn't happen to be visible in the code window, acquiring accurate line numbers for function entries can be awkward. One alternative is to use C-terp's *search* command to position the code window on the target function (making its line number visible). Another is to build in a name-oriented breakpoint structure. A name-oriented breakpoint structure is discussed later in this chapter.

continue cannot be used on a program that has been halted by an error.

Restore, Flip, Window, and Edit

These commands control the window or force an exit to the editor. *Flip*, as mentioned earlier, replaces the debug screen with the program-output screen. Any keystroke will cause a return from the program-output screen to the debug screen. *Window* changes the size of the edit window. *Window* takes a numeric argument representing the number of screen lines that should be committed to the edit window.

Code cannot be edited from debug mode. The editor's cursor-movement keys may be used to change the portion of the program displayed in the edit window. The *restore* option returns the edit window to its original condition. (This is helpful if the programmer is uncertain which breakpoint initiated the debug session.)

Changing code requires that the programmer exit debug mode, abandoning the currently suspended execution. *Edit* moves the user into the editor. *Escape* will end the debugging session and return to the main menu.

Using C-terp

Making the best use of C-terp demands some adjustment in the user's practices if he or she is to exploit the tool's capabilities. The following sections outline approaches that seem compatible with C-terp's capabilities and design philosophy. Surprisingly, even though C-terp represents a radical departure from the conventional compiled development environment, it works effectively with the sort of code-based trace and debug methods discussed earlier in this book.

C-terp is fairly convenient and intuitive when used on small programs with short run-time. A breakpoint can be inserted just inside the main and then it's simply a matter of the user stepping through the entire program. Or, the programmer can use trace to generate a detailed record of the entire execution.

In fact, at least one breakpoint call must be inserted just inside the main if he or she wants to do more than simply hunt for bugs. Without at least one call, the program may never enter debug mode. These ad hoc approaches are reasonable because, for small programs, the volume of trace information and the run-time penalty for restarting a test are relatively small.

When the source begins to approach 1,000 lines, or when the program is computationally intensive (when it executes certain loops thousands of times), greater effort must be exerted to maintain control (preferably dynamic control) of the process.

Although C-terp effectively eliminates the compile-link-load overhead associated with conventional debugging, it doesn't eliminate the run-time penalty for repeating uninformative tests, nor does it magically manage the potentially overwhelming trace output from long runs.

Under C-terp, controlling the process is essentially a matter of triggering controlled exits to debug mode. After the programmer has entered debug mode (and is in the correct vicinity), he or she can use immediate mode, dumpv(), custom snapshot functions, and step instructions to do whatever detailed debugging needs to be done.

The trace mechanism can be enabled or disabled by immediate mode calls to trace. Provided that an initial breakpoint is set early in the program, exits to debug mode can be generated dynamically by judicious use of the continue and step functions of debug mode.

This approach is less convenient in large programs because accurate line numbers are not always readily available (especially not in the rapid-change environment provided by an interpreter).

The following sections illustrate how immediate-mode execution, coupled with code-based control structures like those discussed in Chapter 5, can enlarge the interpreter's powers. The first example presents an extension to the continue command that allows breakpoints to be set by function name. The second example implements a watch mechanism essential to referential tracing.

Selecting Breakpoints by Function Name

C-terp needs a mechanism for selecting (while the program is running) the next breakpoint to be activated. A similar problem (that of how to activate trace statements selectively without modifying code) is discussed in Chapter 5. The method presented here, which is based on function names, is a natural extension of the approach presented in Chapter 5.

If the user includes a breakpoint at the beginning of every function, but makes the execution of that breakpoint dependent on a global variable test, he or she can modify (at each trap to debug mode) the global control variable using the immediate-mode assignment and thus achieve dynamic control over which breakpoints are activated.

If the global is a string, the next breakpoint function can be selected by name.

The skeletal program in listing 10.2 illustrates this technique by exploiting a predefined symbol and the preprocessor to conveniently remove the stop() calls from the production code.

```
#ifdef C_terp
char next[45]="main";
nx(str)
char *str;
{strcpy(next, str); }
#define stop(x) if (!strcmp(next, x)) breakpt()
#else
#define stop(x)
#endif
```

```
main()

{
    stop("main");      /* to give an opportunity to put */

                       /* an initial value in breakptname*/
        foo1();
        foo2();
        foo3();
        foo1();
}


int foo1()
{
    stop("foo1");
}

int foo2()
{
    stop("foo2");
}

int foo3()
{
    stop("foo3");
}
```

Listing 10.2.

Function nx is used interactively to reduce the typing required to change the breakpoint. The debug screen and output screen shown in figures 10.3 and 10.4 illustrate interactive control of execution trace, data monitoring, and next breakpoint. In the command window, dumpv() has been used to list all variables (all one of them). Function tracing has been enabled with trace(). Finally, nx() has been used to set the next breakpoint at foo3().

The structure is significant, even if breakpoints by function name aren't of great importance to the programmer. By replacing the breakpt() call with a trace() or dumpv() call, the programmer can trace or dump variables (or a combination of the two) by function

name. Using an array of global strings for function names with
functions to insert and remove a name will permit the programmer
to name a *set* of functions to be monitored.

```
9     #define stop(x)
10    #endif
11
12
13        main()
14
15        {
16        stop("main");    /* to give an opportunity to put */
17
18                         /* an initial value in breakptname*/
19        foo1();
20        foo2();
21        foo3();
22        foo1();
23        }
```

```
                                              Insert    stop.c
(D/d)isplay Trcbk Flip Continue (N/n)ext-step (S/s)ide-step Edit Restore Window
      expression: dumpv(3):
next: 5led:4 "main"
0
      expression: trace(1): 0
      expression: nx("foo3"): ¦ ¦ 6:         {strcpy(next,str);}
0
```

Fig. 10.3.

```
¦ 19:        foo1();
¦ ¦ 28:      stop("foo1");
¦ 20:        foo2();
¦ ¦ 33:      stop("foo2");
¦ 21:        foo3();
¦ ¦ 38:      stop("foo3");
¦ ¦ 38:      stop("foo3");
```

Type any key to enter debug

Fig. 10.4.

Finding Pointers that Write on Data

With its integral compiler, library trace, and breakpoint functions,
C-terp offers excellent support for searches based on lexical and
temporal proximity. However, the package fails to provide features
that directly support searches based on referential proximity.

Referential proximity is the strongest guide for finding pointer bugs
that write on the wrong data areas. Having a control mechanism

that is sensitive to data references is important. This section describes an automated method based on an adaptation of stop(). The method presented may not be effective in certain cases because it changes the program's utilization of memory and may cause the errant pointer to change targets.

Building a Watch Function

Watch mechanisms are debugging aids that monitor references to a given address and report every change. The call to stop(), if performed at every function entry, creates a frequent and convenient opportunity for testing the value of a selected variable. Each call must simply compare the value it finds with the value found (and left in a global variable) by the last call.

One of the most attractive aspects of this approach is that it can be implemented entirely as modifications to the "debugging prologue" at the beginning of the program. The following fragment details how the preprocessor definition of stop() is changed.

```
#ifdef C_terp
char next[45]="main";
int old = 0;

chg()
{
if (old != target) return 1;
else {
   old = target;
   return 0;
   }
}

nx(str)
char *str;
{ strcpy( next, str); }

#define stop(x) if (!strcmp(x, next) || chg()) breakpt()
#else
#define stop(x)
#endif
```

In this listing, `target` is the variable to be watched. (The user must specify the name of the variable to be watched.) Although, in this example, `target` must be a global variable, that isn't a necessary restriction. The function can be extended to watch locals by passing a pointer to the local (as well as by passing the old value) through a global variable. A function to watch local variables must also be enabled and disabled (perhaps by setting a third global variable while the program is stopped in debug mode), to guarantee that it isn't tested outside its life.

Using this technique requires that the target of the errant pointer be identified. The requirement is reasonable. The programmer shouldn't be interested in conducting a referential search unless he or she has already identified a variable that changes with no apparent cause.

Unfortunately, the act of inserting the watch code may change the target of the errant pointer. Sometimes the change improves matters because it causes the pointer to target an object protected by the interpreter (such as a return address on the stack, or unallocated memory). In some cases, however, the symptoms disappear. When this happens, the programmer must resort to a manual search, generating breakpoints using *continue* and a line number or (if it doesn't obscure the bug) using something akin to `stop()` (as presented earlier in this chapter). At each breakpoint, `printf` should be used in immediate mode to examine the contents of the target variable.

Bottom-up Testing with C-terp

Immediate-mode execution eliminates the need for a driver in bottom-up testing. The programmer simply codes the function and then invokes it with some test arguments. Unfortunately, C-terp doesn't allow access to debug mode unless a program is running.

The solution is to add a main function that does nothing but invoke a breakpoint to the file containing the functions to be tested. When the file is run, main will be halted and the interpreter will enter debug mode. In debug mode, the programmer can exercise the new functions through the *display* option.

Figure 10.5 shows a recursive factorial function being tested interactively.

```
1    main()
2    {
3    breakpt();
4    }
5
6    int fact(n)
7    int n;
8
9    {
10   if (n < 2) return 1;  /* the terminal case */
11   else return n * fact(n - 1);
12   }
13
```

                                                    Insert   fact.c

(D/d)isplay Trcbk Flip Continue (N/n)ext-step (S/s)ide-step Edit Restore Window
        expression: fact(0): 1
        expression: fact(6): 720
        expression: fact(2): 2
        expression: fact(3): 6

Fig. 10.5.

RETURN

Of the four commercial interpreters that I researched while writing
this book, C-terp achieves the best balance between generality
and usability. I did, however, see features in other packages that
would be excellent enhancements for C-terp.

- *A watch function.* C-terp needs support for referential
  tracing. With trace present, creating a watch function
  to monitor assignments to a named variable shouldn't
  be difficult.

- *Hierarchical trace control.* When trace is turned on,
  the user should be able to specify the calling depth
  that will be affected. It would be nice, for example, to
  be able to do a function trace at all levels, but an
  assignment trace only at the current level.

- *Function names in continue commands.* Why not use
  the ever-present symbol table? The programmer
  should be able to mark several functions for tracing or
  breakpoint treatment without writing inline code and
  without referencing line numbers.

- *Some extended examples.* The interplay of C-terp's various capabilities isn't obvious. An extended example in the manual would be a great aid to the new user.

- *A more compact user interface.* The main menu in the package could be compressed into a single status line. Such an arrangement would eliminate many distracting screen swaps.

- *A direct entry to debug mode.* A main menu entry that generates a dummy main consisting of nothing but a breakpoint would make module testing more convenient.

- *A traceback function.* Although C-terp produces an excellent traceback from debug mode, it would be nice (and consistent) to be able to generate the same traceback from an inline function call.

11
Conclusion

Certainly, this book hasn't exhausted the subject of debugging. If you consider that there are hundreds of thousands of programmers, each with his or her own debugging tools and methods, a comprehensive treatment of the topic would eclipse even the multivolume persistence of Donald Knuth. It would certainly exhaust me.

Looking Back

But this book isn't meant to exhaust the subject of debugging. Rather, I have pursued restrained but, I hope, useful objectives:

- to introduce a formal framework for debugging discussions

- to identify fairly universal debugging techniques

- to distinguish between debugging in C, and debugging in other languages

- to introduce the, sometimes, arcane tricks that help to bridge the gap between high-level and machine-level debugging

- to introduce several sophisticated development systems

The Formal Framework

The distinction between lexical, temporal, and referential searches is a useful delineation. Had C-terp designers applied the delineation to their interpreter, they immediately would have noticed the lack of a watch function.

Universal Techniques

Local and global dumps, special-purpose snapshots, stack trace-backs, mile posts, granularity controls, and multilevel switches are all universally applicable debugging concepts.

C's Unique Problems

The C novice who is faced with a pointer that writes on the stack can be compared to the aspiring explorer who has fallen into a deep pit. Newcomers often overlook the pointer's capability to attack the underlying virtual machine. After reading this book, the programmer new to C should know, not only how deep the pit is but also how it was formed.

Arcane Tricks

Stack traces, general-purpose local variable dumps, and checksums demand that the programmer know the compiler and the machine. They are useful but are also extremely implementation-dependent. Although the pointer tricks in Chapters 7 and 8 may not be truly secret—they're close to it.

Sophisticated Systems

By today's measures, source level debuggers and interpreters are sophisticated tools.

Merely "covering the bases," though, isn't enough to justify a book. The true test of this book is whether you are more successful at locating C bugs, and more efficient in your debugging efforts. I hope that the book challenges you to study and learn from the process, to structure your debugging activities, and to bring discipline to debugging, just as you bring discipline to design.

A Curious State of Affairs

After working my way through several interpreter, debugger, and compiler manuals, I was struck by what I consider proof that debugging is the "unwanted child" of programming.

Unquestionably, certain functions are useful debugging aids in any C environment (or, for that matter, in any programming environment). For example, a local variable dump, a stack traceback, and even a "halt-and-ask-what-kind-of-dump-the-user-would-like" function would ease the effort of instrumenting a program. Most of these functions require intimate knowledge of the implementation. In certain cases, most are easier to construct if the user has access to the compiler's symbol table.

Why, then, don't compiler vendors include such functions in their standard libraries? How hard is it for a compiler hack to write a traceback function that knows the names of functions? The answer is "not very." Who has better access to the technical information than the compiler writer? The answer is "no one."

The more perplexing questions are, "Why haven't users demanded such functions?" and "Why hasn't the ANSI committee defined a debugging library?" Sorry, no easy answers for these final questions.

A Challenge to Compiler Vendors

Compiler writers can do more than supply trace functions. A number of relatively simple compiler options could diminish significantly the programmer's task. Compilers should have an option that generates startup code which zeros all of available memory.

Another option should cause the compiler to generate a call to a user-defined function at the beginning of every function. Then it wouldn't be necessary to edit every function to insert or delete the debugging structure. Debugging is an integral part of the programming process; compiler writers haven't completed the development package until they supply debugging support.

A Challenge to the Reader

After you have read this book, I hope that you will return to the task of programming with greater respect for the intellectual challenge debugging offers.

Debugging is not simply the proof that you have done something wrong. It is a necessary step in the process of creating a working program. Until programmers recognize that debugging is a legitimate activity, it is unlikely that there will be much progress in debugging theory, methodology or development tools.

With that in mind, I hope that you will strive to master this genuine offspring of programming, and that you will urge vendors to supply the effective and well-designed tools that you deserve.

Finally, I hope to see, during the next few years, a renaissance of debugging activity that will quickly make this book obsolete.

A
A Resource List

Coding Practice

Kernighan, Brian W., and Plauger, P.J. *The Elements of Programming Style,* 2nd Edition. New York: McGraw-Hill, 1978. A delightful guide to writing readable code, patterned after Strunk and White's classic.

Formal Grammars and Compiler Design

Aho, Alfred V., and Jeffrey D. Ullman. *Principles of Compiler Design.* Reading, Massachusetts: Addison-Wesley, 1977. The classic text in the field, but perhaps not as well suited to self-study as is the Barrett and Couch book.

Barrett, William A., and John D. Couch. *Compiler Construction: Theory and Practice.* Palo Alto, California: Scientific Research Associates, 1979. A readable introduction meant for the college classroom, but equally suited to self-study.

Hayes, Brian. "A Mechanic's Guide to Grammar," Parts I, II, and III. *Computer Language* 2(10):27-35, 2(11):51-60, and 2(12):49-64 (October, November, and December 1985).

Design and Software Engineering

Dijkstra, E. W. *A Discipline of Programming*. Englewood Cliffs, New Jersey: Prentice-Hall 1976.

Kernighan, Brian W., and P.J. Plauger. *Software Tools*. Reading, Massachusetts: Addison-Wesley, 1978. A classic introduction to the programming philosophy underlying UNIX.

Yourdon, Edward, and Constantine, Larry L. *Structured Design*, 2nd Edition. New York: Yourdon Press, 1978. A fairly abstract introduction to large project design. Not everyone will find this a good self-study resource.

Yourdon, Edward, ed. *Writings of the Revolution: Selected Readings on Software Engineering*. New York: Yourdon Press, 1982.

Introductory-Level UNIX Texts

For a more comprehensive listing of UNIX titles, contact any of the book stores listed at the end of this appendix.

Christian, Kaare. *The UNIX Operating System*. New York: Wiley, 1983. Assumes little about the reader's background. A good elementary introduction to UNIX, but not much insight into how to exploit UNIX's capabilities.

Weinberg, Paul N., and James R. Groff. *Understanding UNIX: A Conceptual Guide*. Indianapolis, Indiana: Que Corporation, 1983.

Advanced and Specialized UNIX Books

Foxley, Eric. *UNIX for Super-Users*. Reading, Massachusetts: Addison-Wesley, 1986.

Kernighan, Brian W., and Robert Pike. *The UNIX Programming Environment*. Englewood Cliffs, New Jersey: Prentice-Hall, 1984.

Prata, Stephen. *Advanced UNIX—A Programmer's Guide*. New York: H.W. Sams, 1986.

Introductory C Textbooks

Introductory C texts are plentiful. For a comprehensive listing, see the resource listings cited later or contact one of the book stores listed at the end of this appendix.

Plum, Thomas. *Learning To Program in C.* Cardiff, New Jersey: Plum-Hall, 1983. An excellent self-teaching text for programmers with a strong background in structured languages.

Purdum, Jack. *C Programming Guide*, 2nd Edition. Indianapolis, Indiana: Que Corporation, 1985. A good self-teaching text, especially for those who have little experience with another structured language.

_____. *C Self-Study Guide.* Indianapolis, Indiana: Que Corporation, 1985. A compendium of hard-to-find explanations about the nitty-gritty of C programming. A good second text for the new programmer.

C Reference Works

Harbison, Samuel P., and Guy L. Steele. *C: A Reference Manual.* Englewood Cliffs, New Jersey: Prentice-Hall, 1984. The most comprehensive, useful technical reference available.

Kernighan, Brian W., and Dennis M. Ritchie. *The C Programming Language.* Englewood Cliffs, New Jersey: Prentice-Hall, 1978. The classic (K&R); still an essential for every C programmer.

More Extensive C Resource Listings

Swaine, Michael, ed. *Dr. Dobb's Sourcebook: A Reference Guide to the C Programming Language.* People's Computer Company, 2682 Bishop Dr., Suite 107, San Ramon, CA 94583. 64 pages, $4.95. An extensive listing of C resources, including a comprehensive bibliography of books and periodicals and a complete listing of C vendors and C-related products.

Ward, Terry A. "An Annotated Bibliography on C." *Byte*, 119-120, 382-386 (August 1983). An earlier version of the following bibliography.

_____. "A Guide to Resources for the C Programmer." *Dr. Dobb's Journal.* 9(11):74-86 (November 1984). Lists compiler manufacturers and users' groups and gives a comprehensive bibliography, citing some books and 237 magazine articles.

_____. "A Journeyman's Tool Guide." *Computer Language.* 3(2):138-142 (February 1986). A listing of productivity tools for C programmers.

User's Groups

The C User's Group, P.O. Box 97, McPherson, KS 67460. Maintains a library of more than 100 volumes of public-domain C source code. Publishes a quarterly newsletter and a cross-referenced catalog of library holdings.

Technical Book Stores

Cucumber Bookshop, Inc., 5611 Kraft Drive, Rockville, MD 20852. This store specializes in UNIX and C titles. Write for their "Complete Title List."

Stacey's, 219 University Ave., Palo Alto, CA 94301. A wide range of technical titles.

Uni-Ops Books, 2138 36th Avenue, San Francisco, CA 94116. Phone: (415) 731-2978. Handles Unix and C titles.

The Unix Bookstore, 520 Waller Street, San Francisco, CA 94117.

B
A Full-Featured
Debugging System

This appendix presents a full-featured debugging system that supports: dynamic (almost breakpoint) control of user-defined snapshots, trace frequency and detail, stack checks, and break points called "stop" points.

Programmer's Interface

The debugging system is linked to the executing program by inline calls to one of two functions: `dbginit()` or `dbg()`. Because the debugging system is largly static, it can be precompiled and simply linked each time the test program is recompiled. For example, if you were testing a program in file *tower.c* (under Eco-C88) you would incorporate the debugging system at compile time with the command

   cc tower.c dbg.obj snaps.obj

in which *snaps.obj* contains precompiled code for the user-defined snapshot functions.

Function Interfaces

The `dgbinit()` function initializes the debugging system. Because the function always causes a "stop," allowing initial parameters to

be set, the first executable line of main should always be a call to
dgbinit().

The function call dbg(<stop label>, <detail index>, <trace
format> [, <vars>...]) includes:

<stop label> is a character string identifying the trace statement.
This label is used to "select" stop and trace points. In small functions with only one or two dbug calls, the stop label can be the function name. In larger functions with many dbug calls, it's wise to
distinguish each stop label uniquely. In other words, instead of just
foo, use foo1, foo2, foo3.

<detail index> is an integer indicating the level of detail captured
by the following trace format. Higher numbers are used with specific traces, lower numbers with higher level, more general traces.
The level must always be greater than zero.

<trace format> is a printf-type format-specification string. It may
be the empty string, if no trace information will ever be generated
from this call. If a non-null pointer is provided, the string it identifies
will be used to control the printing of the following argument list.

[, <vars>...] is an optional, variable-length list of variable identi-
fiers as in printf calls. These are variables which will be traced if
this call is enabled as a trace point.

An Example Call

The following call generates a top-level trace at function entry. If
enabled, (a function of granularity, level, trace points and other
controls) the call will trace the procedure parameters:

```
void foo(arg1, arg2, arg3)
int arg1;
char arg2;
char *arg3;

{
dbg("foo", 1, "arg1=%d, arg2=%c, arg3=%04. 4x /%s/",
     arg1, arg2, arg3, arg3);
```

Assuming the following values for the parameters,

```
arg1 = 7
arg2 = q
arg3 = "a string" (stored at 02f4)
```

this entrace will generate the message:

```
foo arg1=7, arg2=q, arg3=02f4 /a string/
```

Although these dbg() calls are no more troublesome to type, they are much more powerful than conventional printf trace statements. When dbg() calls are inserted automatically after every line (with a utility like that shown in Appendix D), the outcome is similar to the effect achieved with an interpreter. Because all debugging calls include the pattern dbg, they can be removed in a single pass with a *grep* tool (you must be careful to avoid this pattern in all your other code). Alternatively, the calls can be written as macros and removed by the preprocessor, as discussed in Chapter 5.

The User Interface

The debugging system is invisible to the user until the executing program reaches either a trace point or a stop point. Potentially, all calls to dbg are trace points *and* stop points. Whether a call qualifies as either depends on the setting of the debugging system's global modes (discussed with the commands which set them). The user interacts with the debugging system through a conventional command interpreter. All commands conform to this structure

<command> [[<arg1>] <arg2>]

in which *<command>* is a question mark (for help) or a four- or five-letter mnemonic; *<arg1>* is either a number (in hexadecimal) or a character; and *<arg2>* is either a string literal or a number in hexadecimal. Commands may be either upper- or lowercase. The next section contains a description of each command, as well as its effect on the behavior of the system.

Debugging Commands

The ? (help) command generates the following command summary:

Command:		Effect:
STAT		reports debugging system status
STOP	n pattern	attaches pattern to *n*th stop point
TRACE	n pattern	attaches pattern to *n*th trace point
SSKIP	n	skip *n* stop points
TSKIP	n	skip *n* trace points
WATCH	n addr	declare *n*th watch address
WATMD	c	watch checking is Off, Stop point only, Trace point only, or Always
LEVEL	n	enable all traces with level below *n*
GRAN	n	enable every *n*th trace point
STACK		produce stack trace
STKMD	c	stack checking is OFF, Stop point only, Trace point only, or Always
LOCAL	n	print locals in *n* most recent stack frames
DUMP	start len	print hex dump for memory block
CRCK	start len	compute CRC on memory block
SNAP	n	invoke *n*th user-supplied snapshot
CONT		resume execution
<Control-C>		exit to operating system

STOP n pattern

Creates a stop point at any dbg call whose label matches *pattern*. Three separate patterns may exist (can be increased easily). In the simplest case, patterns are simple string literals that must match exactly the dbg call's label. Alternatively, if the pattern includes question marks, the stop may match any of a number of dbg labels. The question mark command functions as a wildcard, much as it does in MS-DOS file names. Here, however, the question mark also will match "no character." For example, the pattern foo?? matches

    foo
    foo1
    foo12
    fooey

but does not match foo123. The asterisk (*) will match any pattern.

With an appropriate naming convention, this pattern-matching capability can be used to enable: single debug points, all debug points within a function, all debug points within a program subtree, or all debug points at a given level of the program hierarchy.

The *stop* command changes only the pattern whose number is given. To cancel a pattern, use a *stop* without a pattern.

TRACE n pattern

This command also sets up patterns that match dbg labels, except that these patterns enable trace points instead of stop points.

SSKIP n

The next *n* of otherwise enabled stop points will be suppressed.

TSKIP n

The next *n* of otherwise enabled trace points will be suppressed.

LEVEL n

Sets the trace level to *n*. Has the effect of suppressing all otherwise enabled trace points which have a level parameter greater than *n*.

GRAN n

Sets the trace granularity to *n*. Only every *n*th (otherwise enabled) trace statement will be printed. The argument *n* must always be greater than zero.

WATCH n addr

Sets a watch address. Watch addresses are examined automatically at certain dbg calls (according to the mode selected; see the next command). Whenever an examination reveals that the contents of a watch address have changed, a stop point is forced. A single watch point may be disabled by setting its address to zero.

WATMD c

Specifies which dbg calls are to trigger automatic watch examinations. The options, specified by a single character, are

   O - All watches off. The default condition.
   S - Examine only at stop points.
   T - Examine only at trace points.
   A - Examine at all dbg calls.

STACK

Gives a stack dump like that described in Chapter 8, except that the frame pointer is checked for reasonableness.

STKMD c

This command controls a facility for automatically checking the reasonableness of the stack's frame-pointer chain. This facility offers minimal protection against pointers that write on the stack. The options (specified by a single letter) are identical to those available with *WATMD*.

DUMP addr n

Prints, in ASCII and hexadecimal representations, the *n* byte block of memory beginning at *addr* (like the DEBUG and DDT dump commands).

LOCAL n

Prints, in the same format as dump, the local variables and parameters associated with the last *n* stack frames.

CRCK addr n

Computes a cyclic redundancy check over the *n* byte block of memory, beginning at *addr.*

SNAP n

Invokes one of three user-defined snapshot functions. These functions are defined separately for each program tested.

STAT

Generates a report (similar to the following) that summarizes the condition of the debugging system:

```
TRACE CONTROLS: gran = 2, skip = 3, level = 2
STOPS AT:
  1 tower
  2 tower1
  3 towerex
TRACES AT:
  1 tower??
NOW WATCHING: 1=ffeb 2=0000 3=0000
MODES: watch = S, stack check = T
TRACE CONTROLS: gran = 2, skip = 3, level = 2
```

CONT

Returns control to the program under test; resumes execution.

Machine and Compiler Dependencies

Because it manipulates the stack, much of the code in listing B.1 is machine-dependent. This code compiles under Eco-C88 and runs on a PC-clone (XT). If the code is to be moved to another system, these functions that traverse the stack must be rewritten.

```
stk_dmp()
dbg_init()
advframe()
lcl_dmp()
```

Furthermore, the calls to _format() must be replaced with calls to an appropriate library function in the compiler.

Finally, be warned that crc_16() may behave strangely if the compiler doesn't handle sign extension and type conversions in exactly the same way that Eco-C88 handles them.

Extensions

Although the system presented here is relatively powerful, it isn't the ultimate debugger. In fact, the implementation has been restricted deliberately to help you get it up and running in reasonable time. After you have a version working, use some of these suggestions for easily implemented improvements:

- allow more than one command on a line

- allow shorter command abbreviations

- replace *SYNTAX ERROR* with meaningful error messages

- expand the pattern-matching facility

- allow numbers in alternate radixes

- allow memory blocks to be specified as "start through end," as well as "start plus length"

- redirect command input (from a file)

- duplicate debugger output (to a file or printer)

- improve the effectiveness of the stack integrity check

- automatically perform *crcs*, using a mechanism similar to that which triggers a watch examination

```
#include <stdio. h>
#include <ctype. h>

extern void snap1();  /*defined by the user */
extern void snap2();  /*defined by the user */
extern void snap3();  /*defined by the user */

/*
          Global Declarations used by dbug
*/
#define MAX_LINE 128    /*maximum input line length */
#define STOP_LIST  3    /*just change if you want more */
                        /*stop points and trace points */
#define MAX_NAME_LEN 40   /*plenty for most people */
```

```
#define OFF     0
#define STP     1
#define TRC     2
#define ALL     3

#define NO 0                    /* general-purpose logic values */
#define YES 1
#define OK 1
#define ON 1

#define SILENT 0              /* output modes in stack dump */
#define VERBOSE 1
#define ERR -1
#define HELP 0                /*logical values for commands */
#define STOP 1
#define WATCH 2
#define WATMD 3
#define STKMD 4
#define LEVEL 5
#define TSKIP 6
#define SSKIP 7
#define SNAP  8
#define DUMP  9
#define STACK 10
#define LOCAL 11
#define CONT  12
#define CRC   13
#define GRAN  14
#define STAT  15
#define TRACE 16

FILE *dbg_stream;               /* output stream for debug info */
int dbg_stp_skip;               /* skip count for stop points */
int dbg_trc_skip;               /* skip count for trace points */
typedef char lst[STOP_LIST][MAX_NAME_LEN];
lst dbg_stop;                   /* stop point names */
lst dbg_trc;                    /* trace point names */
int dbg_level;                  /* level of trace detail selected */
                                /* must always be positive */
int dbg_gran;                   /* current trace granularity */
int dbg_count;                  /* how many calls (for granularity) */
int dbg_mon_mode;               /* mode of memory monitor check */
int dbg_stk_mode;               /* mode of stack check. options are: */
                                /* off, stop only, trace only, always */
int *dbg_top_stk;               /* top of stack */
```

```
int *dbg_pt1;              /* addresses of watch locations */
int *dbg_pt2;              /* zero if no watch */
int *dbg_pt3;
int dbg_old1;              /* storage for prior watch values */
int dbg_old2;
int dbg_old3;

/*
This function can be called with a variable number of parameters
like printf. Extra parameters are assumed to follow formatstr in
the parameter list.

Because of the variable list of parameters, the dbg function
should be prototyped as:

  extern void dbg(int, int, char *, ... );

in all source files that will reference it.
*/

void dbg(stop, level, formatstr)
char *stop, *formatstr;
int level;

{
int dbg_out();
void dbg_cmds();
int _format(int (*)(), char *, ... ), stk_chk(), watch();
int inlist();
int interp;

interp = OFF;
/* perform stack check if always enabled */
if (dbg_stk_mode == ALL)
   if (stk_chk() != OK) interp = ON;
if (dbg_mon_mode == ALL)
   if (watch() != OK) interp = ON;

/* see if otherwise a stop point */
if (inlist(dbg_stop, stop)) {
   if (dbg_stk_mode == STP) (void) stk_chk();
   if (dbg_mon_mode == STP) (void) watch();
   if (dbg_stp_skip) dbg_stp_skip -=1;
   else interp = ON;
   }
```

```
/* process enabled traces */
if ((level <= dbg_level) && inlist(dbg_trc,stop)) {
   /* keep track of enabled calls for granularity */
   dbg_count = (dbg_count + 1) % dbg_gran;
   /* update trace skip count */
   if (dbg_count || dbg_trc_skip){
      if (dbg_trc_skip) dbg_trc_skip -= 1;
      }
   else{
      /* if skip count exhausted, check stack ? */
      if (dbg_stk_mode == TRC)
        if (stk_chk() != OK) interp = ON;
      if (dbg_mon_mode == TRC)
        if ( watch() != OK) interp = ON;
      /* now do trace by calling function underlying
         printf and fprintf. Function is documented
         in standard library source code */
      if (formatstr != NULL){
         if (stop != NULL) {
            (void) fprintf(dbg_stream,"\n%s ",stop);
            (void) _format(&dbg_out,formatstr,(&formatstr)+1);
            }
         }
      }
   }
if (interp == ON) {
   (void) fprintf(dbg_stream,"\nSTOPPED AT %s",stop);
   dbg_cmds(stop);
   }
}


/* this function watches up to three memory locations,
   reporting any changes. Prints a message of the form:

   WATCH: label address oldval newval

   whenever a change is detected
*/

int watch()

{
void wtch_rpt();
int rval;
```

```
rval = OK;
if (dbg_pt1)
    if (dbg_old1 != *dbg_pt1) {
        rval = !OK;
        wtch_rpt(dbg_old1, dbg_pt1);
        dbg_old1 = *dbg_pt1;
        }
if (dbg_pt2)
    if (dbg_old2 != *dbg_pt2) {
        rval = !OK;
        wtch_rpt(dbg_old2, dbg_pt2);
        dbg_old2 = *dbg_pt2;
        }
if (dbg_pt3)
    if (dbg_old3 != *dbg_pt3) {
        rval = !OK;
        wtch_rpt(dbg_old3, dbg_pt3);
        dbg_old3 = *dbg_pt3;
        }
return rval;
}

void wtch_rpt(old, ptr)
int old, *ptr;
{

(void) fprintf(dbg_stream,"\nWATCH: ");
(void) fprintf(dbg_stream," %04.4x old = %04.4x, new = %04.4x",
        ptr, old, *ptr);
}

/*
  This is the interactive command interpreter.

*/

void dbg_cmds(where)
char *where;

{
int st, arg1, arg2;
char arg1s[80], arg2s[80];
```

```
void status(), list_list(), synerr(), list_watch();
void snap1(), snap2(), snap3(), fmat_hex(), dbg_help();
void lcl_dmp();
int cmdparse(), chartomode(), crc_16();
char *strcpy();

while (1){
    /* cmdparse returns the type of the command and tries
       to interpret the following arguments as integer or
       string. arg1, arg2 and arg2s are filled accordingly
       Arg2s is guaranteed to be a string less than 80
       after cmdparse.
    */
    (void) fprintf(dbg_stream, "\nDBG>> ");
    switch (cmdparse(&arg1, &arg2, arg1s, arg2s)){
        case HELP:
            dbg_help();
            break;
        case STAT:
            status(where);
            break;
        case STOP:
            if ((arg1 < 1) || (arg1 > STOP_LIST)) {
                synerr();
                }
            else {
                (void) strcpy(dbg_stop[arg1 - 1], arg2s);
                list_list(dbg_stop);
                }
            break;
        case TRACE:
            if ((arg1 < 1) || (arg1 > STOP_LIST)) {
                synerr();
                }
            else {
                (void) strcpy(dbg_trc[arg1 - 1], arg2s);
                list_list(dbg_trc);
                }
```

```
        break;
case WATCH:
    if ((arg1 < 1) || (arg1 > 3))
        synerr();
    else {
        switch (arg1){
            case 1:  dbg_pt1 = (int *) arg2;
                     dbg_old1 = *dbg_pt1;
                     break;
            case 2:  dbg_pt2 = (int *) arg2;
                     dbg_old2 = *dbg_pt2;
                     break;
            case 3:  dbg_pt3 = (int *) arg2;
                     dbg_old3 = *dbg_pt3;
                     break;
        }
        list_watch();
    }
    break;
case WATMD:
    st = chartomode(*arg1s);
    if (st == ERR) synerr();
    else dbg_mon_mode = st;
    break;
case STKMD:
    st = chartomode(*arg1s);
    if (st == ERR) synerr();
    else dbg_stk_mode = st;
    break;
case LEVEL:
    dbg_level = arg1;
    break;
case TSKIP:
    dbg_trc_skip = arg1;
    break;
case SSKIP:
    dbg_stp_skip = arg1;
    break;
case SNAP:
    switch (arg1){
        case 1: snap1(); break; /*user supplied function */
        case 2: snap2(); break; /*user supplied function */
        case 3: snap3(); break; /*user supplied function */
        default: synerr();
    }
```

```
                    break;
                case DUMP:
                    fmat_hex( (unsigned char *) arg1, arg2);
                    break;
                case STACK:
                    (void) stk_dmp(VERBOSE);
                    break;
                case LOCAL:
                    if (arg1 < 1) arg1 = 1;   /* always do one */
                    lcl_dmp(arg1);
                    break;
                case CRC:
                    (void) fprintf(dbg_stream, "\nCRC: %04.4x %x %04.4x",
                            arg1, arg2, crc_16( (char *)arg1, arg2));
                    break;
                case GRAN:
                    if (arg1 < 1) synerr();
                    else dbg_gran = arg1;
                    break;
                case CONT: return;
                default: synerr();
                } /* end command switch */
        } /* end while */
}


/* translates a character into a logical mode selector. Returns
   ERR if a poor selection has been made.
*/

int chartomode(ch)
char ch;
{
int rval;

switch (toupper(ch)){
    case 'O': rval = OFF; break;
    case 'S': rval = STP; break;
    case 'T': rval = TRC; break;
    case 'A': rval = ALL; break;
    default: rval = ERR; break;
    }
return rval;
}
```

```
/* generate a syntax error message on the debugging channel */
void synerr()

{
(void) fprintf(dbg_stream, "\nSYNTAX ERROR");
}

/* print the current watch variables */

void list_watch()
{
(void) fprintf(dbg_stream, "\nNOW WATCHING: 1=%04.4x 2=%04.4x 3=%04.4x",
                          dbg_pt1, dbg_pt2, dbg_pt3);
}

/* print the labels which will cause a stop */

void list_list(list)
lst list;
{
int i;

if (list == dbg_stop)
   (void) fprintf(dbg_stream, "\nSTOPS AT:");
else
   (void) fprintf(dbg_stream, "\nTRACES AT:");
for (i = 0; i < STOP_LIST; i++){
   if (list[i][0])
      (void) fprintf(dbg_stream, "\n %d %s", i + 1, list[i]);
   }
}

/* compares an input string against all entries in the
   stop list. returns true if match found, false otherwise.
*/

int inlist(list, str)
lst list;
char *str;
{
int i, strcmp();
```

```
      for (i = 0; i < STOP_LIST; i++){
          if (list[i][0] == '*' ) return YES;
          if (patmat(str, list[i])) return YES;
          }
      return NO;
      }


      /*
          compares str1 to string in str2, performing limited
          pattern matching. specifically, '?'s in str2 match
          any character (or end of string) in str1. Returns
          nonzero on match. Zero on no match.
      */
      int patmat(str1, str2)
      char *str1, *str2;
      {
      while(*str1 && *str2 && ((*str1 == *str2) || (*str2 == '?' ))) {
          str1 += 1;
          str2 += 1;
          }
      if (!(*str1)){
          while (*str2 == '?' ) str2 += 1;
          }
      if (*str1 || *str2) return NO;
      return YES;
      }


      /* putchar for the debugging stream.
          needed for calls to _format
      */


      int dbg_out(ch)
      char ch;
      {
      return putc(ch, dbg_stream);
      }


      /*
          get a command from the keyboard, parse it into
          its components. Return the logical token identifying
          the command portion. Put the args into arg1, arg2, and
          arg2s.
      */
```

```
int cmdparse(arg1, arg2, arg1s, arg2s)
int *arg1, *arg2;
char *arg1s, *arg2s;

{
char cmdbuf[MAX_LINE];
int cmd_type(), i, n;

/* be sure return values are reasonable */
*arg1 = 0;
*arg2 = 0;
*arg1s = '\0';
*arg2s = '\0';
*cmdbuf = '\0';

(void) gets(cmdbuf);
n = sscanf(cmdbuf, "%s%x%x", arg2s, arg1, arg2);
if (n > 0 ) {
   /* Make command keyword all uppercase */
   for (i = 0; (i < 4) && cmdbuf[i]; i++) cmdbuf[i] = toupper(cmdbuf[i]);
   n= sscanf(cmdbuf, "%*s%s%s", arg1s, arg2s);
   if (n < 1) *arg1s = '\0' ;
   if (n < 2) *arg2s = '\0' ;
   return cmd_type(cmdbuf);
   }
return ERR;
}

/* look up the command word and translate into
   a logical token value */

int cmd_type(str)
char *str;
{
int strncmp();
```

```
    if (*str == '?') return HELP;
    if (!strncmp(str,"STOP",4)) return STOP;
    if (!strncmp(str,"TRAC",4)) return TRACE;
    if (!strncmp(str,"WATC",4)) return WATCH;
    if (!strncmp(str,"WATM",4)) return WATMD;
    if (!strncmp(str,"STKM",4)) return STKMD;
    if (!strncmp(str,"LEVE",4)) return LEVEL;
    if (!strncmp(str,"TSKI",4)) return TSKIP;
    if (!strncmp(str,"SSKI",4)) return SSKIP;
    if (!strncmp(str,"SNAP",4)) return SNAP;
    if (!strncmp(str,"DUMP",4)) return DUMP;
    if (!strncmp(str,"STAC",4)) return STACK;
    if (!strncmp(str,"LOCA",4)) return LOCAL;
    if (!strncmp(str,"CONT",4)) return CONT;
    if (!strncmp(str,"CRCK",4)) return CRC;
    if (!strncmp(str,"GRAN",4)) return GRAN;
    if (!strncmp(str,"STAT",4)) return STAT;
    return ERR;
}


/*
   print the current debugger control status
*/

void status(label)
char *label;
{
char modetoch();

(void)
fprintf(dbg_stream,"\nSTOPPED AT: %s  skip count =%d",
    label, dbg_stp_skip);
list_list(dbg_stop);
list_list(dbg_trc);
list_watch();
/* now list modes */
(void)
fprintf(dbg_stream,"\nMODES: watch = %c, stack check = %c",
        modetoch(dbg_mon_mode), modetoch(dbg_stk_mode));
(void)
fprintf(dbg_stream,"\nTRACE CONTROLS: gran = %d, skip = %d, level = %d",
        dbg_gran, dbg_trc_skip, dbg_level);
}
```

```
char modetoch(md)
int md;
{
char rval;

switch( md ){
    case OFF: rval = 'O'; break;
    case STP: rval = 'S'; break;
    case TRC: rval = 'T'; break;
    case ALL: rval = 'A'; break;
    }
return rval;
}


/*
Generate a command summary
*/

dbg_help()
{
(void)
fprintf(dbg_stream, "\nCOMMANDS:");
(void)
fprintf(dbg_stream, "\n  STAT            -- report debugging system status. ");
(void)
fprintf(dbg_stream, "\n  STOP  n pattern -- attach pattern to nth stop point. ");
(void)
fprintf(dbg_stream, "\n  TRACE n pattern -- attach pattern to nth trace point. ");
(void)
fprintf(dbg_stream, "\n  SSKIP n         -- skip n stop points. ");
(void)
fprintf(dbg_stream, "\n  TSKIP n         -- skip n trace points. ");
(void)
fprintf(dbg_stream, "\n  WATCH n addr    -- declare nth watch address. ");
(void)
fprintf(dbg_stream, "\n  WATMD c         -- watch checking is Off, Stop point only, ");
(void)
fprintf(dbg_stream, "\n                     Trace point only, or Always. ");
(void)
fprintf(dbg_stream, "\n  LEVEL n         -- enable all traces above level n. ");
(void)
fprintf(dbg_stream, "\n  GRAN  n         -- enable every nth trace point. ");
(void)
fprintf(dbg_stream, "\n  STACK           -- produce stack trace. ");
(void)
fprintf(dbg_stream, "\n  STKMD c         -- stack checking is OFF, Stop point only, ");
(void)
```

```
    fprintf(dbg_stream, "\n                          Trace point only, or Always. ");
    (void)
    fprintf(dbg_stream, "\n  LOCAL n              -- print locals in n most recent stack frames. ");
    (void)
    fprintf(dbg_stream, "\n  DUMP  start len      -- print hex dump for memory block. ");
    (void)
    fprintf(dbg_stream, "\n  CRCK  start len      -- compute CRC on memory block. ");
    (void)
    fprintf(dbg_stream, "\n  SNAP  n              -- invoke nth user supplied snapshot. ");
    (void)
    fprintf(dbg_stream, "\n  CONT                 -- resume execution. ");
}

/*
    compute a cyclic redundancy check word for the memory block
    beginning at start and continuing for len bytes. Uses CCITT
    crc 16 algorithm.
*/

int crc_16(start, len)
char *start;
int len;

{
int crc;
int crc_update();

crc = 0;
while (len--) crc = crc_update(crc, *start++);
return crc_update(crc_update(crc,'\0'),'\0');
}

/*
  the shift register simulation
*/

int crc_update(crc, c)
int crc;
char c;
{
long x;
int i;
```

```
x = ((long) crc << 8) + c;
for (i = 0;  i < 8;  i++){
    x = x << 1;
    if ( x & 0x01000000) x = x ^ 0x01102100;
    }
return ((x & 0x00ffff00) >> 8);
}


/* this is just a shell for stk_dmp. It deepens the stack
   so that stk_dmp is always called from two levels below
   the program under test
*/

int stk_chk()
{
int stk_dmp();

return stk_dmp(SILENT);
}


/* this dumps frame pointer and stack addresses. It is as
   described in Chapter 8 except that before going a level deeper,
   that level's frame pointer is checked for "sanity".
   That is, it is checked to ensure that it points at a space
   within the active stack.
*/

int stk_dmp(mode)
int mode;
{
int mark;
int rval;
int *framepointer;
extern int *dbg_top_stk;
int advframe();
void sanityerr();
```

```
    framepointer = &mark + 1;
    /* step over debugging system */
    if ((rval = advframe(&framepointer)) != OK) sanityerr(framepointer);
    else if ((rval = advframe(&framepointer)) != OK) sanityerr(framepointer);
    else if ((rval = advframe(&framepointer)) != OK) sanityerr(framepointer);
    else {
        while (framepointer < dbg_top_stk) {
            if (mode == VERBOSE)
                (void) fprintf(dbg_stream,"\nSTACK: %04.4x-%04.4x %04.4x",
                    framepointer, *framepointer, *(framepointer + 1));
            if (advframe(&framepointer) != OK) {
                sanityerr(framepointer);
                return !OK;
                }
            }
        }
    return rval;
}


/*
    report an error in framepointer
*/

void sanityerr(val)
int *val;

{
(void) fprintf(dbg_stream, "\nSTACK: Bad frame pointer at %04.4x = %04.4x",
            val, *val);
}

/*
    this advances the framepointer along the stack. It checks
    the sanity of the new framepointer before changing the
    old one. If all is well, returns OK.
*/

int advframe(framepointer)
int **framepointer;
{
int *temp;

temp = *framepointer;  /* avoid ** operations */
temp = (int *) *temp; /* advance one link */
if ((temp > dbg_top_stk) || (temp < *framepointer)) return !OK;
*framepointer = temp;
return OK;
}
```

```
void fmat_hex(start, len)
unsigned char *start;
int len;
{
int i, k;
char *temp;
char buf[20];

for (temp = buf, k = 0, i = 0; i < len; i++, k++, start++, temp++){
    if (k == 16) {
        k = 0;
        *temp = '\0';
        (void) fprintf(dbg_stream, " %s", buf);
        }
    if (k == 0) {
        (void) fprintf(dbg_stream, "\n%04.4x", start);
        temp = buf; /* reset ascii output pointer */
        }
    (void) fprintf(dbg_stream, "%c%02.2x",
            (k % 4) ? ' ' : '-', *start);
    *temp = (isprint(*start)) ? *start: '.';
    }
*temp = '\0';
(void) fprintf(dbg_stream, " %s", buf);
}
/* dump n frames of local variables and parameters */

void lcl_dmp(n)
int n;
{
int mark;
int *framepointer;    /* points to current frame pointer */
int *endpntr;         /* next frame pointer, space between (-2)*/
                      /* is locals and parameters */
extern int *dbg_top_stk;
int advframe();
void sanityerr();
```

```
framepointer = &mark + 1;
/* step over debugging system */
if (advframe(&framepointer) != OK) sanityerr(framepointer);
else if (advframe(&framepointer) != OK) sanityerr(framepointer);
else if (advframe(&framepointer) != OK) sanityerr(framepointer);
else {
   while ((framepointer < dbg_top_stk) && n--) {
      endpntr = framepointer;
      if (advframe(&endpntr) != OK) {
         sanityerr(framepointer);
         }
      fmat_hex((unsigned char *) (framepointer + 2),
            2 * (int) (endpntr - framepointer - 2));
      framepointer = endpntr;
      }
   }
}


/*
   this routine must be called once at the beginning of main
   to initialize the debugging system. Always causes a stop.
*/

void dbg_init()

{
int i;
void dbg_cmds();

/* empty out stop list */
for (i = 0; i < STOP_LIST; i++) {
   dbg_stop[i][0] = '\0';
   dbg_trc[i][0] = '\0';
   }
(void) strcpy(dbg_trc[0], "*");
   /* default is enable traces in all functions */
```

```
/* give defaults to other modalities */
dbg_stp_skip = dbg_trc_skip = 0;
dbg_level = 0;
dbg_gran = 1;
dbg_count = 0;
dbg_mon_mode = dbg_stk_mode = OFF;
dbg_pt1 = dbg_pt2 = dbg_pt3 = 0;
/* for output to a file, change this to an fopen statement */
dbg_stream = stdout;

dbg_top_stk =(int *) *((&i) + 1);   /* see the discussion in Chapter 8 */
dbg_cmds("init");
}
```

Listing B.1.

C
Assembly Language Functions

These three assembly language functions are used by the memory-initialization program in Chapter 7. All are nonstandard functions; using them will damage severely the portability of your code.

This intdos() is nonstandard in its handling of register values. The intdos provided with Eco-C88 is more universally available, efficient, and elegant than this version. But this version, which avoids the extra complexity of unions of structures, may improve the accessibility of the manipulations of Chapter 7.

After you have figured out what is happening, rewrite the code in Chapter 7 to use the standard intdos.

```
;
;   intdos -- c interface to operating system
;
    include pro.h               ; the Eco-C88 standard prologue
;                                 just contains magic for the assembler
$b$prog segment public 'code'   ; what follows is part of code segment
    public _intdos              ; the only symbol other programs will need
_intdos proc                    ; note the leading underscore
    push bp
    mov bp, sp
    mov bx, word ptr [bp][4] ; address of register array now in bx
    mov ah, byte ptr [bx][2] ; get bl, bh first and save in stack
    mov al, byte ptr [bx][3]
    push ax
    mov ah, byte ptr [bx]       ; now get other register values
    mov al, byte ptr [bx][1]
    mov ch, byte ptr [bx][4]
    mov cl, byte ptr [bx][5]
    mov dh, byte ptr [bx][6]
    mov dl, byte ptr [bx][7]
    pop bx                  ; get bx data
    push es
    push ds                 ; just in case
    int 21h
    pop ds
    pop es
    push bx                 ; save return value
    mov bp, sp             ; compute address of output array
    mov bx, word ptr [bp][8] ;
    mov byte ptr [bx], ah   ; put ax in array
    mov byte ptr [bx][1], al
    pop ax                  ; now get b stuff and put in array
    mov byte ptr [bx][2], ah ; now copy other results to array
    mov byte ptr [bx][3], al
    mov byte ptr [bx][4], ch
    mov byte ptr [bx][5], cl
    mov byte ptr [bx][6], dh
    mov byte ptr [bx][7], dl
    pop bp
    ret
_intdos endp
$b$prog ends
    end
```

Listing C.1.

```
;
;    getseg -- returns the current data segment pointer
;
        include pro.h

$b$prog segment public 'code'
        public _getseg
_getseg proc
    mov ax, ds
        ret
_getseg endp
$b$prog ends
        end
```

Listing C.2.

```
;
;    fillmem
;
;        this function fills an arbitrary block of memory
;    with the specified character. Block identified by
;    segment and length.
;
        includepro. h

$b$prog segment public 'code'
        public _fillmem
_fillmem         proc
        push    p
        mov     bp, sp
    mov bx, word ptr [bp][4] ; get new segment
    mov cx, word ptr [bp][6] ; get count
    mov ax, word ptr [bp][8] ; and value
    push es                  ; save current segment
    mov es, bx               ; change segment (di always refers to es)
    mov di, 0                ; begin at zero offset
    rep stosb                ; store al, increment di, decr cx until
    pop es                   ; cx is zero. then restore ds
    pop bp                   ; and bp
    ret
_fillmem         endp
$b$prog ends
        end
```

Listing C.3

D
A Poor Man's Ctrace

The *ctrace* utility processes a C source file, inserting calls to the debugging system shown in Appendix B (or to another system with a similar interface). The program is structured as a text filter—it expects the source file to appear at standard input and writes the modified file to standard output. The program accepts a single option that controls how frequently debugging statements are added to the source.

The syntax for invoking the program is

```
ctrace [option] <source.c >dbg.c
```

in which *option* is one of the following:

Option	Effect
-a	which inserts a debugging call after almost every statement.
-o	which inserts debugging calls after almost every lefthand curly brace.
-f	which inserts a single call at the beginning of each function.

The debugging calls added by this program are of the form

```
dbg("fooXX", n, "");
```

in which foo is always replaced with the name of the function containing the call and XX is a two-digit number indicating the relative position of this call within the function. In each function, the calls begin with *00* and increment sequentially. You can think of this number as a *line number*, even though it doesn't correspond exactly to lines of source code.

The second argument (n) indicates the nesting level in effect at the call. Calls outside the control of any while or if will replace n with 1. Calls inside the scope of a single control structure will replace n with 2. Each additional level of control-structure nesting increases n by 1.

The very first call in function main is replaced by a call to dbg_init.

Caution

This program doesn't really understand C—the program simply looks for certain patterns in the text. These patterns depend heavily on the way in which the source code is formatted. To use this program successfully, your code must observe the following rules:

- the first executable line of a function should follow an empty line. This is natural for functions with local variables, but somewhat awkward in functions without local variables

- opening (lefthand) curly braces should be the last significant (noncomment) character on the line

- the keyword else always should be the first significant symbol on a line

- break and return statements should be on a line by themselves, with the break or return keyword appearing first

Listing D.1 complies with these rules. Other popular coding practices also comply with these rules (except for the blank line requirement).

Variations

The line numbers appended to the function name in each call aren't particularly useful as a guide because these numbers don't correspond to line numbers in the file or function. By replacing ejectline() and printdbg() with the following versions, you can create a program which prints a listing of your source, annotated with the same "line numbers" that are used in dbg calls. Equipped with this numbered listing and a load map, you will be able to use the debugging system quite effectively.

Functions ejectline and printdbg should be replaced with:

```
void ejectline()
{

(void) printf("    %s\n", holdbuf);
}

void printdbg(str, line, level)
char *str;
int line, level;
{

(void) printf("%02d ", line);
}
```

When added to the source, all debugging calls appear flush-left. The resulting modified source is extremely difficult to read because the program's indentation is obscured.

The debugging calls are most helpful if you make all corrections and modifications directly in the expanded source (as opposed to modifying the original and resubmitting it to *ctrace*). You can use this work strategy and still have readable code if you run the modified source through a *pretty printer* (a utility that reformats source code). The suggested procedure is:

1. Draft and enter code.
2. Process with *ctrace*.
3. Process again, to get numbered listing.
4. Process unnumbered *ctrace* output with *pretty printer*.
5. Debug and modify using the *pretty printer* output.

```
#include "stdio.h"
#include "ctype.h"

#define MAXLINE 256
#define ALL 0
#define BRTOO 1
#define FONLY 2

#define EMPTY 0
#define FULL  1

#define NEWFUNC 0
#define OPENBR 1
#define LINEEND 2

#define SEMI 1          /* lexical token values */
#define LBRACE 2
#define RPAREN 3
#define ELSE 4
#define CASE 5
#define FILEEND 6
#define OTHER 7
#define RBRACE 8
#define RETURN 9
#define BREAK 10

#define YES 1
#define NO 0
#define ON 1
#define OFF 0

int level;     /* curly brace level of current line */
int fline;     /* line number (within current function */
char funcname[MAXLINE];  /*current function name */
char lhbuf[MAXLINE];
char holdbuf[MAXLINE];
char linebuf[MAXLINE];  /* current stripped source line */
int cmtlvl;    /* current number of open comment levels */
int lookahead;
```

```
/* library functions referenced */
extern void exit();
extern int strncmp();
extern char *strncpy();
extern char *strcpy();
extern char *gets();
extern int strcmp();

/* functions defined in this file */
int findpoint(), nexttoken(), firsttoken(), nextline(), lasttoken();
int getlhline(), readline(), text();
void printdbg(), updatefunc(), updatelvl();
void ejectline(), findbblnk();

main(argc, argv)
int argc;
char **argv;
{
int st;
int mode;

mode = ALL;

/* Process command line options */

if (argc == 2){
   switch (toupper(argv[1][1])){
      case 'A' : mode = ALL; break;
      case 'O' : mode = BRTOO; break;
      case 'F' : mode = FONLY; break;
      default:
         (void) fprintf(stderr,"\nUnrecognized option %s",argv[1]);
         exit();
      }
   }
/* findpoint() reads - and copies to stdout - all stdin until */
/* a debugging call point is reached. Then it returns the type*/
/* of the call point. As findpoint reads code, it updates */
/* global indicators level, fline, and funcname    */
```

```
lookahead = EMPTY;
fline = Ø;
level = Ø;
funcname[Ø] = '\Ø';
cmtlvl = Ø;

while ((st = findpoint()) != FILEEND) {
    switch (st){
        case NEWFUNC:
            findbblnk();
            printdbg(funcname, fline, level);
            break;
        case OPENBR:
            if (mode != FONLY) printdbg(funcname, fline, level);
            break;
        case LINEEND:
            if (mode == ALL) printdbg(funcname, fline, level);
            break;
        }
    fline += 1;
    }
}

/*
    findpoint -- process code up to the next possible
                 site for a debug call.
                 updates all global indicators.
*/

int findpoint()
{
int st, tk;

do {
    if ((st=nextline()) == FILEEND) return FILEEND;
    if (level == Ø) {
        if (lasttoken() == RPAREN) {
            updatefunc();
            st = NEWFUNC;
            }
        else st = OTHER;
        }
```

```
      else if (lasttoken() == LBRACE) {
         if (nexttoken() != CASE) st = OPENBR;
         else st = OTHER;
         }
      else if ((lasttoken() == SEMI)) {
         tk = nexttoken();
         if ((tk != ELSE) && (tk != CASE) &&
            (firsttoken() != BREAK) && (firsttoken() != RETURN))
            st = SEMI;
         }
      else if ((lasttoken() == RBRACE) && (nexttoken() == RBRACE))
         st = SEMI;
      updatelvl();
      } while (st == OTHER);
return st;
}


/*
   nexttoken   -- looks ahead to next executable token.
*/

int nexttoken()
{

if (getlhline()== FILEEND) return FILEEND;
   /* scan foward enough to get lookahead line */
if (!strncmp(lhbuf,"else",4)) return ELSE;
if (!strncmp(lhbuf,"case",4)) return CASE;
if (!strncmp(lhbuf,"default",7)) return CASE;
if (!strncmp(lhbuf,"break",5)) return BREAK;
if (*lhbuf == '{') return LBRACE;
if (*lhbuf == '}') return RBRACE;
return OTHER;
}


/*
   firsttoken -- returns type of first token on current line
*/
int firsttoken()
{
```

```
if (!strncmp(linebuf,"return",6)) return RETURN;
if (!strncmp(linebuf,"else",4)) return ELSE;
if (!strncmp(linebuf,"case",4)) return CASE;
if (!strncmp(linebuf,"default",7)) return CASE;
if (!strncmp(linebuf,"break",5)) return BREAK;
if (*linebuf == '{') return LBRACE;
if (*linebuf == '}') return RBRACE;
return OTHER;
}
/*
   getlhline -- fills lookahead buffer with next line
                of executable text, stripped of leading
                blanks and comments.
*/
int getlhline()
{
int st;

st = readline(lhbuf);        /* get a stripped line */
while (!lhbuf[0] && ( st != FILEEND)){
   ejectline();          /* if non-executable, print original */
   st = readline(lhbuf);    /* and get another */
   }
lookahead = (st == FILEEND) ? EMPTY: FULL;
return st;
}


int readline(buf)
char *buf;
{
char lastch, *tmpin, *tmpout;
int quote, singlequote;

quote = OFF;
singlequote = OFF;
lastch = ' ';
if (gets(holdbuf) == NULL) return FILEEND;
tmpin = holdbuf;
tmpout = buf;
while (isspace(*tmpin)) tmpin++;    /*speed over leading whitespace */
if (*tmpin == '#') {    /* screen out preprocessor lines */
   *tmpout = '\0';
   return !FILEEND;
   }
```

```
while (*tmpin){
   if (cmtlvl){
      if (!strncmp(tmpin, "*/",2)) {
         cmtlvl -= 1;
         tmpin += 2;
         }
      else
         tmpin++;
      }
   else if (quote == ON){
      if ((*tmpin == '\\') && *(tmpin + 1)) tmpin += 2;
      else if (*tmpin == '\"') {
         quote = OFF;
         tmpin ++;
         }
      else tmpin++;
      }
   else if (singlequote == ON){
      if ((*tmpin == '\\') && (*tmpin +1)) tmpin += 2;
      else if (*tmpin == '\'') {
         singlequote = OFF;
         tmpin++;
         }
      else tmpin++;
      }
   else if (*tmpin == '\"') {
      quote = ON;
      tmpin++;
      }
   else if (*tmpin == '\'') {
      singlequote = ON;
      tmpin++;
      }
   else if (isspace(*tmpin) && isspace(lastch)) tmpin ++;
   else if (!strncmp(tmpin, "/*",2)) {
      cmtlvl += 1;
      tmpin += 2;
      }
   else {
      *tmpout++ = *tmpin;
      lastch = *tmpin++;
      }
   }
```

```
*tmpout = '\0';
return !FILEEND;
}

/*
   ejectline -- prints the last read line on stdout
*/

void ejectline()
{

(void) puts(holdbuf);
}

/* advance current line one */

int nextline()
{

if (lookahead == FULL){
   lookahead = EMPTY;
   (void) strcpy(linebuf, lhbuf);
   }
else {
   if (readline(linebuf) == FILEEND) return FILEEND;
   }
ejectline();
return OTHER;
}

/*
   updatelvl -- scans the line buffer, counting braces
*/

void updatelvl()
{
char *temp;
```

```
    temp = linebuf;
    while (*temp){
        switch (*temp++){
            case '}' :
                level -= 1;
                if (level < 0) level = 0;
                break;
            case '{' :
                level += 1;
                break;
            default:
                break;
            }
        }
    }


    /*
        lasttoken -- recognizes a limited set of line-ending tokens
                     assumes the line is devoid of comments
                     (as it would be thanks to readline).
    */

    int lasttoken()
    {
    char *temp;

    temp = linebuf;
    while (*temp++);   /* find end of string */
    --temp;
    while (isspace(*(--temp))) ;   /*back up past trailing white space */
    switch (*temp){
        case ';' :
          return SEMI;
        case ')' :
          return RPAREN;
        case '{' :
          return LBRACE;
        case '}' :
          return RBRACE;
        }
    return OTHER;
    }
```

```
/*
   updatefunc -- update function name from current line
*/
void updatefunc()
{
char *temp;
char *end;
int len;

temp = linebuf;
while (*temp++);   /* scan to end of line */
while (*(--temp) != '('); /* back up to function name */
end = temp--;
while (!isspace(*temp) && (temp != linebuf)) temp--;
if (isspace(*temp)) temp +=1;
len = end - temp;
(void) strncpy(funcname, temp, len);
funcname[ len ] = '\0';
fline = 0;
}


/*
   printdbg -- generate a dbg call
*/

void printdbg(str, line, level)
char *str;
int line, level;
{

if (!strcmp(str,"main") && (line == 0))
   (void) printf ("dbg_init();\n");
else
   (void) printf("dbg(\"%s%02d\", %d, \"\"); \n", str, line, level);
}


/*
   findbblnk -- process lines until a blank line or
                a closing brace is found
*/
```

```
void findbblnk()
{
int st;

do{
   st = nextline();
   if (lasttoken() == LBRACE) level += 1;
   } while (!text(holdbuf) && (st != FILEEND));
}

/*
   text -- returns true if the holdbuffer has something
           besides whitespace in it
*/

int text(buf)
char *buf;
{

while (isspace(*buf)) buf++;
return (!(*buf));
}
```

Listing D.1.

E
sdb Command Summary

Program Invocation

sdb [–w] [–W] [objfile [corefile | –]]

Options	Effect
–w	allows changes in object file
–W	suppresses missing file warnings

Variables: specified as <procedure>:<variable>,<instance>

Dump Variable	<variable>/[<count>][<length>][<format>]
Set Variable	<variable>!<value>
Give Variable Address	<variable>=<format>
Dump Stack	t
Dump Stack (top line only)	T

Source Code

Select File or Function	e <object name>
Search Forward	/<regular expression>/
Search Backward	?<regular expression>?
Print Current Line	p
Print and Advance One Line	<carriage return>
Print Last Line Executed	l (lowercase el)
Print Window	w
Scroll Window	z
Scroll Window (clean)	<end of file character>
Move Current Line (absolute)	<line number>
Move Current Line (relative)	+<count> or –<count>
Print List of Procedures and Files	Q

Breakpoints

Set Breakpoint	<line number>b[<attached commands>]
List Active Breakpoints	B
Delete a Breakpoint	<line number>d
Delete All Breakpoints	D

Monitor Points

Announce Execution	<line number>a
Watch Variable	<variable>$m<count>

Execution Control

Run (no args)	[<passcount>]R
Run (with args)	[<passcount>]r <args>
Continue, setting temporary breakpoint	
–Ignore Interrupt	<linenumber>c[<passcount>]
–Forward Interrupt	<linenumber>C[<passcount>]
–Resume in Interrupt Handler	<control-C>
Begin Execution at	
Nonsequential Location	<linenumber>g[<passcount>]
Single Step (follow calls)	s[<repeat count>]
Single Step (over calls)	S[<repeat count>]
Invoke Function	<function name>(<args>)
Invoke Function with	
Formatted Output	<function name>(<args>)/<format>
Kill Program	k
Exit Debugger	q

Machine Level

Dump Registers	x
Dump Memory	<address>/[<count>][<length>][<format>]
Set Memory	<address>!<value>
Monitor Address	<address>:m<count>
Disassemble Memory	use Dump Memory with l or i format
Single Step (ignore interrupts)	i
Single Step (forward interrupts)	I
Print Current Instruction	X
Print Address Map	M

Miscellaneous

Get Command Input From File	<filename
Execute System Command	!<command>
Turn On Verbose Mode	<level> v
	(level can be 1 or 2)
Turn Off Verbose Mode	v

Length Codes

b   byte
h   two bytes (half word)
l   four bytes (long)

Format Codes

c   character
d   decimal
u   decimal, unsigned
o   octal
x   hexadecimal
f   single-precision fp
g   double-precision fp
s   string
a   character array
      (a is one less dereferencing operation than s)
p   pointer to procedure
i   symbolic disassembly
I   nonsymbolic disassembly

Bibliography

Cooper, Doug, and Michael Clancy. *Oh! Pascal!* 2nd Ed. New York: W. W. Norton, 1985.

Dale, Nell, and David Orshalick. *Introduction to Pascal and Structured Design.* Lexington, Massachusetts: D. C. Heath, 1983.

Harbison, Samuel P., and Guy L. Steele, Jr. *C: A Reference Manual.* Englewood Cliffs, New Jersey: Prentice-Hall, 1984.

Hayes, Brian. "A Mechanic's Guide to Grammar," Parts I, II, III. *Computer Language* 2(10):27-35, 2(11):51-60, and 2(12):49-64 (October, November, and December 1985).

Pattis, Richard E. *Karel the Robot.* New York: John Wiley, 1981.

Plum, Thomas. *Learning to Program in C.* Cardiff, New Jersey: Plum-Hall, 1983.

Purdum, Jack. *C Programming Guide.* Indianapolis, Indiana: Que Corporation, 1983.

Schneider, G. Michael. *An Introduction to Programming and Problem Solving with Pascal.* 2nd Ed. New York: Wiley, 1982.

Index

More Computer Knowledge from Que

Que Order Line: **1-800-428-5331**

All prices subject to change without notice.

FOLD HERE

_____

_____

_____

_____

Que Corporation
P. O. Box 50507
Indianapolis, IN 46250

REGISTER YOUR COPY OF
DEBUGGING C

Register your copy of *Debugging C* and receive information about Que's newest products relating to programming languages. Complete this registration card and return it to Que Corporation, P.O. Box 50507, Indianapolis, IN 46250.

Name _____

Address _____

City _____ State _____ ZIP _____

Phone _____

Where did you buy your copy of *Debugging C*?

_____

How do you plan to use the programs in this book?

_____

_____

_____

What other kinds of publications about programming languages would you be interested in?

_____

_____

_____

_____

Which operating system do you use? _____

THANK YOU!

DC-8611

FOLD HERE

_____

_____

_____

_____

Que Corporation
P. O. Box 50507
Indianapolis, IN 46250